MW01632861

MASTERS OF THE ART

MASTERS OF THE ART

A Fighting Marine's Memoir of Vietnam

Ronald E. Winter

BALLANTINE BOOKS • NEW YORK

Published in the United States by Presidio Press, an imprint of The Random House Publishing Group, a division of Random House, Inc., New York.

PRESIDIO PRESS and colophon are trademarks of Random House, Inc.

Originally published in hardcover in a slightly different form in the United States by Carlton Press, New York, in 1989.

ISBN:0-7394-6519-8

Cover design: Carl Galian
Cover photograph: U.S. Marine Corp

Printed in the United States of America

To Heather,
For reminding me
that there is also music

Prologue

I moved slowly down the walkway, outwardly anxious, wanting to rush ahead, but blocked by the mass of people before me. Secretly, I was happy with the slow pace of the crowd, because I was not really sure how I would handle what was waiting.

The darkness to my left kept growing, the sense of being pulled into gloom and death was stronger with each step, and soon I had to stop anyway. There were too many panels, bearing too many names I remembered, and I wouldn't pass any of them without a brief pause, to reflect, to remember.

After a while it was almost over. There was only one left.

I stopped, knelt, wiped some accumulated grime off the name, and used every bit of strength I had to keep my emotions in check. Marines don't cry. He had taught me that. But it wasn't supposed to end like this. None of it was supposed to end like this. We were supposed to be the victors. And, given everything we had done, I still couldn't understand why we weren't.

We hadn't lost. We hadn't been beaten. So why had I spent the last decade and more hearing us referred to as losers or suckers who had fought for a lost cause every time the subject came up?

Maybe it was because the country and the media just didn't know what had really happened. Maybe it's time they learn.

This book is about war and fighting, about people who do

the fighting even when they aren't sure why, and about staying true to a cause, even if it is not popular.

It is about life, and death, and futility, and hope. It is about surviving and teaching. But above all, it is about a group of men who joined forces in 1966 in North Carolina and stayed together for the most part until 1969.

It is about their actions, individually and collectively, in that time. They, or we, were United States Marines, assigned to what became Medium Helicopter Squadron 161 (HMM-161). We were commanded most of that time by Lt. Col. Paul W. Niesen, who was promoted to full colonel and named Marine Aviator of the Year in 1969, just after our time together ended.

But that was after Parris Island, after North Carolina, and after Vietnam. Most of us were quite young back then, in our late teens or early twenties, and those who survived are now grown men, working in a different environment than the one we trained for and went to in 1968. We've gone on to other endeavors, and we don't even look much like we did then.

But—outside of my family—the people I met in 161, and one other, have had a greater impact on my life than anyone I have encountered since.

This book is intended as a reminder of what we did there, because it was significant. It was lost temporarily in the larger picture of the war, the protests, Watergate, and the fall of Saigon in 1975.

But it will not remain lost. There was too much that was too important and should be passed on. It is for the survivors, and about them, but it is also about those members of 161, and one other, who didn't survive, because their deaths should not go unnoticed.

Some of the incidents are sad, some are tragic, some are funny, but all are true and represent my best recollections, aided by Marine Corps records and the recollections of other former members of 161.

This isn't intended as an exact history. It is a tribute.

Because back then we lived together, worked together, fought together, looked out for each other, and didn't let each other down. Finding people who live up to that standard in the years since we last saw each other has been hard to do. But I haven't forgotten, the others haven't, either, and I won't let them down now.

But first, I have to tell you how it started for me. And I have to tell you about Starbuck.

PART I

Chapter 1

My first impression of Sgt. Robert F. Starbuck was a worm's-eye view of the soles of his boots. They came crashing through the double swinging doors in the middle of the Parris Island Recruit Receiving Barracks at about 3:00 a.m. January 14, 1966.

I was sitting on the floor of a squad bay along with eighty-four other recruits, having been told to do so by the sergeant major of Parris Island, who had left us there only a minute before.

Then there was a rumbling noise, like thunder, or maybe a herd of buffalo on a rampage, and Starbuck kicked through the door, both feet off the floor. He saw us sitting there and his face turned to a twisted, red picture of pure anger.

"Get up, get the fuck up. Get on your goddamn feet. Who told you maggots to sit down? Get up!" His voice had the depth of a bottomless well and the pitch of an acre of gravel.

Starbuck was six feet tall and about 185 pounds. He had legs like tree trunks and a perfectly V-shaped upper body, with wide shoulders and a narrow waist. His head was shaved damn near as closely as ours were, *because he wanted it that way.* Starbuck looked like what I'd expect a U.S. Marine drill instructor to look like.

I'm sure that thought went through my mind at the time, but it took second place to one other thought.

He was pissed! Somebody made the mistake of trying to say, "But the sergeant major told us . . ."

"Shut your hole, maggot. I don't want to see your green teeth or smell your rotten breath."

That was just the beginning. Right behind Starbuck was a short black corporal named Jonathon L. Sparks, and he was carrying a footlong piece of iron pipe. A long, lean staff sergeant, whose name I can't remember, rounded out the trio.

They were all yelling like madmen, and nothing could be said or done correctly.

It was a setup of course. We had arrived on the island at about midnight, after a bus trip from Charleston, South Carolina, where I had gotten off the train that had brought me from the North. There I joined what was to be the rest of my platoon. A few guys who thought they were smarter than everyone else had been drinking in the back of the bus on the way. They paid later.

When we stopped at the receiving barracks, a drill instructor named Sergeant Wilson came on board, laughed a minute with the driver, and then turned on us like a wolverine.

"You maggots have ten seconds to get off this bus," he bellowed. *"I'm going to count down from ten. Anyone left when I get to zero is going to die. Now move!"*

Talk about people scrambling. The fun was abruptly over. He kept counting, and believe it or not we all made it. Outside it was more of the same. "Line up. Stand straight. Close it up. Toe to heel. Dick to tail. Asshole to belly button."

The terminology was unquestionably different than anything I'd been exposed to previously.

The country needed a lot more Marines in 1966 than it had, thanks to Vietnam, and there was no delay in processing us. In the next three hours we stripped, showered, had all our hair cut off, identification pictures taken, and uniforms issued. We were given seabags for stowing our extra uniforms and other gear, and we packed away our civilian clothes. All contraband was confiscated, and I sneaked a small laugh when they found a pack of rubbers in one guy's pocket.

"What the hell do you think you're going to do with these here?" was the obvious question.

A few recruits who had arrived from New York City together had knives and razors, but they went in the garbage, too. Then it was into that long squad bay, and a friendly talk from the sergeant major. He had a chest full of medals, hash marks—telling how long he'd been in—running from his cuff up to his elbow, and the stripes he'd accumulated running from his shoulder down to his elbow.

"Sit down men," he said in a quiet voice. "It's been a long night. You must be tired."

He told us of the challenges facing us, how difficult they would be, that many others had come to Parris Island just like us and made it through. He told us to keep trying and never quit, and we could make it, too. He seemed like a really decent guy. Our seabags were on the tables in front of us, so we wouldn't have to hold them while we were sitting on the floor listening to his steady voice.

I started to feel mellow. I felt so warm, so good. It had been 12 degrees above zero when I left Albany, New York. It was about 70 degrees now. I was going to like this place.

"I'm going to leave you now," he said quietly. "In a few minutes your drill instructors will come and take you to your barracks. They'll show you where to sleep and start your training in the morning."

What a great bunch of guys, I thought. I can't wait to meet them.

"This is the last time you'll be spoken to in a normal tone of voice until you graduate," he added. It should have been a warning, but I didn't pick up on it.

"Just remember, you can make it."

A definite warning. I still didn't pick up on it. I remember thinking, this isn't so bad. I remember asking myself, what about all this breaking you down business I kept hearing about?

I actually thought that, except for the physical training, the worst was already behind me. I thought the DIs would come out, shake our hands, welcome us to Parris Island, and be happy we were there.

I mean what the hell, that was the impression I got from civilians on the way down who congratulated us on serving our country. And now look. Here was the sergeant major of Parris Island telling us what wonderful things to expect in the next few months. I was pleasantly tired, ready for a good night's sleep, and primed to go out there and show them what kind of Marine I could be.

God was I stupid. That was when the rumbling started. That was when the floor started shaking. That was when Starbuck came blasting through those doors, and life as I had known it ended forever. And I clearly remember that within seconds, my thoughts had changed to one simple question.

How in the hell did you get yourself into this?

Chapter 2

The sun was bright, the sky so blue it hurt your eyes to look up, and a nearly comfortable mid-October warmth was taking the chill off the air.

It was just after 8 a.m., Monday morning, and downtown Troy, New York, hadn't really started to come alive yet. There was some traffic, but not the kind you'd see in a few hours when the shops opened. I had taken the Traction Company bus down to the city from Wynantskill, the small town east of Troy where I lived. I did that most days, and usually rode to the stop on Fulton Street, across from Frear's Department Store, a huge steel-and-marble wonder that was partially torn down in a 1970s burst of redevelopment fever. There I normally transferred to another bus that would take me to college in Albany.

But this day I had gotten off early, at the stop on Third Street, just past Proctor's Theater, where I used to go to the movies with my friends. I walked to the corner and faced the U.S. Post Office. The steps leading into the building were wide, beginning to cast off the night chill and absorbing the heat from the sun. If they weren't exactly inviting, they weren't throwing any obstacles in my way, either.

I walked up, went inside, and for the first time in all the times I had been in that building, didn't stop to look at the mural of the Headless Horseman chucking a pumpkin at the fleeing Ichabod Crane. It took up all the space over the windows where the workers sold stamps and took packages. When I was younger I would stand there in awe, mesmerized by that chaotic scene, and just stare while my mother attended to her business at the windows. But that day I didn't even give it a glance.

Instead, I walked up a stairway to the second floor, then down a hall. The gold paint on the door read UNITED STATES MARINE CORPS, RECRUITING STATION. WALK IN.

A sergeant was there, a Staff Sergeant I would later learn. He was a bit taller than me, lean, with friendly yet wary brown eyes. He had close-cropped dark hair flecked with gray, stripes on his arms, and medals on his chest. He looked at me with a mixture of curiosity and friendliness.

"Good morning. Have a seat. How can I help you? Do you want some coffee?"

And so it began.

When I graduated from high school in 1965, it seemed that my life was set for at least the next four years. I had a college to attend, a scholarship to help me through, and a summer job to earn extra money.

But in retrospect, everything I did after graduation turned me in the direction of the U.S. Marine Corps, and eventually to Vietnam. It was just heating up back then, yet I felt, and still do, that I was destined to be there.

Wynantskill was a small town, about ten miles east of Albany, New York, and bordering Troy. I lived in a rambling house with a wraparound front porch and a small front yard, but big side and back yards. The driveway ran along the left side of the house, with a half-acre lot next to it that we used for baseball and football games.

We moved into that house two days before my tenth birthday, and I stayed there until I left for the Marines. An old garage stood at the end of our property, about one hundred feet from the street, and attached to it were an old workshop and chicken coop. Along the way the workshop and chicken coop were torn down.

My father, brother, and I spent a lot of time trying to salvage the garage, but we ultimately tore that down, too. The house had been some kind of showplace when it was first built. It had flowers along the sides of the yards, a small goldfish pool that we never used on the side lawn, and grapes growing on two arbors, one on the property line on the side yard and another that climbed up the side of the back porch.

My bedroom was on the second floor overlooking the back porch roof, and I could exit the house that way—out the window, over the roof, and down the grape arbor—if I was so inclined.

The house was on a dead-end street that went up the side of a hill, with the hill continuing up for another five hundred yards or so after the street ended. The bottom of the street made a T-intersection with Main Street, and the intersection was flanked by gas stations. A Gulf station was on the left, going downhill, and a small grocery store, first called the RKO and later the IGA, was to the left of the Gulf station at the bottom of a street parallel to the one I lived on. Right after graduation the store owner hired me as a stock clerk and bag boy, full-time for the summer and part-time when I went to college.

That job was my introduction to the wider world beyond school, and especially to the Marine Corps. The produce manager, a husky guy named Jack, was a former Marine who had flown as a crewman in cargo planes. He was a tough guy when he had to be, easygoing most of the time, and I had a lot of fun working with him.

Jack's accounts of being in the Marines were regularly bolstered by an honest-to-God recruiter, who wore his uniform and medals to work every day and lived on the street that ran alongside the store. He'd stop in the store several times a week for some bread or milk, or "Just to say hi," and he never neglected to mention that the Marines had a good job and some great training for a near-man like myself.

Just to make sure I didn't miss the hint, my girlfriend's father had served in the Marines on Guadalcanal in World War II.

He didn't say much, but he did make a point of showing me his medals one day, neatly encased on the wall.

And then there was Dad. Dad and I were very much alike as I was growing up. We were both stubborn, didn't like taking any crap from anybody, didn't know how to back down or back off, and wouldn't have even if we did know.

That made for some interesting confrontations as I progressed through my teenage years. When a disagreement erupted between us, there was no middle ground. Dad had his point of view, I had mine, and compromise was a dirty word. Dad usually won out, mainly because he was Dad, and even in the middle of a fight I respected the fact that he was in charge.

As I got older and stronger—I was very much into lifting weights, doing sit-ups, push-ups, and calisthenics—the confrontations got physical, at least on Dad's end. Almost to the day I enlisted, he made sure I understood that he was in charge, physically and otherwise.

Dad had taught us a lot about working—besides tearing down the old coop and workshop, we completely renovated the interior of our house—and while we got a lot done, it was that work that brought about one of our more intense confrontations.

Our biggest job during those years involved digging out the cellar. It originally had about five feet of headroom, two huge old cisterns where rainwater was stored, and a massive cast-iron coal furnace. Dad wanted a nice basement with a family room.

We started digging it out when I was twelve, and the project continued even after I left. We dug up the floor, carried the dirt and rock out in buckets, dumped it all into an old mason's wheelbarrow, and pushed the load to the edge of our lot next door, filling in low spots.

I knocked the cisterns down, and we replaced the old coal-burning furnace with a modern natural gas system. My main job was to swing a sledgehammer while Dad or my brother held a bull point, an eighteen-inch steel rod with a pointed end. The pointed tip of the bull point was placed on a seam in the rock, I'd hit the top with the sledge, and eventually we'd pry apart the layers of shale rock below the old floor. I swung that sledge for years and missed the top of the bull point only one time, and then recovered quickly enough so my brother just got skinned knuckles.

Swinging the sledge became "my" job, and it became my trademark. I was swinging the sledge in the garage one day, a month or so before I joined the Marines. I was breaking up pieces of the cement floor and Dad was loading them into the wheelbarrow. I wasn't speaking because I was mad at Dad for some reason or another. He wasn't speaking because he was mad at me for some reason or another. Finally, when he decided he'd had enough, Dad brought his fist up from the floor and nailed me right on the jaw. But, aside from my head whipping to the right, I didn't move. I just stared at him.

Getting smacked by your "Old Man" was commonplace in my circle of friends. Our fathers worked in factories, steel mills, or on construction jobs, and most had gone through World War II and grown up in the Depression. They believed in "spare the rod and spoil the child," and applied it whenever they felt it was necessary.

Standing up to a shot from your father, neither crying nor getting knocked down, was considered one rite of passage into manhood among my friends. I'd taken quite a few punches to the chest or shoulders in recent years without reacting, but this was the first flush on the jaw punch that hadn't leveled me. All those years of work had toughened me, and I think we both realized then that our relationship had moved to a new level.

I figured that it was time for one of us to be moving on. There was no confusion over who that would be. This was Dad's house, the place he'd bought to spend the rest of his life in. He'd had his share of moving around and now he was settling in.

I was the rebel, the rambunctious one, the one who was aching to be out in the world, my own man and my own boss. I knew I wouldn't be going at just that moment, but that punch had a major impact on me, physically and otherwise, and it was just a matter of time.

The job at the grocery store also had a major impact on my outlook on life, and on Dad's view of the proper father-son relationship.

I had quickly developed the air of independence that comes with handling responsibility and receiving a weekly paycheck. I earned enough to pay for my books and school expenses, some for a bank account, and even had enough left over for fun. I had my girlfriend and a buddy with a car.

Hot summer nights after work were good times for double dates, with a six-pack of beer. I'd work hard all day, then go out that night, hook down a few cold beers, and wrestle around on the backseat of a 1963 Chevy. And I got paid for doing it! Life that summer was all I could ever hope it would be.

When September came and I started commuting to the state university in Albany, I had undergone some substantial changes. After thirteen years of confinement in the public schools, chained to books and studies, a single summer of work had spoiled me.

Western Civilization held no mysteries for me, sociology didn't make the list of "things I am interested in," and I had a real problem relating to others who seemed to live only to study. I couldn't understand how some juniors or seniors, who had done nothing with their lives previously except attend school—and were in college courtesy of their parents' bank account—could claim at the ripe old age of twenty to know for sure that they wanted to be brain surgeons or psychoanalysts.

Nonetheless, when summer ended and school started, Dad expected a return to the pre–high school graduation norm. I was to stay in nights and study. I was to work and attend classes and that was that.

Dad was a foreman at an army arsenal in Watervliet, New York, and my mother had sold Stanley Home Products as long as I could remember. They made a comfortable home for themselves and their four kids. But there was no money for luxuries such as living on campus. So it was stay home, work, commute, and do as I was told. But taking all those orders from Dad didn't sit too well with me.

So I fooled them. Boy did I fool them.

I turned eighteen on October 10, 1965. A week later on a Sunday night, I had an especially intense argument with Dad. He and Mom were worried because they felt I was seeing too much of my girlfriend. They figured I'd end up getting married before I was really ready and were determined to head that off.

They were on the right track, of course—parents aren't as uninformed as they sometimes seem to an eighteen-year-old. But they took the wrong approach in dealing with the situation. They forbade me to see her.

I'd had other girlfriends, but this one was special, and forbidding me to see her would never work. I wasn't going to take that lying down! We were in the living room, watching television, but the argument lasted for at least an hour and obliterated any interest anyone else might have had in *The Ed Sullivan Show.*

A gold-colored swivel chair was nestled in a corner between the doorway to the front hall and the archway into the dining room. In earlier and better times I used to sit in the chair with my feet tucked under me, grab the molding on the door or archway, and push as hard as I could to see how many times I could spin that chair around.

That night I just sat there, listening—or not listening—answering sometimes, generally getting more and more sullen as the argument progressed. Dad's famous last words were, "You want to join the Marines? Go ahead! I'll sign the papers."

I didn't answer, and I didn't tell him I was already old

enough to do it even if he didn't want to sign the papers. On Monday I didn't go to college. I went to the Marine Corps recruiting station in the post office. I had assumed my recruiter friend from the store worked there, because he always said his office was in the post office. It turned out that he worked in the Albany Post Office. But that didn't matter. The sergeant on duty in Troy was just as friendly and just as willing to help me fill out the enlistment papers.

He scheduled me to go to Albany on Tuesday for my physical and other tests. I spent a good part of the day in the recruiting office, hung out downtown when I was done with the forms, and went to my girlfriend's house later in the afternoon. I told her the news, she did give me some assurances of undying affection and devotion, and after a while I took the bus home.

The bus left me off at the bottom of my street around 6:30 p.m., the same time I'd usually get home from school. I was walking up the street toward the house when Dad backed his '63 Chevy Impala out of the driveway.

It was Monday, and as always he was on his way to go bowling. He pulled over and asked where I had been.

"I joined the Marines," I told him with that half-innocent and half "I know this is going to be a shocker" look.

Dad flipped. I had seen him mad before, but now he was really pissed!

"Get up to the house," he yelled. Well, maybe it was more like he thundered or roared.

He took off for his bowling league, and I started over to the grocery store to spread the news. But Dad turned around, blowing his horn at me as I crossed the Gulf station lot. He picked me up, even though it was only a hundred yards up to the house, and started yelling at me immediately, continuing in the driveway, through the back porch, and into the kitchen, where my mother was cooking dinner.

Dad had served in the U.S. Navy in World War II on the

aircraft carrier *Princeton.* He had been on board when it was sunk in the Battle of Leyte Gulf, and he was blown into the ocean by exploding bombs after making his way to the hangar deck from six decks farther below. Dad spent three hours treading water in the Pacific, with sharks below and Japanese Zeroes above, before being rescued.

Dad knew about combat. He had seen how Marines looked after weeks of fighting on the islands that were taken during the war. He'd told me of seeing a hard, tough Marine who had been in fierce fighting come aboard and break down crying when he was given fresh eggs to eat.

"They'll use you for cannon fodder," he kept yelling. Mom was aghast. She had a stunned, frightened look on her face as we burst through the back door. She kept asking, "What's wrong? What's wrong?"

"Go ahead, tell her—go ahead," Dad yelled.

I tried to do it gently, make it seem upbeat rather than something to worry about. It didn't work.

I had really given my mother a major disappointment a year earlier when I told her I didn't want to become a lawyer. That had been her dream since I was in the seventh grade, all because of an essay we had to write on the theme "what I want to be when I grow up."

I said farmer, because I had fond memories of my grandfather's dairy farm in Center Brunswick, New York, where I lived until I was ten. Even though he no longer had cows when I was a kid, he still had apple trees and hay fields, a barn, and a stream running through the property with fish in it and willow trees along its banks.

I'd also worked for other local farmers in my teen years, helping with haying and milking chores, and I liked that, too. Natural selection.

I also picked dentist and lawyer because I'd heard they both paid well and figured they'd look good if anyone thought being a farmer wasn't a smart career choice. Unfortunately, the essay was used by elementary school guidance counselors to determine my college entrance course selection in high school.

Mom locked onto the lawyer bit because I think she liked the idea of having a lawyer in the family. She didn't take it well nearly five years later when I finally told her that law school really wasn't in my future.

Now I told her quietly, "I joined the Marines, Mom." She didn't take that well, either. The argument with Dad raged for another few minutes, and then he left for his bowling.

My father had bowled on Monday nights for as long as I could remember, and that night was no exception. I ate dinner in silence, talked with my brothers and sister for a little while, and went to bed.

It was 3:00 a.m. when I heard the car door slam. It wasn't quite 3:01 a.m. when I heard that angry tread on the back steps, across the back porch, through the kitchen, dining room, front hall, up the stairs, down the hall toward my room, and *bam*—through my bedroom door.

"Wake up! Get up! Get out of that bed."

There didn't seem to be any point in telling him I was already awake.

"Where are those goddamn papers? Give them to me. I'm ripping them up. You're not going in the Marines. Get downstairs."

My room, which I shared with my younger brother, had two beds, a dresser, a small stand for my record player and records, and an old easy chair and footstool that had been Dad's. My papers were in a manila envelope on the chair.

He grabbed them and ripped them up.

"That's what I think of your Marine Corps!"

That pissed me off. But my father stood five-feet-eleven-and-a-half inches tall and weighed in around 160. He had a punch that could send you flying, and even though he hadn't knocked me down that day in the garage, it still hurt. He used to get a kick out of bending a beer can in half with his thumb and one finger, either hand. I'm talking tin cans here, with a seam down one side, not these modern-day, wimpy aluminum beer cans.

It was another test of manhood in our house to be able to bend a beer can one-handed. In contrast to Dad, my mother was four-feet-eleven-and-one-half inches and weighed in around 110.

I got a little of both and finally hit five-feet-seven-and-a-half inches, 125 pounds. I was in good shape, could do more than 100 push-ups, 25 chin-ups, and sit-ups forever, and press about 20 percent more than I weighed. I was a finalist two years running in the annual Troy High School physical fitness contest, which was based on the Marine Corps physical readiness test, and in gym class I could outwrestle people who outweighed me by forty pounds or more.

When I was sixteen I got into a schoolyard fight with a kid who threw a cherry bomb in my face. He was a year younger, but quite a bit bigger than I was, and he knew how to box. I swung at him and missed, he hit me four times across the forehead, and then landed a right cross along the left side of my face. I remember my brain exploding, first in an incredible shower of light and then a split second of blackness.

The punch knocked me off my feet, and I can recall arching toward the black pavement. The whole area was covered with that blacktop, and it tore the hell out of both of my arms behind the elbows when I landed. They were scarred for years, and my nose was broken for the umpteenth time.

From my vantage—or disadvantage—point on the ground, all I could see were thick, hairy legs approaching, and it looked as though he was going to stomp me. But as quick as I had landed, I bounced, rolled, pushed him back, and stayed away from him long enough to regain my breath.

Then I kicked him in the groin as hard as I could. That pretty much ended it. I went home bloody, and then to the hospital for stitches where the cherry bomb had hit my mouth. The emergency room intern didn't believe my nose was really broken, and by the time the swelling went down and someone believed me, it was permanently crooked. It hasn't changed.

The other guy didn't go home for quite a while until his pain subsided, and we generally figured it came out even. The important thing was, I didn't back away from the pain, and I could take a punch.

But my father in a rage was something else to see. I don't think I ever would have raised a hand to him anyway, just out of respect, unless I thought I was going to be seriously hurt, but there was no way I was going to challenge him that night.

He was a picture of white-hot fury, and he was on a roll. I sat at the kitchen table as he raged.

"I busted my balls for you," Dad yelled. That was significant because Dad hardly ever swore in front of the kids, and when he did he didn't say "balls."

"I had a lousy score tonight because of you."

You didn't screw up Dad's bowling score. In the end, Dad figured he had convinced me not to join the Marines, and I secretly vowed that I was going to get my physical the next day come hell or high water.

Chapter 3

Tuesday morning came and I went to Albany to take the physical.

Tuesday night came and I returned home. I had failed! After all that had happened, I failed the damn physical because I had flat feet! I was devastated. I believed I had absolutely no other options to consider except being a Marine. I knew I had flat feet, but I used to walk ten miles or more at a stretch with no discomfort and not even a blister. I just couldn't believe it.

I never told Dad. I just tried to pick up the pieces of my first college semester and go on. But it didn't work. I couldn't get interested. I started skipping classes. And somehow, it all didn't seem final. Somehow I knew I would still be a Marine.

Vietnam was calling, I swear I could hear it. I listened intently every time I heard it on the radio or stopped what I was doing when I saw something about it on TV. I even dreamed about it.

It would be more than two years before I would go there. But when I did, it didn't seem like a strange place. And it shouldn't have. I had already seen it in my dreams, and they were accurate.

In December I got a call from the recruiters. There might be a way, they said. I could go to Syracuse and take the physical over. I'd just have to tell a little white lie. Well, actually two little white lies. One, that I had never failed a physical before, and two, that I had never been turned down for military service.

No sweat. I approached Dad a little more calmly this time. I told him college wasn't working out, I had no training to do any other kind of work just then, and I still really wanted to be a Marine.

After a while he relented. "All right," he said. "But wait until after the holidays."

I did, and on January 6, 1966, I met the recruiter in Troy early in the morning, around 4:00 a.m. We drove to Syracuse, stopped at a phone booth, and I picked out a local address to use on the enlistment forms. Then I went through the paces again.

In Albany the doctors checked your arches by making you stand with both feet on the ground, shoulder-width apart. Then the doctor walked past and looked at your arches.

In Syracuse they told you to take your right foot in your right hand while balancing on your left, and then walked behind you to check the arch on the foot that was off the floor. So I arched my foot as the doctor passed. I did the same thing for the other foot. And I passed.

I fooled them. This time I really fooled them.

We arrived back in Albany in midafternoon, just as a group of recruits was getting its final instructions before heading off to Parris Island. John Messick, a good friend from high school, was there waiting to leave. John was about my height, heavier, in good shape, with dark hair and glasses.

He was one of the funniest people I have ever met and had a wisecrack to fit every situation. I didn't know he had enlisted because I hadn't seen him since the previous June. If I'd known, we might have gone in together on the buddy system. But it was too late.

I would see John only occasionally in the next four years, even though we both ended up in helicopter squadrons and even though we went to many of the same places. The first time was in April 1966, when we were home on leave after boot camp. John was one gung ho Marine then. The next time was in March 1968, at the Marine Corps Air Facility in New River, North Carolina.

He had just come back from Vietnam, and I was a month away from going. The air facility was part of the Camp Lejeune complex that surrounded Jacksonville, North Carolina, and was situated next to Camp Geiger, the infantry-training base where everyone went after Parris Island. Across Route 17 from the main gate to Camp Geiger was a bar called the Seven Seas. It was a Polynesian/Japanese place run by a former Marine, and as bars in that area went, it was an okay place to hang out.

I was sitting there one Friday afternoon sipping a beer at the horseshoe-shaped bar. As I put the glass up to my mouth, I saw Messick on the other side, doing the same thing, looking right back at me. We had quite a reunion, but John was different. He was an older and wiser man, as I was soon to become.

That afternoon in Albany two years earlier, I had said good-bye to him and promised to look him up at Parris Island, not knowing that such things just aren't done.

When he left for his trip to Parris Island, I headed home with the good news. All I really remember is my mother lying on the couch, turning over, and softly crying. Later on she composed herself and tried to be interested. I had enlisted for four years and was guaranteed a chance at an aviation job assignment. I told her I would try out for a flight cadet program and have a chance at flying jets. She tried to be interested. But my good news was bad news for Mom. Mothers are like that.

I was scheduled to leave Albany on January 12, 1966. I spent the week before taking care of business. I went to the university and withdrew from my courses. I had an audience with the dean, and he tried with everything he had to change my mind. He did a good job, but he just didn't understand. I had to go.

In the years since, I have come to a better understanding of what the dean was trying to tell me. People who have been in war often have a vision that others do not. But passing that vision on can be difficult. I don't know why it was so important to me to join the Marines.

It may have been my upbringing, listening to tales of my father's exploits or those of my friends' fathers. It may have been something genetic, passed down to me from the Scottish Highlanders of Clan Gunn, a warrior clan, themselves descendants of Viking raiders who settled in the Orkney Islands around A.D. 900, and moved south to the northern mainland of Scotland a century later.

It may have been all of those things, but it was manifested in one central concept—I never wanted to look at myself in the mirror as a young man, or an old man, and know inside that I ran from a worthwhile challenge, as hard or dangerous as that challenge might be. No matter what else can be said or believed, all these years later I am convinced that my decision back in 1966 was the right one, and I can't even begin to consider who or what I might have become if I hadn't been a Marine and gone to Vietnam.

I know that the military isn't for everyone, and I fully appreciate and respect those Americans who worked in the defense plants and farms keeping the military armed and supplied. But for me, anything else would have been something less. I knew that in 1966, even if I wasn't able to articulate it. I never wanted to have to justify myself to anyone.

I tried telling that to the dean, who didn't have to go to war, but we may as well have been talking in different languages. We shook hands and I left. The rest of the week I spent time with my girlfriend, partied with my friends, and worked so I'd have some extra traveling money.

I didn't go to church on my last Sunday at home, which again disappointed Mom, and suddenly it was Wednesday morning, 6:00 a.m., and time to go.

"Keep your mouth shut and do what you're told," everyone said.

Dad drove me to Albany in his Chevy. It was still dark, and he had an easy-listening station playing on the radio. We didn't talk much. I thought it was because he was mad, but later I would find out that he just couldn't say anything because he was too choked up.

I don't remember much about my thoughts, just that I was feeling lonely already, but was determined to show the world. I was going to be a Marine, and the best Marine there ever was. Then we were there, we shook hands, and I told my dad good-bye.

The next few hours were a blur of forms, oaths, lining up, and being singled out. There were too many of us for the airplane out of Albany's airport, so they picked six of us, all of whom had a little college, to go to Parris Island by train. Instead of a few hours on a plane, ours was a two-day trip, first to New York City and then down the Coast Line Railroad, and we would be on our own the whole way.

Everyone else left for the airport and a sergeant marched us to the train station a block away. On the way I could've sworn I saw my father's car go by. But that didn't make sense. It was a little before noon, and he was supposed to be to work at 7:30 a.m.

Dad hardly ever missed work, even if he was sick, and I figured I was just seeing things. Some of the other guys had family members waiting to say good-bye to them. I was alone, and I kind of wished someone was there to say good-bye to me, too. I didn't realize then just how emotional that would have been, and why no one could face it.

I figured it out two weeks later. I was on Parris Island and got two letters, one from Dad and one from my sister Nancy. She told me how strange it was without me at home and how she still found herself setting a place for me at the table. Dad said he missed me, told me to do a good job, and mentioned that it *was* his car I saw in Albany.

He couldn't bring himself to leave like that, and he'd stayed around until he saw me marching away. But he couldn't bring himself to park and say one more good-bye, either.

It was pretty tough, finding out just how much a son means to a father, and just how much love is between them, even when it doesn't seem that way.

I wasn't the oldest member of our family, but I was the first to leave the nest. All my thoughts had been centered on what was happening to me, and I didn't realize the effect it was having on the rest of the family. I thought about those letters long after lights out, lying on my bunk in the darkness, staring up at the ceiling.

I hadn't made any close friends yet, and for the first time in my life I was completely on my own. I felt sad, and incredibly homesick. There were a million things I wished I had said, and a million more I wished I could say.

But I was two weeks into my Parris Island training. The drill instructors told us the only way off that island was as a graduated Marine or in a coffin, and I intended to be a Marine, the best there had ever been. So I put the letters away and buried my sadness. It was a trick I learned right there, and it came in handy many more times in the future.

I put my emotions in a little vault, with strong walls that couldn't break, and went on with my work. Family and friends were behind me. Vietnam was waiting, patient and volatile. There was no turning back, and I could never go home again—at least not as the same person who had left.

All that existed before, all that had seemed so important, had already become insignificant when compared to the Marine Corps—and Starbuck.

Chapter 4

The drill instructors didn't wait to start our training. It began right there, in the receiving barracks, the second they arrived.

The first thing I learned was to jump when they said jump, and ask how high on the way up. The scene was complete bedlam. The three drill instructors were shouting instructions, often purposely contradicting each other to add to the confusion, and somehow managed to assign a number from one to eighty-five to each of us in alphabetical order, for identification purposes.

We were standing at attention, and the perfect position was continually drummed into us. "Chest out, stomach in, shoulders back, chin up, eyes level and straight ahead, heels together, toes at a 45-degree angle, thumbs along your trouser seams."

They called us maggots, ladies, fools, motherfucking hogs, and names that it must have taken a linguist to conjure up. The lean DI went outside, Sparks stood by a door at one end of the squad bay, and Starbuck started calling out names.

"When I call your name you *will* answer with a loud 'Yes sir,' you *will* grab your seabag in your right hand, and you *will* run to the hatchway and take your assigned position on the yellow footprints outside."

Well, it would have been nice if it had worked that way. But it seemed that no one could respond fast enough. That's where Sparks came in. He stood by the door—hatchway—

with that pipe in his hand, and if a recruit didn't run fast enough, Sparks would "motivate" him.

"You better move, fool. You better move or I'll *kill* you. Don't you eyeball me, boy. Get out! *Get out!*"

Anyone who grabbed his seabag in his left hand got an extra dose.

For the first time in my life I was glad my name came at the end of the alphabet. I had been assigned number eighty-three and a chance to watch what was going on. Sparks emphasized his commands by slamming his pipe on a table conveniently placed nearby. He had a wild look in his eye and I swore he really meant he'd kill someone.

When Starbuck called my number I answered, had a grip on my seabag, and was headed for the hatchway before the last syllable had ended. Sparks yelled something at me, but I was going too fast to hear it. I think his yell was more out of habit than necessity, and I kept going full speed.

Outside the scene was the same. The lean DI was telling each recruit as he emerged from the receiving barracks, "Put your right foot on the right footprint, and your left foot on the left footprint."

About once every third person he'd go into a spasm. "I said your *left.* Do you know which foot is your left foot? The one that looks like the one on the ground."

"No. Your other left. Your *military left.*"

Finally we were all lined up outside, in our first formation, and they gave the order.

"*Forwaaaard.* March."

No one in that crowd knew how to march. At least not like Marines march, and they march very well.

If anyone did know, it was obscured by the clumsiness around them. The drill instructors called us mob, they called us herd. They didn't call us platoon, Marines, or anything remotely resembling a formation that knows what it is doing.

We put our seabags over our right shoulders and headed down the street in the dark, stumbling, walking into each other, trying to get used to the feel of combat boots and uniforms, and to carrying that seabag without dropping it. The drill instructors herded us like sheepdogs with a flock.

Platoon 214 had arrived.

Our barracks was four blocks away. They harassed us all the way. Even in the dark they picked out the people who screwed up or stood out for one reason or another.

The DIs already were taking on godlike qualities. They were tough, mean, all-powerful, and could see in the dark. Who the hell was going to mess with someone like that?

The barracks in the 1st and 2nd Recruit Training Battalions on Parris Island at that time were old, World War II–vintage, two stories high, and shaped like a giant H. The two sides of the H contained squad bays, the cavernous rooms where an entire platoon was housed. There were four squad bays, so a series, four platoons that would go through the training together, lived in one building.

The bar in the middle of the H contained four heads—bathrooms—with showers, toilets, and sinks, offices for the platoon commanders and company gunnery sergeant, and the DIs' huts. One DI hut, or house—it actually was only a room with a desk, a bunk, a locker, and file cabinets in it—was located adjacent to each squad bay, so the drill instructors were in constant contact with their platoons.

Our squad bay was on the second floor. We were hustled up the stairs—excuse me, ladderway—and assigned bunk beds inside. I lucked out and was assigned a top bunk.

The bedlam continued. We stripped to our shorts and undershirts. They wanted us to get some sleep before the night was over, so our bed-making lesson was delayed until morning. We stood at attention at the foot of our bunks—they were bunks or racks, but definitely not beds—and counted off, shouting out the number that had been assigned to us as our turn came up. That routine made sure each recruit was where he was supposed to be, and continued through our last day on the island.

We learned new commands: "Prepare to mount," which meant standing by the side of the bunk, ready to jump in on command. "Mount" meant getting in the bunk and lying faceup at attention until given the command "At ease."

After each command we responded in unison.

"Prepare to mount—aye-aye, sir."

"Mount—aye-aye, sir."

The final command was "Sleep."

But it was quite some time before the final command was given. Instead, we practiced preparing to mount and mounting, about a dozen times or more until we got it right. Then we practiced lying in our bunks at attention for another dozen times or so.

It was only about two hours to dawn, so our sheets and pillowcases remained folded on the bunks. We used our blankets for pillows. When they were finally satisfied, the DIs gave us one last instruction.

"When the lights come back on you *will* stand at attention at the foot of your bunks. You *will* hold your sheets in your left hand and you *will* hold your blanket and pillowcase in your right hand."

"Sleep."

"Sleep—aye-aye, sir."

The lights went out and I sank into the warmest, deepest sleep I can ever remember. I don't think I dreamed.

Chapter 5

I felt the lights go on. I didn't hear the switch being thrown, and for a second I didn't hear anything else. But the light was right above me and it came on suddenly, accompanied by a sharp pain shooting through my eyes.

It couldn't have been more than five minutes since I had gone to sleep, I thought, and I wondered in that split second why the lights had been turned on again.

Then all hell broke loose. It was actually two hours since I had closed my eyes, and I was about to endure my first wake-up at P.I. A second after the light flashed on me, Starbuck and Sparks cut loose, making enough noise for ten people.

"Get up! Get up! Get out of those racks."

They were yelling and Sparks was banging his pipe on the metal bed frames. The lean one was there, too, running a broomstick around the inside of a metal garbage can, adding to the din. As if that weren't enough, they started tossing the garbage cans, technically known as shitcans, down the middle of the squad bay. Nobody slept in that morning.

I was lucky once again. Each squad bay had double swinging doors in the middle, just like the ones in the recruit receiving barracks. They opened from the hallway that led to the offices and the DI hut where the drill instructors emerged each morning when it was time for reveille. Down by the doors the DIs were tipping racks over if their occupants didn't get out fast enough. But my bunk was at the far end of the squad bay, so I was spared the initial onslaught. Nonetheless, my turn was about to come, along with everyone else's.

Remember that last instruction, about sheets in one hand and pillowcases and blankets in the other? No one else did.

I was standing at attention at the foot of my bunk when I remembered, and dived for my sheets. But it was too late.

"Get back here, fool," Sparks yelled. "Nobody told you to go back there."

Because no one remembered that instruction, we were ordered to lift our seabags over our heads and hold them there. They weighed about sixty pounds, not a lot, but I was glad I had lifted weights.

It's one thing to lift sixty pounds over your head. It's another to keep it there. I did, but after a while recruits all around me were starting to buckle. I kept my arms extended over my head and locked my elbows so they wouldn't bend. We held on and held on and held on. Sweat was pouring off of us, but they still wouldn't let us put those seabags down.

All the while the DIs kept up a constant stream of shouting, insulting abuse. They patrolled the squad bay between the two rows of bunks, and two rows of recruits facing each other. They waited for someone to make the fatal mistake of looking directly at them. When it happened they jumped.

"Don't you eyeball me, boy. What the fuck you looking at me for? Do you like me, boy?"

God help you if you said "No, sir."

"You don't like me?"

Anyone who made the mistake of saying *no* also made the second mistake of changing the answer and saying, "Yes, sir."

"You do like me, boy? Well, I'll tell you something, Private. Liking leads to loving, and loving leads to fucking. But you ain't going to fuck me, boy. . . ."

A recruit from Tennessee also made the mistake of saying *you* to Starbuck.

"You?" Starbuck blasted. "Do you know what a *ewe* is? A

ewe is a fucking female sheep. Do I look like a fucking *ewe* to *you*?"

There was no way to answer.

The whole point was to keep at us, keep us confused, and not give us a minute to think. I didn't realize it at the time, but they had already broken us. They had complete control over us, everyone was scared shitless, and they were watching us, seeing how we responded.

Not everyone handled it well. One of the guys who had come down from Albany with me went into a daze, dropped his seabag, and started stumbling around. He finally fell on the floor and I thought they'd ease up on him.

Sparks dumped a bucket of water on him. That got him going again, but scared me.

"Jesus Christ," I thought, "these people really don't care if we die here."

After a long, long time quite a few people couldn't keep the seabags up. My elbows were locked and my mind was focused on anything other than the pain. I didn't give up.

They finally gave us a break. They let us put the seabags down. Then they told us to lift our locker boxes over our heads.

The locker boxes were wooden, with metal hinges, nearly three feet long, about two feet wide, and one and a half feet high. Luckily for us they were empty. But our arms were tired from lifting the seabags, and once again some recruits had trouble holding them up.

One of these was the recruit who slept in the bunk below me and who was standing next to me. He started to waver and his locker box crashed onto my hand, scraping and cutting it. I was bleeding from my knuckles, but I wouldn't drop the box.

Starbuck was out there calling everyone who couldn't hack it a pussy, at the very least. I didn't want his wrath coming down on my head. Sparks noticed me though, especially after my hand started bleeding, and he kept getting on my case. I handled it pretty well. But I didn't want to. I didn't want him to notice me. I wanted to be anonymous.

It seemed like forever, but finally they said we could put the locker boxes, or footlockers as they also are known, back under our bunks. Then they told us we could get dressed. We were going to go to breakfast—morning chow.

I had this impression of Marines and how they looked in uniform from recruiting posters and other literature. That's not how we looked after we were dressed.

In the first place, all of our uniforms were brand-new and hadn't been ironed or starched. What you see in recruiting posters are Marines in pressed, starched uniforms. We hadn't been issued our formal dress uniforms yet.

Some recruits would be gaining weight in the next couple of months, and some would be losing. You couldn't get fitted for a dress uniform until your weight stopped fluctuating. So we had green dungaree working uniforms called utilities.

Recruiting posters show Marines with the top button of their utility shirt unbuttoned and a clean white T-shirt underneath. They show them with hats—covers—that fit and also are starched to hold a sharp-looking shape.

We had to button up all the buttons on our utility shirts, right up to our necks. Our covers weren't starched and didn't look sharp at all. Our belts were too long and the ends flopped like limp rags in a hurricane after we tightened them.

Real Marines wear steel springs, called blousing garters, around the top section of their boots. Their trousers are tucked up under the springs, which makes them look sharp, fit right, and not interfere with your circulation.

We didn't have them and were told to tuck the bottom of our trousers into our boot tops, which caused a lot of friction on our calves and ankles.

The result of not having all the things that make Marines look sharp was that we looked pretty sloppy. Damn sloppy.

The word *nerd* wasn't in widespread use back then, but it suited us perfectly.

That's the way it was supposed to be. A new recruit on Parris Island is given nothing with which to develop a sense of false pride. New recruits can't do anything right, and even if they do, they're told they're wrong. Everyone snarls at them, and they look and feel like they're ten feet lower than whale shit. That's the way it has to be.

If they are to be called Marines, they have to earn the right. We set out to earn that distinction right away. We learned that recruits who stand in front of doors yell "Gangway!" whenever anyone who is not a recruit comes through. We learned to sidestep through chow lines, to hold our metal tray in front of our face until food was to be put on it, and to hold our silverware properly. We learned that we didn't have to take every type of food offered in the chow line, but we had to eat everything we did take.

We learned the terminology. Bathroom—head; wall—bulkhead; door—hatchway; stair—ladderway; ceiling—overhead; boots—boondockers; underwear—skivvies; working uniform—utilities; hat—cover; window—porthole; floor—deck; and on and on.

Much later I was to learn that in the real Marine world there is a descriptive addition to every term we had been taught. It was "fucking" head and "fucking" overhead and "fucking" bulkhead and "fucking" deck and "fucking" everything else. Fuck became a noun, pronoun, adjective, adverb, subject, predicate, and direct object.

It was so commonplace and used so frequently that its shock value vanished. But that came much later and wasn't part of the training at Parris Island.

In our first days there we started to learn how to march, and we learned to call everyone "Sir." We also learned that on Parris Island everything is "Outstanding!"

Not outstanding, as in "Well done." Outstanding as in "Out-fucking-standing, Private." I found out on Parris Island that there is a way to make every word uttered, even those originally intended as a compliment, come out as criticism.

If you did something wrong, said something wrong, wore something wrong, or even looked wrong it was "Out-fucking-standing, Private."

Later, in the outside world, I would encounter sergeants who could even make the word "Marine" sound bad. They'd say, "Come here, Muhreen." "Get over here, Muhreen." "What the fuck you doing, Muhreen?"

It always came out like there was something slimy dripping off it. But at Parris Island, since we weren't Marines, we had to settle for "Out-fucking-standing."

About three days after we arrived, S.Sgt. G. C. Hale replaced the lean DI. Staff Sergeant Hale was taller than Corporal Sparks, but shorter than Sergeant Starbuck. He was the senior DI and had been in the Marines for nearly twenty years. Starbuck had about seven years in and Sparks just over four.

Staff Sergeant Hale said he was going to retire after our platoon graduated. We also were the last recruits to be trained by Starbuck, who had orders for Vietnam when we were through. Corporal Sparks would be around Parris Island for a while longer. Hale and Starbuck were Reconnaissance Marines, or Recons, while Sparks was an infantryman.

All three were tough as hell, and all three were very, very good at being Marines. Many people who have graduated from Parris Island will tell you that, at the end, they respected their drill instructors. That's true for me. I respected and liked them all by the time it was over. But in that first week they terrified me.

The few minutes I had to myself, which usually came just before I fell asleep each night, I could only ask, "What the hell have you gotten yourself into?"

I did everything just as I was told. I moved when and how I was told and spoke only when ordered. I did my best to be inconspicuous, but to no avail. Sparks had noticed me that very first morning. And when we left the barracks the first time to go to chow, I saw him point me out to the other DIs.

I didn't know what that was to mean. But I didn't want to find out. I wanted to stay out of their way, because I felt that to be noticed was to invite their wrath when I screwed up. And sooner or later everyone screws up.

Chapter 8

"Look at it. Miles of dick, standing right there in front of you."

It was all I could do not to laugh as the leathery-faced Woman Marine gunnery sergeant dressed down a platoon of women recruits at the rifle range mess hall. She wasn't being gentle about it.

They had come through our chow hall, and while in formation outside after eating had been checking out some of the guys, who were standing nearby in their formations checking out the girls.

"You like that, girls?" she bellowed. *"Well forget it! There might be miles, but you're not going to get a single inch!"*

I couldn't believe what I was hearing and felt sorry for the WMs. I still remembered my upbringing that said you didn't swear in front of women, nice or otherwise. But I also thought that was the funniest thing I'd ever heard. I think I would have burst out laughing if that gunny hadn't looked like she'd kick my ass all over the island if I did.

So I kept a straight face while inside I was having a hemorrhage. It had started inside the mess hall, when the women first started down the chow line. They were the only women we saw during our time on the island, and they caused quite a stir.

A cute blonde was stopped in front of a recruit who was dishing out potatoes. He looked at her and she looked at him, and you could see they were interested in each other. But that

Chapter 6

There is a distinct disadvantage to being a short Marine recruit. A lot of Marine recruits are not short. The Marines who guard embassies, the Marines whose pictures are on recruiting posters, the Marines who march at the Marine Barracks in Washington, D.C., are generally six feet tall at least.

As previously noted, I was five-feet-seven-and-a-half inches and topped the scales at 125 pounds. That meant I stood out.

First off, everyone wants to see if you've got enough heart to hang in there with so many bigger guys and become a Marine. Then the drill instructors and other personnel at Parris Island have their pet names for you. One of their favorites is feather merchant. Another is short round, which describes a bullet or shell that falls short of its target.

Those of course are in addition to the ever popular maggot and a litany of similarly derogatory scatological, social, and physical terms that the DIs used to describe all recruits.

As a short Marine recruit, I couldn't be a squad leader on Parris Island because they put the tall recruits up front. But the drill instructors made up for that in a way I hadn't even known existed. It came as a result of our Initial Strength Test.

In addition to being run all over that island, filling out forms, taking another physical, and getting a bunch of shots the first few days we were there, we also started one morning by taking that test.

We did sit-ups, push-ups, squat thrusts, agility tests, running, and chin-ups. That test gave the DIs an idea of each recruit's strong and weak points, and also weeded out those who were either too fat and weak to keep up with regular training or too skinny and weak to keep up with regular training.

Those recruits were sent to STB, the Special Training Branch, a real ball-buster of a place out by the rifle range where they got "fat bodies" and "skinny bodies" into shape. STB was not to be confused with the CCP, the Conditional Custody Platoon, a real ball-buster of a place out by the rifle range where they sent people for a few days or weeks if they screwed up real bad. STB and CCP made platoons going through the regular training cycle seem like heaven.

Recruits at STB stayed there until they either put on enough weight or took off enough weight and had developed sufficient strength to keep up with the normal training routine. Recruits at CCP stayed there until they became "motivated" to join a regular platoon in training.

When I took the test, I maxed most of the categories and did more chin-ups than anyone else in the platoon. Then, because Sparks was so pleased with my performance, he called me back to demonstrate chin-ups for the rest of the platoon, and I repeated the same number.

I was able to do that because at home my workout routine included three types of chin-ups—palms facing me, palms facing away from me, and behind the neck. I did 15 repetitions of each kind and repeated each type three times per workout, which means I did at least 135 chin-ups each workout.

So doing a second set in my Initial Strength Test was no big deal. Except, once again I was in the limelight. Sparks was really pleased because it was making him look good. So they picked me to be a house mouse! I'd never even heard the term before, but I was going to hear a lot of it in the next few weeks.

A house mouse had to clean up the DI's hut, which included sweeping, emptying ashtrays, washing coffee cups, and making the bunk for the DI who stayed on overnight duty. A house mouse also had to run errands for the drill instructors. A house mouse had to get dressed twice as fast as everyone else because the workload was doubled.

Each morning as soon as I had made my bunk, I also had to make the DI's bunk before the rest of the platoon was dressed for morning chow and be ready for whatever else might come up. The last thing in the world I wanted just then was to be constantly in the DI's line of sight. But that's what I got.

They each had a different way of getting your attention. Staff Sergeant Hale, for instance, would merely yell, "House mouse, front and center."

I'd respond, "Aye-aye, sir," and make tracks for the center of the squad bay.

Sparks would yell, "House mouse!"

I'd reply, "Here, sir," and he'd yell, "Get up here, fool."

Starbuck had a unique way of doing things. He'd yell, "House mouse," and I'd respond, "Here, sir."

Then Starbuck would yell back, "I know where you are, Winter. *I don't care where you are. Get up here*!"

As a result of all that attention I learned some things about being a Marine very quickly. For instance, Sparks felt it was his duty to make sure I learned as much about the proper positions and commands as could be taught indoors. He taught me the attention position, parade rest, at ease, left-face, right-face, and about-face.

Everything came easily to me except that "about-face" command. It requires a person to put the toe of their right foot behind the heel of their left foot, pivot to the right on the right toe and left heel, and end up facing in the exact opposite direction, at the perfect attention position with their heels together and toes facing outward at a 45-degree angle.

Right. For what seemed like forever, every time I tried that maneuver either my heels didn't come together at all or they faced odd angles, or something went wrong. And each time Sparks was right there.

"You trying to make me look bad, fool?"

"No, sir!"

"Then you better practice 'til you get it right! Understand?"

"Yes, sir!"

All the while he was explaining it to me, Sparks would have his fingers wrapped around my Adam's apple, massaging it none too gently.

"Something's wrong with your collar, crazy," he'd say.

"Sir, Private Winter will fix it, sir," I'd respond.

I started practicing my movements back by my bunk every chance I could, because I figured I wouldn't have a throat left by the time I graduated otherwise.

While all this was going on, the platoon was progressing through its training cycle. I had planned on being on Parris Island for twelve weeks, but again, Vietnam intervened, and the training cycle had been cut to eight weeks to process more recruits. They told us that in World War II the cycle had dropped to six weeks to keep up a fresh flow of replacements.

Ultimately, Vietnam would chew up more Marines than either World War II's island beachheads or Korea's three years of insanity, but in 1966 no one knew that.

I made some friends there. A guy named Joe DeSeve came down from Albany on the train with me, and we got along pretty well. In about our fourth week a recruit named William Laing joined our platoon.

He lived in Florida and had come to P.I. a month ahead of us. But Laing had been set back several weeks in his training, because of a phone call. Unfortunately, it wasn't authorized. Laing was walking a tour of guard duty near a phone booth, figured no one was watching, and slipped inside to call home. He got caught, set back, and was assigned to our platoon. Staff Sergeant Hale brought him in one day, introduced him by telling us that Laing had paid the price, and if we voted favorably, he'd let Laing join us. Naturally everyone said let him in, as if we really had a say in the matter, and Bill Laing became a permanent part of Platoon 214.

We got to be friends because of a laundry mixup. Two recruits from the platoon would take our clothes to the base laundry every few days and bring them back that night, freshly washed and dried. Each recruit's clothes were identified by laundry numbers—the same numbers one through eighty-five that had been assigned to us the first night—stamped inside them.

Somehow, while the utility shirts and trousers were being distributed one night, I got Laing's utility trousers and he got mine. While we were both slim, and our waists were about the same size, he was several inches taller, meaning his trousers were too long for me and mine were too short for him.

Laing brought up the problem right away. Starbuck brought it to the platoon's attention right away, and we all checked our laundry to see who had Laing's clothes. I did, we exchanged, and a friendship was formed.

At one point we planned to visit each other's homes once we got out in the regular Marine Corps, and Bill was looking forward to having a date with my girlfriend's sister, but for a lot of reasons that was never to be.

We continued on with our training, Sparks continued on with his individual instructions, and things stayed that way until our third week. Then something happened that deprived the platoon of Sparks' leadership and made Starbuck the central figure in our training.

Sparks left! No one knew why and we didn't know that he would return, we were just told one day that Sparks was gone, and we were introduced to his replacement. This DI was older, acted like he really didn't want the assignment, and the platoon didn't respond well to him.

Since Starbuck had natural leadership qualities, anyway, the platoon gravitated toward him, even if he was tough as hell. We'd also realized that Starbuck yelled a lot less if we followed orders correctly.

Starbuck had one standard that he said we all had to live up to if he was going to consider us Marines. "When you leave here, I want to know that I can count on you if you end up in a foxhole with me in Vietnam."

That recognition, that ability to be accepted by regular Marines, especially those who were as dedicated and professional as Starbuck, was what we strived for at Parris Island. Well, that was what most of us strived for.

There is a saying in the Marine Corps that "there's always that 10 percent." It means that despite the best efforts of the recruiters and DIs, there would always be some "shitbirds" who didn't want to learn.

Platoon 214 had its 10 percent. But they had to deal with Starbuck. One especially incurred his wrath, and at the same time set the stage for a confrontation that cemented my loyalty to Starbuck permanently.

Chapter 7

Not everyone in Platoon 214 was there because he wanted to be. A few were reservists, on duty for only six months, and some were draftees, among the first in the Marine Corps since Korea. Being in one of those categories immediately put you on bad terms with Starbuck, because he lived the Marine philosophy that nothing is more important than being a Marine.

Starbuck drilled this into us constantly with life stories, such as his decision to leave college to join the Marines. His decision to become a Recon, because that was the toughest duty, also was brought up regularly. Starbuck didn't like people who played the angles, always looked for the easy way out, took credit for work others did for them, or were egotistical grubbers who wanted everything for themselves and didn't make a significant contribution to the human race.

Fitting nicely into this category was a six-foot, 200-pound recruit who had a real bad attitude. The guy pissed Starbuck off right away. The guy was a bully, always pushing other recruits around when the DIs weren't looking. Although the recruit was large, he also was mostly shapeless fat. I tried to stay out of his way, but my confrontation with him came one night in the head, while we were passing in the narrow hall that led past the sinks and toilets and ended in the huge shower room.

It was just after Sparks had left, and Starbuck had the duty. We were allotted one hour of limited free time every night to shower, shave, shine brass, boots, and shoes, and write letters home. The squad bay was divided into two sections, the starboard side to the right of the hatchway to the DI hut, and the port side to the left.

Each night the DI on duty would command, "Port side into the head—starboard side free time."

Every night they alternated the side that went into the head first. After a half hour the DI would yell, "Clear the head," give the forty or so men in it about a minute to get out, and then send the opposite side in. On the night in question, the port side had gone in first, and Starbuck had given the command to clear the head. There was nothing that pissed Starbuck off more than somebody not obeying an order when it was given, or acting like Parris Island was some kind of resort where you did things at your own speed.

The fat recruit had exhibited the trait of not responding when an order was given, and Starbuck noticed it right off. After the port side had cleared the head, Starbuck ordered, "Starboard side into the head," and we all headed in.

Since my bunk was at the end of the squad bay, I was one of the last ones in, and as I entered the hall, I saw the recruit strolling out of the shower.

The fact that he was supposed to be back at his bunk already didn't even seem to faze him. He decided to take up the whole hall, leaving only enough room for me to step aside. But I didn't like the idea of being pushed around, so I kept coming. And he kept coming.

I could see the look on his face change, first from calm self-assurance, to anger—and then to doubt as I kept coming. This all took place in less than three seconds and we kept advancing, and then—*kabooom!* I'd heard that sound before, not too long ago, and here it was again, with the same source. Starbuck!

Directly across the hall from the entrance to the DI hut was a set of double doors that led into the hallway in the head. The doors had glass windows so the DIs could keep an eye on the head as well as the squad bay. Starbuck had been watching, and waiting. He didn't like that big recruit, and just as we'd gotten within fighting range, he came blasting through again.

He swept me aside and headed for the recruit. "You want to push somebody, maggot? Try pushing me! Go ahead, try me!"

Starbuck's face was red, his eyes were flashing, and he was coiled, like a rattlesnake ready to strike. The recruit shrank from him, even though he was taller and outweighed Starbuck.

He sent the guy back to the squad bay with orders to run in place forever and turned to leave. As he passed, Starbuck glanced down at me. I hadn't moved from the edge of the wall where I'd been thrown, and I was standing at attention. I looked at Starbuck's eyes, expecting to catch holy hell for instigating a fight, but I saw something else instead.

Grudging respect is probably the closest description. I don't know if I would have won that fight. I might have gotten my ass kicked. But that didn't matter. I wouldn't have backed down, and because of that I learned something else about Parris Island.

Being a Marine is as much a matter of the heart and mind as it is the body. Being big helps, but there was a place in the Marine Corps for a smaller man with a lot of heart. And for the first time, I knew I had the qualities to graduate from Parris Island. My determination to do the best job I could was cemented that night. And for the first time, I wasn't terrified of Starbuck.

In the following weeks there would be many more lessons from him.

While Starbuck didn't mind getting physical occasionally, there was much more depth to him, and as time went by on Parris Island he taught us lessons that ranged from the practical to the philosophical. He taught us how to march and how to shoot, but he also taught us about life.

There were quite a few teenagers in the platoon, and some still were suffering from adolescent acne. He taught them what foods to eat, which ones to stay away from, and how to clean their skin and pores to avoid pimples. He taught us how to shave, once down and again back up with the double-edged Gillettes we were issued, to make sure we got all the whiskers. He gave us more than one lecture on what to expect from wives and girlfriends when we became Marines and would inevitably be sent overseas.

Starbuck taught us about our social life after Parris Island, too. "If you're out on liberty, don't give the MPs any shit. If you're in a bar and they come in, mind your own business, drink your beer, and shut up. If they ask for your ID card, give it to them, and don't run your sewers [mouths] or you'll end up in the brig for the night."

Starbuck also taught us self-reliance, pride, and dignity. He taught us to set goals for ourselves, short and long term, and not to waver from them until they were reached. He taught us a sense of moral and ethical responsibility. And there was one other lesson, an important lesson, one that I've sometimes thought I'd forgotten, only to remember in a time of need.

He said, "When things are so bad that they're too tough for everyone else, I smile, because then, they're just right for me."

I knew it was a mind game, a way of coping with the harsher aspects of life. But then, life has plenty of harsher aspects, and we all need to have some way to deal with them. Otherwise, we're left to the mercy of emotions that can cripple us when we need most to be strong.

Starbuck relayed that lesson during a lecture on something else and I'd remembered it, not knowing I'd have to apply it soon in my own life. But it came in handy just a few weeks later as I walked fire watch late at night. Fire watch was a walking tour of the squad bay, the head, and the hallway by the DI's hut, divided into two-hour shifts and ran from lights out until reveille.

Every two hours a recruit would wake up his replacement, and the recruit who got the last shift had to wake up the DI. My tour was from midnight to 2:00 a.m. I walked through the head, making sure no one was in there smoking a cigarette when he wasn't supposed to be. I went out through the squad bay, listening to night sounds, wondering about all those people, who they really were and how they'd gotten to Parris Island with me.

Some guys stirred, rolled over, talked in their sleep, or cut farts. It was winter and the windows and doors were closed tight. We'd had the first snowfall in recent memory a few days earlier, and lots of cold rain. But shutting up the barracks made them smell like a stable, especially at night. The sleep talking was interesting. One guy called out, "Mom? Mom?"

Another guy was mumbling, "I want some ice cream."

It was dark, the only illumination coming from streetlights outside and dim red bulbs by the exit hatchways.

"These guys are supposed to be tough," I was thinking. "They want to be Marines. So how come they want ice cream and their mothers?"

I walked out in the main hallway and then back into the head. I went to a window in the section where the sinks were located and watched the roadway that led to the recruit receiving barracks and the causeway that led to the outside world. Four buses came blasting in, all loaded with new recruits, just like I'd been a few weeks earlier. It seemed like a lifetime ago.

"Poor bastards. They don't know what they're in for," I thought.

Later, back in the head, I watched the empty buses leave. For the first time in a while, I wanted to be going with them. I'd received what amounted to a Dear John letter from my girlfriend. It hadn't been entirely unexpected, but it wasn't a nice experience regardless. In fact, I felt pretty lousy. I felt like a jerk.

This had all started because my folks forbade me to see her, and like a smart-ass I'd taken things to an extreme. Now she couldn't even wait eight weeks for me to come home. It was lonely there that night, as are all late-night guard posts, and I had a strange kind of longing inside. Perhaps I should have handled things differently, with my family, with my girlfriend. I really didn't know.

My thoughts were interrupted by the doors from the hallway swinging open, and Starbuck came into the head, dressed in his skivvies, going to take a piss. I snapped to attention and figured I was in deep shit for screwing off.

"Carry on, Winter," Starbuck snorted.

I moved out into the squad bay and then into the hallway by the DI hut. I was glad he hadn't yelled, and frankly, I didn't think it was appropriate to stand around while a DI was taking a piss. I mean, after all, they were next to God in our lives, and of all the things that have been written, spoken, or painted about God, no one has mentioned how He takes a piss. I guess it's just one of those things you don't talk about.

Starbuck came out and I snapped to attention again.

"At ease," he growled.

"Homesick?" He said it with a sneer, and that gravelly voice. He made you feel that any form of homesickness was the worst type of disease imaginable.

"Yes, sir. Got a Dear John letter."

Starbuck had his own ideas about love and the Marine Corps. He had a girlfriend somewhere, and I think she was a woman Marine. A few days earlier another drill instructor had called loudly to Starbuck while we were marching by on the company street.

"I hear you got a letter," the DI had said. "You going to get married?" he'd asked.

"Yeah," Starbuck answered, "in about twenty years."

The point was made. The Marine Corps came first. Everything else was secondary. That night he made the same point to me.

"Forget it, Winter. There are other things to think about now."

I said, "Yes, sir!" without really meaning it. But after he left, while I continued my measured pace through the dark barracks, I thought long and hard about what he'd said.

I realized then that the brotherhood I was entering was a strict and unyielding group in ways I hadn't anticipated. The Marine Corps came before all else and answered only to the orders of its senior officers and the President of the United States.

To be a Marine, in the strictest sense of the word, you have to be willing to forsake family and friends, be ready to move to faraway places on practically no notice and face the possibility of sudden and violent death. The Marine Corps is held up to constant scrutiny and receives far more than its fair share of criticism, often from those who can't qualify as a Marine.

But Starbuck's lesson was obvious. To be a Marine, you take it all without complaint and continue on with your mission. That is why you become a Marine.

So I continued my watch, trying to emulate his toughness, remembering that lesson he had taught us earlier. I kept walking, trying to apply it.

Eventually it worked. By the time I woke my replacement, I had put the letter behind me, buried it in that vault, and started looking to the future. It was uncertain, bound to be dangerous, and I didn't know where it would take me.

But it was better than dwelling on the past. That was the first time I applied his lesson. It has come back to me many times as the years have slipped by. Occasionally, it still does.

didn't matter. The woman gunnery sergeant caught the look going between them and showed immediately that she was as tough on her recruits as our DIs were on us.

"You like that, sweetheart?" she yelled at the blonde. "Well, forget it! The only thing he wants from you is pussy. He wants to fuck you. But he ain't going to. Now move!"

Everyone had stopped what they were doing during this exchange, and that girl's face turned about fifty shades of red. She moved out quickly. That afternoon showed me that no one escapes the wrath of the DIs on Parris Island, and as harsh as it seemed, it actually made life out in the real Marine Corps somewhat easier.

After being exposed to that place, I figured anything had to be easier. As difficult as it was, however, it was during the second week of training that I realized that even on Parris Island life could fall into a routine. From what began as a series of endless days filled with shouting, marching, constant misery, and the pain of being turned into a Marine, physically and mentally, a pattern developed.

After we learned the routine, and the DIs knew who among us were motivated and trying hard, the days and weeks began to slip by. First it was the initial training phase, with marching instruction and classes on military history, the M-14 rifle, the .45-caliber pistol, and the proper way to wear the various uniforms.

We learned the rank structure. Enlisted men are ranked E (for enlisted) 1 through 9. An E-1 is a private, an E-2 is a private first class, an E-4 is a corporal, an E-5 a sergeant, up to E-9, a sergeant major or master gunnery sergeant.

Officers were ranked O (for officer) 1 through 10, an O-1 being a second lieutenant and an O-10 being a four-star general. There were tests, constant physical training, the obstacle course, the confidence course, running forever it seemed, drown-proofing—a term used to describe swimming techniques, so we'd be able to survive hours in the ocean if anything happened while on ship—hand-to-hand combat training, and bayonet drills.

Starbuck was there through all of it. Sometimes leading the runs, usually going backward faster than we were running forward, sneering at us, ridiculing our weaknesses, taunting us to do better than we ever thought we could. Other times he'd be in the background, watching, listening, while Hale or Sparks led the platoon.

He never missed a trick and sometimes seemed to materialize out of thin air when someone was goofing off. We got lectures, sometimes from the DIs, sometimes from other instructors or officers. But Sparks gave us a breather once after he returned to the platoon, and allowed us to laugh when he was giving two recruits from Georgia a hard time.

In the eight weeks we were on Parris Island we moved four times. First, on the night we arrived there, then to a barracks by the rifle range, where we lived for a week while we served on mess (kitchen) duty, then to another barracks for two weeks while we learned how to shoot M-14s and .45s, and finally back to a barracks in the 2d Battalion training area for our final two weeks of training.

Sparks noticed that two of the recruits always ended up bunking with each other.

"You two in love?" he asked one day.

There were immediate denials.

"Well then, I'd better not come out here at night and hear any springs squeaking or anybody telling anybody else that something feels good!" Sparks said.

By that time we had been on the island nearly two months and were allowed to laugh.

Hale also had some good ways to illustrate how we were expected to handle the other problems we encountered as recruits. Occasionally a recruit would be so disheartened by the tough regimen that he'd try to escape through the salt flats that lie between the island and the mainland. In addition to reports of sharks and alligators, there also was quicksand in those salt flats, and several recruits had drowned in a nearby stream a few years earlier on a training exercise.

Hale told us, "If anyone is thinking of escaping, come tell me. I'll draw you a map. I'd rather you got to the mainland because they'll catch you in Beaufort anyway, and I don't want to be there in that mess looking for you."

Hale had a point.

"How far do you think you'll get with bald heads and wearing green utilities?"

Hale said only one recruit had ever run away from the island and not been accounted for. It may have been that the guy really made it and was hiding out somewhere, Hale said.

"But I think he got caught in the quicksand and drowned, or he got carried away by a shark or alligator and eaten."

That was enough for us. But a few weeks later, when we were assigned guard duty, a new recruit did try to run away. One of our guys caught him, and we heard that the runaway was sent to the brig.

During the initial training phase I had another glimpse of the brotherhood that is the Marine Corps, in an incident that also solidified my respect for Starbuck. We were at the sick bay, getting some shots, after which a navy corpsman was drawing blood samples from our arms.

There is supposed to be a link between the corpsmen and the Marines, since they depend on each other in combat. But this particular corpsman must have had a sadistic streak.

He told us, "Grab your right arm at the elbow joint with your left hand, and bring your right fist up to your shoulder."

The point I guess was to force your veins to bulge so he could find them with the needle when he took the samples. Naturally someone forgot or just wasn't paying attention. We had been standing in line, with that solitary corpsman taking samples one at a time, and finally the private who didn't follow directions got his turn. Then the corpsman decided to play DI.

"Can't you follow directions, Private? Don't you understand orders, Private? What are you, Private, some kind of shitbird?"

The recruit initially tried to answer, but the real problem was not with what the corpsman was saying, it was with what the corpsman was doing. He'd punctuate each question with a jab of the needle into the recruit's arm, then withdraw it, leaving a stream of blood.

"I can't find your vein, asshole! Here, let's try this spot. Oh, sorry, how about this spot?"

It went on like that for a minute or so, and the recruit looked like he was going to pass out. He kept saying, "Please, sir, please don't do that."

He was looking bad, and everyone was mad, but we had been instructed to call everyone at Parris Island "sir" and not give lip to anyone, so no one said anything.

The incident came to a sudden end, kind of the way World War II came to an end—with a major explosion. The explosion was Starbuck, who had been out of the room for a minute, but had slipped quietly back in and in an instant had seen what was transpiring.

Starbuck descended on that corpsman like a tidal wave.

"What the fuck are you doing to that recruit? Get that fucking needle out of that man's arm!"

It was great! In two seconds that corpsman went from smirking to terrified! He looked at Starbuck's face and saw what we had all come to recognize in the last ten days. If you pissed that man off, you could see your destiny in his eyes. It was short, and extremely unpleasant.

A navy doctor, hearing the commotion, came running in, took one look at that recruit's arm, and hustled that corpsman out of there with Starbuck towering over him all the way.

Another corpsman took over, cleaned off the blood, and coolly finished taking samples. It was a nasty experience, especially for the recruit, but that day we saw a glimpse of what most of us had been seeking when we came to Parris Island.

We weren't Marines yet; we were a long way from it. But at least we were on the bottom rung of the ladder and working our way up. That was better, Starbuck often pointed out, than not being on the ladder at all. It was certainly better, he said, than being a "squid," as sailors were called, or "doggie," as they still referred to soldiers, and a hell of a lot better than being what he called a "scumbag civilian!"

Starbuck came back after a while, checked on the recruit, and gave us a short talk on the fact that no place on earth is perfect, and you have to expect assholes no matter where you go. Then he chewed us out for slouching too much, made us double-time run back to the barracks, and ordered a round of push-ups just for good measure.

But Starbuck's reaction in the sick bay was what everyone remembered, and we took his "punishment" with an inspired attitude.

After three weeks of the initial training phase, we were sent to the rifle range on the far side of the island for three weeks. We were housed in newer barracks, which were more open, with two platoons in one squad bay.

We were assigned to one week of mess duty at the rifle range mess hall. Our normal 5:00 a.m. wake-up was pushed up an hour so we could be at the mess hall, with morning chow ready to go, when the other platoons come in. It was dirty, tiring work and wasn't made any easier by the fact that we were getting an hour less sleep each day.

The mess cooks at the rifle range had what they called the "tunnel," a two-by-two-foot space between rows of back-to-back stoves in the galley. Recruits who incurred their wrath were ordered to crawl into the tunnel and clean up all the grease back there. Only one recruit in our platoon was sent down the tunnel.

I was assigned as a DI waiter, because on P.I. the DIs didn't have to get their own meals, or their own coffee, or glass of milk, or anything else if they had a recruit to do it. Being a DI waiter was okay, but often the DIs in charge of different platoons would hassle the recruits they didn't know in a form of insider-DI competition.

God help the recruit who screwed up, cause there'd be two kinds of hell to pay—from the DI who was busting on you as well as from your own DI for embarrassing him. Hale, however, devised a way to bust on some of the other DIs, using recruits in our platoon.

He started spreading a tale that he let his recruits call him "Gus" instead of "sir." During the noon meal one day he called a recruit over to a table where several DIs were eating.

"What do the recruits in Platoon 214 call me?" Hale asked the private.

"Gus, sir!" was the immediate response.

The other DIs just looked at Hale, their eyes bugging out and their mouths open. They couldn't believe it. Of course, no one told the other DIs that Hale had instructed us the night before to give that answer if we were asked.

While there were some light moments, work at the mess hall was nearly nonstop. After each meal all the tables and chairs were pushed to one side and the entire mess deck, the area where the troops ate, would be washed and rinsed completely, as was the entire galley area.

All pots, pans, and dishes were scrubbed clean, and the place was set up for the next meal. It was a lot of work, yet Marine Corps mess halls are the epitome of cleanliness.

To avoid getting stuck with swabbing duty after the meals, I volunteered to work in the spud locker and the salad locker. That's where the potatoes get peeled and salads for the next meal are prepared. It was good duty, because unlike cartoon displays of potato-peeling in the service, the job really is done by a large machine instead of a hapless private with a knife.

Also, a corporal was in charge of the spud locker, and since he had recently been busted back to corporal from sergeant for hitting another higher-ranking sergeant in a fight, he wasn't opposed to giving us some slack time between meals.

The corporal said if we gave him the money, he'd buy batteries for his transistor radio, and we could listen to it if no one was around. That was a big deal, because we hadn't had contact with the outside world, except for letters, since we'd arrived.

So the three of us who were in the spud locker pooled our funds—we got paid at Parris Island, but most of the money was kept on the books and we were allocated only enough to buy necessities—and the corporal made good on his promise.

To this day the one song I remember from that time is B. J. Thomas singing "I'm So Lonesome I Could Cry." It just seemed very appropriate back then. The corporal also had a good sense of humor and one day decided to use it on one of the guys in our platoon.

The recruit had a perpetual bemused expression on his face, primarily because that was the way his face was formed, but the DIs thought he was always laughing at them. That pissed them off.

One Saturday they made him run all over the island, chased by a jeep, to "motivate" him and wipe the smile off his face. He was definitely motivated by the end of the day, but his expression never changed.

That same recruit became the corporal's target because of the simple biological function of taking a leak. One thing you learned to do early on at Parris Island was to control your bladder. There generally were set times throughout the day when a platoon could make a head call en masse. The DIs didn't like having their training schedule interrupted by anybody with weak kidneys, and they also wanted us to develop a sense of discipline, even in our bathroom habits.

It took a real emergency to get to a head if it wasn't an authorized head call. But the recruit went to the corporal and asked, "Sir, request permission to make an emergency head call."

Well, that was it for the spud locker corporal.

"Is it a real emergency, Private?"

"Yes, sir!"

"Do you know what an emergency vehicle sounds like, Private?"

"They have sirens, sir!"

"Can you make a sound like a siren, Private?"

The recruit obliged with a passable siren wail.

"Private, if this is an emergency, I want you to turn on your siren, keep it going all the way to the head, all the time you're in there, and all the way back. Do you understand?"

"Yes, sir!"

"Permission granted."

So off went the young recruit, running all the way across the mess deck, through the galley, and into the head at the rear of the mess hall wailing like an ambulance.

And he came back the same way. Everybody was dumbfounded at first, and then cracked up laughing. The recruit may not have liked what he had to do, but at least he got to go to the head. The only bad part of the whole incident was the fact that the corporal got chewed out royally for it.

It was a fact of life that Parris Island drill instructors could give recruits all the hassles they wanted. It was their job. But, as that navy corpsman had learned a month earlier, anyone else caught trifling with a DI's recruits was headed for trouble.

Even though the corporal got hassled, that emergency head call was only one of a number of incidents during our training that broke the strain of constant pressure and taught us how to laugh even in adverse situations.

That same corporal figured in another unexpected situation while we still were on mess duty, this time involving a lance corporal and instructions on making Jell-O. It's hard to screw up Jell-O, but that guy did. It was green and so hard that you couldn't stick a fork into it, much less a spoon.

It couldn't be served, so we played basketball with it. Eventually an irate master sergeant discovered what was going on and we were ordered to throw it all out. Nonetheless it was fun while it lasted, especially when we put a limited amount of it out on the chow line and watched other recruits try to eat it.

Occasionally there were other incidents on the island that from a distance seem funny. But while we were there, they weren't funny at all. Each of the DIs had his own style of punishment if the platoon screwed up. And one person screwing up was sufficient justification for the whole platoon being punished. We were being taught to work as a team, and everyone learned to look out for themselves and each other at the same time.

For example, Starbuck came out of the barracks one extremely cold morning after ordering us to fall out with black gloves on for marching instruction, known as close order drill. They said we were enduring one of the coldest winters on the island in twenty years, and we'd even had a snow squall. That snow actually made me homesick.

But as a result of that cold, our rifles, especially the metal parts, could just about give a recruit a case of frostbite when bare hands came in contact with them. Therefore, the luxury of marching with gloves on was one not to be carelessly thrown away.

Each drill instructor had a unique quality to his voice and a unique way of giving commands and calling cadence while we marched. Starbuck would start his command as he came down the sidewalk on his way to the company street.

"Plaaaattooooon! AAAAAttennnntion!"

On that morning Starbuck gave the command, looked the platoon over, and saw a sea of black-gloved hands—except for one.

"Forget something, Private?" he asked.

"Sir, the private forgot to wear gloves, sir!"

I was hoping maybe he'd send the guy back in for his gloves.

"Take them off," Starbuck ordered.

"Put your right glove in your right front field jacket pocket, and your left glove in your left front field jacket pocket."

We spent the next several hours marching around the parade deck with cold rifles and cold hands. The next time out everyone wore gloves.

Hale often ordered a mass exercise session in the event of a screwup, but with a twist. Looking miserable on the drill field was usually good for a bunch of push-ups.

Hale would order, "Push-ups, ready—begin. Continue until I get tired. And I'm not doing any."

Hale also liked to have us do side-straddle hops—jumping jacks—in our squad bay if he was unhappy with us, with the unusual command, "Side-straddle hops. Forever. Ready—begin."

Hale even made the whole platoon get into the shower room at one time and do side-straddle hops. We didn't all fit in there and were knocking each other senseless, but he made his point.

In our second week at the rifle range, Sparks returned to the platoon. We never were told what he was gone for, but Sparks was sporting new sergeant chevrons.

Although any spontaneous show of emotion was frowned on there, the whole platoon cheered when Sparks entered the squad bay and announced that he was back. We had never gotten used to his replacement, and although Sparks acted as though we had broken some kind of code for cheering—he demanded to know whether he had to go back "to get my stick" to straighten us out—you could see he was pleased with our reaction.

One of the first things Sparks did on his return was check out my "about-face."

I did it perfectly, and my Adam's apple was saved.

Sparks also had unique ways of calling attention to what he was teaching. If he was giving a lecture, Sparks would prowl up and down the squad bay telling recruits, "Eye-fuck me, eye-fuck me, boy! You want to learn something that can save your ass in Vietnam, or you want to die?"

But it was his replacement who had the most unusual games for us to play if we screwed up.

"Flood and air raid" was one of his big favorites. In the flood, everything on the floor—deck—had to be moved up to the top bunk. This included two sets of footlockers, seabags, boots, and people. In the air raid, everything that was on the top bunk, including two people, had to get under the bunk.

The DI would yell "Flood," and everyone would scramble to get everything on the top bunk before he got pissed off. Then he'd yell "Air raid," and everything would be thrown under the bunks.

He'd go on like that for an hour, and it was exhausting! His games were one of the reasons we were so happy to see Sparks return.

But Starbuck was the most physical of the DIs and had the most unusual games. Outside, if someone missed a movement on the drill field, Starbuck would order him to do push-ups. If the recruit was a wise-ass, someone who was always screwing up, Starbuck would step on his hands while he was exercising, just to make sure the lesson was learned.

But he also had one other way of making sure a lesson sank in, especially if a recruit broke a cardinal rule, such as disobeying an order or lying to him. He'd deck you.

A recruit who bunked directly across from me caught the full force of Starbuck's ire during mail call about a week before graduation. Mail call preceded free time, which meant it also preceded the head call, so nobody was allowed to go to the head during mail call.

Starbuck had a set routine. He'd walk up and down the squad bay with the letters in his hands. He'd call a name, the recruit would answer, and Starbuck would order, "Get up here!"

The recruit would then come to attention in front of Starbuck, the letter would be held out, the recruit would slap it between his two hands in a clapping motion, step back one step, say "Aye-aye, sir!", do an about-face, and, at an order from Starbuck, run back to his bunk.

Starbuck didn't like any distractions during this time. But the private had to take a piss. Behind all of our bunks, each recruit had a galvanized steel bucket. They had been distributed early on, and contained "782 Gear," which included cartridge belts, canteens, tent poles, tent pegs, and related equipment.

The gear was distributed either on our cartridge belts or in packs, so the buckets usually were empty. Once in a great while, if we were being rewarded for something, the DIs would let us pull the buckets out from behind the bunks and sit down on them for a few minutes.

But the private had to take a piss! And there was a lot of mail that night!

So when Starbuck went to the other end of the squad bay, the private snuck behind his bunk and pissed in his bucket. But he didn't make it all the way back out front without Starbuck seeing him. All of a sudden Starbuck was there, glaring down at him.

"What were you doing behind that bunk, Private?"

"Straightening my footlocker, sir."

Starbuck's face went deep red, and he suddenly threw the mail he was holding all over the squad bay.

"I'm going to ask you one more time, Private. What were you doing behind that bunk?"

"Straightening my footlocker, sir!"

There was a deathly silence. Then Starbuck's right foot shot backward, smashing into a garbage can positioned between my bunk and him. He dented it and it flew into my shins.

But while everyone was watching that happen, Starbuck had simultaneously brought his right fist upward in a short but extremely powerful punch that caught the private right in the solar plexus.

He went up in the air and came down on the floor between the bunks. He couldn't catch his breath, his face was mottled purple, red, and white, and he was just short of crying.

"You were grab-assing [fooling around] back there, weren't you?" Starbuck roared.

"Yes, sir."

"You should have admitted that in the first place," Starbuck said as he walked away. He then continued with the mail call as though nothing had happened.

The private threw the piss in his bucket out the window later during free time. It may seem like a harsh punishment, but actually I figured he was lucky. If Starbuck had ever found out what was really going on back there, he probably would have poured that bucket of piss all over the private.

Mail call seemed to create the correct formula for discord, and a few nights later it came my way. I was called to receive a letter and required to perform the standard procedure—slap the letter between your hands, step back, say "Aye-aye, sir," and do an about-face.

Well, I did everything except the "Aye-aye, sir!" and Starbuck noticed.

"Forget something, Winter?" he asked in that deep growl.

"Sir, Private Winter forgot to say 'Aye-aye, sir!' "

"Well, maybe this will help you remember!" he said. And with that I got a kick from one of those big boots of his, right in the ass.

He hit me across the butt with the inside of his foot, though, so while the kick literally lifted me off the floor, it didn't hurt that much. But as I was taking off to run back to my bunk, I glanced out of the corner of my eye and, out in the hallway, in full view of what had just happened, stood our platoon commander, Lieutenant Pulaski.

It could have been very bad news for Starbuck because the DIs were absolutely forbidden to hit recruits. But Pulaski just walked away as if he hadn't seen anything. Starbuck later walked down to my bunk, stood in front of me, and asked, "Did that kick hurt you, Winter?"

"What kick, sir?" I responded.

Starbuck just looked, with the same kind of look he'd given me that night in the head, smiled, and walked off without saying anything further.

What the hell? I figured that if I could take a shot in the chin from Dad, I wasn't going to let a kick in the ass spoil Starbuck's career.

Chapter 9

And then it was over! For all of the pain and aggravation, the wrenching process of changing from a civilian to a Marine finally came to an end.

We returned from the rifle range and were given two more weeks of instruction, our final training phase. We marched to the Elliott's Beach section of the island for our first bivouac, took some tests, and graduated.

At Elliott's Beach, I was interviewed by the DIs for possible meritorious promotion to private first class and was notified two days before graduation that I had been selected. That honor was bestowed on less than 10 percent of the graduating recruits, and I was very proud. I felt that I could look my family in the eye and say I had done a good job. I also felt that I was living up to my mental promise to Starbuck, to be the best I could be.

In the last two weeks we were given final fittings for our formal uniforms, and I discovered that I had gained thirteen pounds at Parris Island. I would spend the next four years within a few pounds each way of 138.

The platoon was relieved that we finally were allowed to wear starched utility uniforms, open at the throat, could blouse our trouser legs so we didn't look like dummies, and starch our covers so they looked sharp, and were issued our dog tags, the identification tags on a silver chain that said who we were so our remains could be identified if we were killed.

Starbuck kept up his unique brand of instruction, telling us one time that dog tags "used to have a slot in them, so they could slide them over your top teeth on the battlefield, kick you in the bottom jaw so they'd be locked in place, and keep going."

He also touched on a matter that I was close to, lecturing us once on encounters we ultimately would have with people back home, those who had negative attitudes about the military, and Marines in particular.

"Whenever I hear those people bragging, I just look them in the face and say, 'Me? I'm just a Marine! All I do is fight and get drunk!' " A few recruits laughed at that, but Starbuck snarled, "Shut up!"

Some people may have believed that image of Marines, but Starbuck had already taught us that there was so much more. Starbuck had definite ideas on how we should appear in public, telling us a Marine should keep good posture, walk with hands out of pockets, no cigarettes dangling from our lips, looking straight ahead, not eyeballing everything along the way.

Yet a Marine keeps alert, so he knows what is before him when he reaches it. He said a Marine doesn't back down when challenged, minds his own business when he should, and speaks the truth when called upon. A Marine is disciplined, principled, and can do the job in half the time, with nearly nothing for tools, while others with all the tools never finish.

I would later learn that not every Marine lives up to that credo. But at that time and in that place, I wanted to believe Starbuck. From the reactions around me, I figured most of the remainder of the platoon wanted to also. By the time I left that island, I was absolutely convinced that it was better to die a young Marine, having reached that pinnacle in life, than to live to one hundred as a lesser form of humanity.

The night before we graduated I was picked out of the platoon and asked to go to the base public affairs office to do a radio commercial about my training at Parris Island. Before I got to do my recording, however, Starbuck told me that my family had arrived at the base and was waiting for me at the battalion reception center.

"You don't really need to be on the radio do you, Winter?" he asked.

"No, sir!" I answered, knowing full well what was expected before I spoke.

In a minute I was in a car being driven by a DI from another platoon, on my way to see the family I had left two months earlier. I was really anxious to see their reaction. The reception area was in a stone building with wide stone steps. I ran up the stairs into a large reception hall and stood for a minute, looking around.

A drill instructor approached me and asked, "Looking for someone, Private?"

Maybe it was because I had been promoted to private first class. Maybe it was because of the radio commercial, or maybe because I was graduating in the morning. Maybe I was just getting cocky. But I didn't come to attention, and I had a slight smile on my face as I said, "I'm looking for my parents, sir!"

God, did that guy jump!

"Lock them up, Private! Wipe that smile off your face! Since when do you stand at ease when you talk to a drill instructor?"

He reamed me for about a minute and then told me to check out a small room adjacent to the main reception hall. I did as I was told, in correct military manner this time, and still couldn't find my family. I turned to leave the small room to go back to the large room, and the DI who had hassled me was entering with my mother on his arm.

He gave me a look, and I locked into the attention position without a word, and he said, "Here's your son, ma'am."

He gave me another look, like, "Don't slip up again, maggot!" and left.

Outside, Dad, Nancy, and my younger brother Larry were waiting.

"You should have seen what we just saw!" Dad said after we greeted. "Some drill instructor was giving a guy a real working over. Boy, if that had been my son he was talking to, I'd have kicked his ass!"

I just looked at Dad for a minute. Then I realized how much I had changed, at least physically. My own parents hadn't recognized me! Which in a way was a relief, because if they didn't know me, then at least no one else did, either!

I didn't appreciate being chewed out in public, but that was Parris Island, and that was the Marine Corps. You don't ever forget who you are, or what you are.

"That *was* me, Dad!" I said.

He just looked, and for a minute didn't believe it.

We had a nice reunion, Dad laughed about the changes I had gone through in such a short time, and about my getting reamed by the drill instructor. Then they returned to their motel on the mainland in Beaufort and I returned to the barracks to spend my last night as a Marine recruit.

Graduation day was clear and cold, and to accommodate the parents and other relatives who came, the ceremonies were held inside the base theater. I was disappointed because we had practiced for an outside graduation, and I wanted the thrill of marching past that reviewing stand, a Marine at last.

I was singled out at the ceremony along with the others from our series who had been meritoriously promoted, and, finally, we were addressed by the commanding officer as "Marines."

Later we took pictures of the family and their new Marine in front of the Iwo Jima statue, and I showed them our barracks, the mess hall, the rifle range, everything that had been part of our training there.

We ate at the base snack bar, bought some souvenirs at the post exchange—PX—and talked about my future. Mom was still pretty unsure about it all, but Dad was proud, really proud.

We had a meeting of the minds there, I think. He told me that my barracks looked just like the ones at Camp Sampson in New York where he had trained after joining the navy. He told me how his stomach had been as hard as rocks after his boot camp from all the running and sit-ups they'd done.

I showed him the obstacle course and the confidence course, and all the time kept looking for Starbuck so I could introduce them. I wanted Dad to meet Starbuck more than anything, but once the graduation was over, he disappeared.

Hale didn't, however, and I convinced him to have his picture taken with me, and Sparks stayed around for a while, too. The family also got to meet him before they had to leave.

But Starbuck didn't show up even that night, our last at Parris Island. The platoon talked a bit and got some last-minute instructions. Buses were scheduled to take us to Camp Geiger in North Carolina the next morning for a month of infantry training.

I figured all the drill instructors would be there to see us off. We went to chow, returned, straightened up the barracks for the last time, and stowed all of our gear in our seabags. I kept looking for Starbuck.

He never came.

Hale was there to see us off. He walked us right up to the door of the bus. And I kept looking for Starbuck until the motor started and the driver put the bus in gear. I was finally headed off that island, a much different person than the one who had entered such a short time before.

I couldn't call Starbuck my friend, because that wasn't allowed, and it wasn't the way things were done. He wasn't a confidant or a drinking buddy. He was a leader, and a teacher. He was rough, but in the two months I knew him, Starbuck in his own way had shown me how to handle a lot of life's rough spots.

He taught me to stand up to the things you can change,

and to handle the things you can't change with dignity, pride, and fortitude.

The bus started moving. Staff Sergeant Hale was the only one of our three drill instructors on the sidewalk below. On impulse, I opened a window, and in front of a half dozen other DIs yelled, "Good-bye, Gus!"

Hale laughed, smiled, and waved, while the other DIs just looked startled. The bus turned the corner, and I finally understood.

Starbuck wasn't coming. It just wasn't part of his view on the Marine Corps. You do your job, then look to the future and go on to something else. He had his next assignment.

Vietnam was his destiny, too, and Starbuck was already on his way. But I'd wanted to say thank you. And even if Starbuck had given me the standard response, "Don't thank me, Marine, it's my job!," I would have told him, "Thanks for doing it well."

I'd only wanted to tell Starbuck good-bye.

I never saw him again.

PART II

Chapter 10

The next nine months alternately seemed to drag on forever, or fly by so fast I couldn't keep up with them. After Parris Island, I spent one month up at Camp Geiger for infantry training. Thousands of Marines were stationed at Camp Geiger, and the base was overflowing. We were sent to a small annex near the rifle range.

Most of the time we were at Geiger, mostly the month of March, it was cold and it rained—a perfect introduction to the life of an infantryman. We were exposed to a tremendous number of infantry skills while there, however.

I learned to assemble and disassemble the M-1 rifle and the M-60 machine gun, and how to fire both of them. We fired flamethrowers and rifle grenades, threw hand grenades, and learned to use 3.5-inch rocket launchers, which had replaced the older-vintage bazookas. We were taught how to use compasses and read terrain maps, then we were sent out in the woods and swamps to demonstrate what we knew.

The day and night compass courses were our introduction to the type of terrain and conditions we would encounter in Vietnam, and I soon found I could function well in the swamps. We learned how to camouflage ourselves so we could remain hidden, and were introduced to infiltration and surveillance techniques.

We learned how to handle explosives such as mines, detonation cord, and blasting caps, how to set up day and night ambushes, the intricacies of street fighting in "Combat City," and fired what were called the "John Wayne" courses. These consisted of trails with a series of pop-up targets and obstacles that we shot at with our M-1s.

We walked the trails in patrol formations with our rifles held in front of us, diagonally across our chests about shoulder height—a position that was called "high port"—so we could fire from the hip or shoulder with equal speed in any direction.

On the John Wayne course, a corporal instructor performed a feat of marksmanship that I have yet to see equaled. A large ditch, some twenty to thirty feet deep and about fifty feet across, was on the left side of the trail. The corporal took an M-1, loaded an eight-round clip, and pointed out a stick, about a half inch in diameter and a foot long, lying on the far bank.

He walked back along the trail, reversed himself, and came toward the ditch again. When he was opposite the stick the corporal spun, aimed the M-1 from the hip, and began firing. Each round struck just below the stick, knocking it up in the air, effectively making it "walk" up the bank! He was firing the rifle in the semiautomatic mode, meaning the trigger had to be squeezed for each shot, and as the bolt pulled each spent shell from the rifle chamber, it would eject it in a short arc.

What was even more amazing than the corporal's marksmanship was that the last round had been fired from the rifle before the shell from the first bullet hit the ground! That corporal was a good example of the caliber of instructor that I encountered at Camp Geiger.

We learned that the life of an infantryman is not pleasant, and many skills must be learned if one is to have a decent chance of survival in combat. We learned under adverse conditions, the weather being one of them, which only added to the reality of our training. I liked most of the training, despite the hardships.

But there were two aspects of my training at Camp Geiger

that I didn't like. One was a place called the gas chamber. It was a small, one-room building. In it an instructor wearing a gas mask would lecture groups of Marines on different types of gas and how they would affect the infantryman who encountered them in combat without wearing a mask. Before entering the building we already had been given a lecture on some of the more sophisticated forms of biological warfare, including nerve gas.

During a lecture on tear gas we were issued masks and given instructions on how to wear them, but there were too many Marines and not enough masks, so I didn't get mine until the demonstration on how to wear and tighten them was over.

Then, as I was trying to figure out the mask I was given, and before it fit securely, an instructor popped a tear gas grenade right underneath the bleacher where I was sitting. We were supposed to yell "Gas," take out our masks, put them on, and not run away, which could lead you right into an enemy ambush.

Nope! My mask didn't fit, the gas went right up inside it, my eyes were stinging horribly, my nose and mouth hurt, and my skin felt as though it was on fire.

I ran like hell right into the woods and didn't care if someone did shoot me, it had to be better than that gas. As it turned out, several people were in the same boat I was and no one noticed me, but that experience set me up for the gas chamber, which I entered after lunch.

The building was filled with CS gas, which had some nasty physical effects on anyone who breathed it. But we were wearing our masks, and mine now fit.

That is, we were wearing the masks until the instructor told us to take them off. That was the part I didn't like.

We not only had to take them off, we were supposed to sing a complete verse of "The Marine Hymn."

Hah! No one got past "From the halls of . . ." before that stuff started hitting us. It locked up your muscles, displaced your body's oxygen, and gave you the sickest feeling imaginable.

When they were sure everyone had a good dose of it, the instructors opened the door and everyone ran out into the air, where the effects were doubled. There were four platoons in my infantry training company, and we went in the building a squad—thirteen men—at a time. I was in the fourth squad to enter the building and couldn't figure out what was so wrong with all the others who came running out.

From the outside they could be heard banging on the walls and yelling before the door opened and they blasted out of there. They ran right past us looking like people who had gone mad.

I found out why. A few minutes later I was banging on the walls like everyone else. I had tried to hold my breath and fool them, but to no avail. You can't sing and hold your breath, and I think I got a double dose.

As I ran into the air my skin started burning, my nose started dripping, my eyes were running, and everyone was yelling. I was in charge of my squad since I was a PFC, and we all ran right past our company lieutenant without slowing down a beat and without saluting. He just shook his head and kept walking.

I have hated anything to do with gas ever since, and even the mention of it has been sufficient to have me scrambling for my mask.

When we were hit with tear gas on the perimeter at Quang Tri, Vietnam, more than two years later, I came out of a dead sleep instantaneously and had my mask on before I even was fully cognizant of what was happening.

I guess you could say the training was successful.

Besides the gas chamber, another place I hated in Camp Geiger was the mess hall. It had the worst food I have ever encountered, and whether it was by design or not I don't know. What I do know is that it was preferable to eat cold

C rations out on maneuvers rather than to hope for a decent meal in the Camp Geiger mess hall.

The tables always had jars of peanut butter and jelly on them, bread was available at the end of the chow line, and nearly everyone just made sandwiches whenever we ate there.

By the time I finished training at Camp Geiger, I had a good basic background in infantry tactics. We had staged mock battles at night, and we had learned how to go over rolled concertina wire and under stranded barbed wire, avoid trip mines, and stay down while machine guns were firing over our heads.

I was scheduled to go to the naval air station at Jacksonville, Florida, in April for basic training as an aircraft electrician, but regardless of what job any Marine is assigned to, all Marines are infantrymen first. Those who were to have infantry assignments trained slightly longer at Geiger and would take further advanced training at Camp Pendleton in California before going to Vietnam.

But when I left Geiger, I felt confident that I at least knew the basics of combat and survival if I ever ended up in the jungle.

From Geiger it was back home for twenty days. It was still cold in New York in early April, and that was quite a departure from the warmth of the South. Even the cold rain in North Carolina seemed warm compared to the lingering snow and below-freezing nights at home.

The weather wasn't the only thing that was different. Most of my friends from high school were either off at college somewhere or had entered the service themselves.

My best high school friend was a guy named Bob Soloyna, who because of his huge size and incredible strength had been nicknamed Rock. Bob was almost ready to join the navy, but we enjoyed a few times together while I was on leave. We also contacted John Messick, who was home on leave for part of the same time I was, so we spent one last memorable night drinking and raising hell.

John was as gung-ho as could be, so was I, and I think we had most of our friends bewildered somewhat by our behavior. Basically they agreed that we were "brainwashed." We spent part of a Saturday evening at our old hangout, a place called the Villa Valenti, and then moved on a short distance up the road to another place called the Excelsior House.

The Excelsior House had been the starting point for the rock group Buddy Randell and the Knickerbockers, who ultimately made one very successful record called "Lies" and then were never heard from again. The Excelsior House also was a good place for a fight, and a friend of John's, a very large friend of John's, got into one that night.

Soloyna, John, myself, and a few other guys provided backup, but the whole thing came to a quick end when we heard the cops were coming. Marines or no Marines, you didn't mess with New York State troopers back then, any more than you should now, and we split before they arrived.

One nice part of that leave was the new car my older brother had bought while I was away. It was a 1966 Mustang GT, with a 289 engine, four-barrel carburetor, three-speed shift on the floor, bucket seats, and convertible top. He let me use it quite a bit, if I'd drive him to work in the morning. He had a job as an apprentice at the army arsenal in Watervliet, where my father worked.

I saw my now ex-girlfriend a couple of times, but most often spent time driving around, sometimes with a friend, sometimes alone, just looking over where I had come from and remembering a bit.

The Mamas and the Papas had released their hit "Monday, Monday," and I heard a lot of it that month. When my leave was over, I was ready to get back to the Marine Corps. I still missed my family, and everyone was sad when it was time to go. But I had changed, and the world I had left was changing, too. I couldn't be there to change with it, and frankly I didn't want to be.

I said my good-byes and boarded the plane for Florida. At least it would be warm.

I was stationed at the Naval Air Station, Jacksonville, Florida, assigned to the Marine Air Detachment. There is practically nothing I remember about the place that I liked, although I did make some good friends there, especially Allen Herlocker, who ultimately would accompany me to Vietnam and remain a friend ever afterward.

My school was twenty-two weeks long and consisted of teaching the basics of electricity and how it related to aircraft. I was assigned to the school because it had been part of my enlistment guarantee.

I agreed to sign up for four years, and the Marine Corps agreed to send me to an aviation school. Of course, if I flunked out it was my fault, and I could then spend four years in the infantry, but that was a chance you had to take.

Oddly enough, once I got to Florida, I decided I probably would have liked the infantry better. Our basic routine in Florida was to get up at 6:00 a.m., clean the barracks, make our bunks, go to chow, fall out for morning formation at 7:00 a.m., and march to the classes a few blocks away, which started at 7:30.

We broke for an hour at noon and were back for classes until 4:30 p.m., when the day was basically over, unless you were on duty. Duty assignments rotated every fourth day and every fourth weekend, which meant everyone could expect to be on duty one night each week and one weekend each month.

That wasn't so bad. What I didn't like about Florida was that the troop handlers, who had much the same jobs as the instructors in Camp Geiger, didn't seem to share the inspiration that the infantrymen did and didn't seem to be as dedicated.

More than once during a personnel inspection I noticed

that my shoes and belt buckles were shined much better than those of the person inspecting me, and I noticed that my uniform was much more squared away. I didn't intend to develop an attitude about that, but after a while I found it hard to respect people who were telling me one thing and practicing another.

It was so hot in the classrooms in Jacksonville that we were in constant danger of falling asleep during lectures. There were strict regulations against falling asleep, but instead of doing something smart, like installing air-conditioning or letting us get an extra hour of sleep each night, the instructors would shoot water at students from squirt guns or pour it over their heads out of buckets, and then require extra duty.

I did have some good times, but one of the best of those nearly got me killed. On a warm night in midsummer three of us were drinking beer on the railroad tracks leading from Jacksonville to the air station, because we weren't twenty-one and couldn't drink legally, and in the midst of our revelry we almost got hit by a train.

It started when I found some Schaefer beer in a cooler in a 7-Eleven store. That was back when the Schaefer Company was family-owned, and one of their breweries was located in Albany. It had been my favorite beer, and I was so happy about the find that we got a twenty-one-year-old friend to buy a case for us.

Since we had nowhere else to go, we sat up on the tracks drinking until it was gone. Somewhere along the way a train came by and was nearly upon us before we all tumbled down an embankment to avoid it. That was the height of my experiences in Florida. I was pretty happy when fall came and I finished my training there.

Most of the guys in my class wanted to be attached to jet squadrons, which were considered to be less strict than the "ground-pounder" bases where infantry regiments were stationed. I guess that was the "smart" thing to do.

I didn't want to play at being a Marine, however. I was

therefore happy when my request to be stationed at a helicopter base was granted. I left Florida in October and did a quick ten days at home. Not much had changed there, so I said some good-byes and headed back to North Carolina.

I came back to Camp Lejeune, rode past Camp Geiger, and went through the gates of the Marine Corps Air Facility, at New River, North Carolina. There I entered the world that would be my home for nearly three more years and met the people with whom I would share it. And there I began preparing for Vietnam.

Chapter 11

The bar was noisy, smoky, dimly lit, and filled with the sound of a local band playing country-and-western music. It was typical of the bars found in Jacksonville, North Carolina, in 1967.

If you wanted rock 'n' roll, you could get it at some of the bars in the middle of the downtown area, but those on the backstreets and along Route 17 catered to country tastes.

It was a frosty Friday night in early December, and the atmosphere in this particular bar mimicked the weather outside, especially to the four of us: Dale Bush, Jeff Sass, Anselmo "Al" Munoz, and myself. The place wasn't friendly because it was a bar where locals hung out, and we were the only Marines there.

It was on a side street, one door from the railroad tracks that went through a portion of Jacksonville, and was as close as a place could get to being off-limits and still permit Marines inside. We were standing at the bar, talking among ourselves and keeping an eye on the local talent, when Munoz decided it was time to dance. That's what got it all started.

He had picked out a good-looking girl sitting with a couple of other girls at a table in the middle of the floor.

"Think I'll go ask her to dance," he told us.

We took bets on whether Al would get turned down, and he walked, or should I say limped, up to her, catching her halfway to the dance floor, where she was headed with one of her girlfriends. She didn't appear to have a date and looked like a reasonable prospect for a dance at least.

"Would you like to dance?" was all Munoz said.

It wasn't just that she turned him down. She turned him down with attitude, and a poor attitude at that.

Munoz, a lanky Texan who was very handy with his fists, probably would have let it lie if she'd just said "No, thank you" nicely.

But she didn't, so Munoz looked at her for a minute, then extended his tongue and made a lapping motion and sound, kind of like a dog at a water dish.

"Don't you dare do that to me!" she shouted.

He promptly repeated the gesture.

The girl took it badly, thinking, properly so, that there was some devious sexual connotation to his actions, and she promptly hauled off and smashed Munoz across the face.

That really got things started!

A local guy whom I dubbed Sir Galahad was sitting at a nearby table and jumped up, just like he was in a Foghorn Leghorn cartoon, or maybe *Gone with the Wind,* yelling in a thick Southern drawl, "We don't treat ouah women like that around heah!"

To which Munoz replied with an expletive.

Everyone at Galahad's table jumped up to defend Southern Womanhood, and we were already moving to Munoz's side to add another chapter to Marine Corps history. It never really got to be much of a fight, however, because someone called the cops and the MPs.

They took pity on Munoz because they figured a guy in a cast probably wasn't really causing that much trouble.

The cast?

Munoz had gotten that a month earlier, on November 11, 1967, to be exact, one day after the Marine Corps' birthday.

It happened as he was leaving the annual Marine Corps Birthday Ball, or more specifically the Birthday Brawl, in our squadron hangar at New River late on the night of the tenth. Five guys accosted Munoz, who figured the odds were just about even and took them all on.

He decked three of them immediately and had a fourth on the ground in a ditch, choking him with the guy's own tie. Then the fifth one jumped into the ditch to help his buddy and landed on Al's ankle, breaking it.

I missed all of that because I had come down with the flu earlier that day and didn't go to the brawl. Another member of our group, Doug Braman, brought a keg of beer and a huge chunk of cake back to the barracks for me so I wouldn't miss out on the fun, but even so I didn't drink very much.

I woke up early and clearheaded the next morning and found Munoz hobbling around the barracks. I walked to sick bay with him, and the doctor said he'd broken his ankle, hence the cast.

It would have been better for everyone if we had just gone looking for another place to drink that night a month later, but we didn't. After the MPs left with a warning to stay out of trouble, we went back inside and continued drinking beer.

Sir Galahad and his group kept eyeballing us, and we kept insulting them. Finally it was closing time, and we were primed to take the whole bunch of them on outside. But they wouldn't leave.

After taunting them a bit, we said "To hell with it," went outside, and got into Bush's car. We were just about to pull away when Sir Galahad came out looking as though he was really going to fight us and, oh, how sorry he was that we had gone!

But we hadn't!

Munoz, sitting in the passenger seat up front, simultaneously opened his door a crack and rolled down the window.

"Hey, asshole!" he yelled.

"Who, me?" Sir Galahad replied. I couldn't believe he actually answered.

"Yeah, you. Asshole. Come over here!"

I also couldn't believe the guy was dumb enough to come

over, but he did. He leaned down, right alongside Munoz's door, looked inside, and *wham!* Munoz smashed him right in the forehead with the door.

Galahad backed up onto the sidewalk, his face covered by both hands, which were holding his head, and Munoz quickly jumped out after him with the rest of us right behind.

Munoz gimped up onto the sidewalk, tapped Galahad on the shoulder, and the dummy lowered his hands. Munoz smashed him right in the face. Then all of his buddies came to his rescue, roughly eight of them as I remember. But they weren't Marines, and they weren't fighters. In less than a half minute they were all running down the street.

All except one of them, who was running his mouth about what he was going to do to us. He hadn't realized that whatever he may have planned, we weren't into talking and had already done it to his friends. He suddenly realized he was alone, facing the four of us, with his mouth still running, but it suddenly slowed to a few words that trailed off into the night.

Munoz was on the far left, with Sass next to him, Bush next to Sass, and me next to Bush on the far right. I looked down at Munoz with the thought in mind, "I'll take him," and Munoz looked back at me, nodding.

I took this to mean, "Okay, he's yours," but I later found out that Munoz was thinking, "I'll take him."

So I swung with my right, connecting with the guy's jaw just as Munoz swung with his left, connecting with the other side of the guy's jaw. He went down, and all of his friends came running back toward us with renewed vigor.

Someone grabbed me from behind in a full-nelson hold, and I called for Bush to help, but he was already engaged with a couple others. So I dug my thumbs underneath the earlobes of the guy holding me, nailing him right in a sensitive pressure point. He yelled, loosened his grip, and I stepped forward, bent down, and smashed him in the balls with a backward chop from my elbow.

That put him out of action, but before we went any further the cops and MPs were back. They separated us and tried to get both sides of the story. Galahad kept yelling that he wanted us all arrested, which pissed off the cops because they don't like being told what to do. Ultimately they told the civilians to get out of there, checked to make sure we were carrying our liberty cards and were authorized to be in town, and then told us to head back to base and stay out of trouble.

This all may have seemed unnecessary and something that could have been avoided. But, in fact, it was a typical Friday night in Jacksonville, and similar incidents were repeated nearly every weekend, regardless of whether we stayed in the area or went elsewhere.

We now were part of Marine Medium Helicopter Squadron 161 and were learning that it was necessary to depend on each other, on the job or off. We were members of a squadron that wasn't even a full-fledged unit at the New River Air Facility when I first checked in during October 1966. I was assigned to a still-forming squadron referred to only as Sub-unit 1, which we were told would someday become HMM-163.

When my leave in October 1966 was over and I checked into the barracks that became my home for eighteen months, it was only half filled. I don't know who I met first there. It was probably someone from the avionics section, which included all the aviation electricians and electronic technicians, hence avionics.

But making friends there was easy because nearly everyone was new. My circle of friends included Roger Gangi, who had gone through Jacksonville, Florida, a few classes ahead of me and who came from farther west in upstate New York; Doug Braman, a mechanic from Connecticut; Munoz, and Abelardo Leal, both from Texas, who had, along with Sass and Braman, learned the basics for their Marine jobs at the naval air station in Memphis, Tennessee; and Bush, an electronics technician who also came from upstate New York.

There were plenty of others who came to that unit, before and after I did, and on December 18, 1966, we received the designation HMM-161 and that unit's flags after it completed its first successful tour in Vietnam. In military jargon the unit was regrouping in the States, but in fact we were all brand-new.

We were commanded by Lt. Col. W. D. Watson, and most of our officers and senior NCOs transferred in from other units. We started receiving new CH-46 helicopters and began learning everything there was to know about them.

The CH-46 Sea Knight was the second-largest helicopter in the Marine arsenal, smaller only than the CH-53 Sea Stallion. It had two large rotors on top—one in the front and one in the rear—rather than one large one on top and a small one on the side. The rotors spun in opposite directions to offset each other's torque and keep the aircraft flying straight.

It had two jet engines, two transmissions, a cockpit large enough for only the pilot and copilot, and a small passageway back to the rear cabin, which was large enough to carry more than a squad of fully armed Marines, or two internal fuel tanks to boost its range, or a wide variety of cargo.

Since the front and rear rotor blades meshed at a high RPM, a synchronization shaft ran down the length of the rear compartment, above the cargo area, between the fore and aft transmissions. It kept the blades from hitting each other and chewing the aircraft up in flight. For combat purposes the pilots had armored seats, armor was installed around the engines, and two .50-caliber machine guns were installed, one on each side, for further protection.

Some squadrons in Vietnam went so far as to designate one aircraft a gunship. In those cases extra .50-caliber machine guns were installed farther along the sides, an M-60 machine gun could be installed on the rear ramp, and one squadron even rigged a frame to allow the pilots to fire two additional M-60s forward.

We were told that we would go to Vietnam in 1968, although exactly when we weren't sure. On July 7, 1967, Lt. Col. Paul W. Niesen, a square, solid six-footer who tipped the scales at around 250 or so, and who was nicknamed Tiny, of course, took command.

Lieutenant Colonel Niesen was highly proficient, both as a pilot and specifically as a pilot of CH-46 helicopters. His presence added a new dimension to the squadron history.

Niesen would lead us, inspire us, and become something of a legend among us in the nearly two years he would be our commanding officer. But in the meantime, we had to deal with an often-hostile world that had a lot of problems with the war in Vietnam and usually liked to focus that feeling on the people who would be, or were, fighting it.

I wanted to think that the fight we had that night in Jacksonville was just a fluke, the kind of thing that happens when civilians clash with military personnel in a service town bar. But it wasn't.

Yes, there were times when we went looking for it, but there were many more times when it was impossible to avoid, when just the appearance of a short haircut and a military bearing would start the questions, and ultimately the insults.

We weren't people who took insults lightly. Even at home I couldn't escape it. There was a night in the spring of 1967 when I went back home for a weekend, accompanied by Doug Braman, and realized that my real home was now my unit, not the place I had left more than a year earlier.

Doug had been in New River about two months when I showed up. Something about his swagger and his wise-ass way of looking at the world seemed to mirror my attitudes, and we became friends almost immediately. Within a few months we began making the "swoop" home from Camp Lejeune on off-duty weekends, once every six weeks or so.

"Swooping" was a slang term describing the practice of heading out at the end of the workday on Friday, usually around 4:30 p.m., driving ten, eleven, or twelve hours to points north, south, or west, arriving sometime in the early morning hours Saturday, staying up all day, and partying all Saturday night.

Sleep usually lasted from around 3:00 a.m. Sunday morning to 9 or 10, and at around 3:00 p.m. the reverse trip started. Since there was so little to do on weekends at base or in Jacksonville, swooping was popular.

Those without cars tried to hitch rides with friends who had them, or at worst could go to "the circle," a traffic rotary at the main Camp Lejeune complex where Marines with cars waited to hook up with riders going their way, asking for gas money as the price of the ride.

Coming back from the North, a repeat performance was played out on Sunday afternoons in New York City on Eighth Avenue and Forty-second Street, on the corner across from the Port Authority Building. There, riders and rides again teamed up, again for gas money, usually five or six dollars, and headed back to Camp Lejeune.

Mondays at New River were devoted to getting through the day, and then trying to catch up on a whole weekend's sleep on Monday night.

One weekend Braman and another electrician, Jeff Harnly, joined me in the trip to New York. Harnly had a Volkswagen and we squeezed into it, gear and all, and took off. We hit Albany around 2:00 a.m. and hit a bar at 2:01. We stayed 'til closing time, 3:00 a.m., and then went to my parents' house in Wynantskill. We woke my mother up at 5:00 a.m., had breakfast, and stayed up the rest of the day.

Saturday night we went to the Villa Valenti, and somewhere around midnight my brother got into an altercation. It wasn't major, but my brother let the guy shove him around, which pissed me off. So I intervened, telling the other combatant, "If you want to push him, you've got to get through me."

It seemed to end momentarily, but a few minutes later, as I was standing alone by the jukebox, I suddenly found myself surrounded by about seven guys, all with smug looks on their faces, figuring, I guess, that I was hopelessly outnumbered.

But I didn't back off from my earlier comments, and I also didn't figure on surviving that one intact. At least I had already targeted the recipient of my first punch. I might be on my way down, but at least one face was going to get smashed up first.

Suddenly Doug was there with me, shoulder-to-shoulder, back-to-back. And even though the odds were nearly four to one, they backed off. Way off. I even got an apology later.

Doug and I talked about that a lot of times in the years that followed, and we both figured there was no way we could have taken on that many guys at once, especially if they knew what they were doing. But the thing that mattered was our attitude. We figured we were going to get hurt, but "So what?"

They figured that even with overwhelming odds in their favor, some of them were going to get hurt, and they didn't want to pay the price. I was willing to face the odds regardless of the punishment, because I felt my personal and family honor was at stake. If I was willing to face up to the odds, no way was Doug going to let me do it alone.

These confrontations, that nearly everyone in the squadron seemed to be involved in sooner or later during this period, were indirectly preparing us for events that were coming. We were still slated for Vietnam in 1968, and as Starbuck had taught us, there is no way to be nice in war.

In a very short time people would be trying very hard to kill us, and in quite a few cases they would be successful. Only a very positive and very tough mental attitude would be of help in surviving. Anything soft or anything less could only contribute to the danger level. So we learned to turn to each other for support, and we learned to depend on each other.

But while our outside experiences were indirectly preparing us for one aspect of war, our work and training were directly contributing to our ability to perform our jobs under the extreme stress of combat as well as the only slightly less stressful flying atmosphere Stateside.

Our commanders made sure that everyone in our squadron became highly trained in his primary job assignment, in addition to those he might encounter in an emergency, and the Naval Air Technical Training Command classrooms on base were constantly full. During the eighteen months I was stationed at New River, I was trained in every aspect of the CH-46's electrical and instrument systems, all of its communications and navigational systems, and its electro-hydraulics, and I even took courses on basic jet engine theory and how to repair flaws—such as bullet holes—in the helicopter's frame or metal skin.

Virtually everyone else in the squadron was doing the same thing. While those of us who were permanently in the squadron were learning how to do our jobs better, we also were training replacement pilots for Vietnam. New River had a building that housed simulators—mock cockpits used to simulate actual flight—and they too were in constant use, as were our helicopters.

Early in 1967, I got my first chance to become part of the flight crew and jumped at it. The first time I went up I didn't have the slightest idea what I was supposed to do. But as the months and my training progressed, my familiarity with the helicopter and its functions grew steadily.

In mid-1967, I was judged competent enough to fly on test flights, which usually involved tests of instruments or systems that had failed in flight, had been repaired, and couldn't be written off as fixed until they had been tested in actual flight.

During some test flights, the pilots allowed crew members to fly in the copilot's seat and occasionally even gave us "stick time," meaning they showed us how to operate the controls and let us take over for a while. Even here there was a method to the madness, because if both pilots were wounded in combat, someone would have to get that aircraft safely on the ground—or everyone would die.

While I learned my job, others, such as Doug, Al Munoz, and Leal were training to be crew chiefs. They started out as mechanics, then after more schooling and experience tested for the first mechanic's position, meaning they were assigned to a specific helicopter as a right-hand man to the crew chief.

Finally they took the crew chief's test. Our squadron had some excellent crew chiefs. Nearly all started out new, took advanced schooling at New River, and put in thousands of hours working and flying before they took the test.

A crew chief was responsible for anything and everything that happened in that helicopter behind the pilot and copilot. He was responsible for identifying any malfunctions that occurred in flight, the conduct of passengers, regardless of their rank, the conduct of other crew members, and ensuring that the pilots were aware of anything that might affect their flying, such as aircraft approaching from blind spots behind them.

It was an awesome responsibility, but 161's crew chiefs, many not even twenty-one years old, handled it as though they had been born in a '46.

Our flying simulated combat conditions as closely as possible, using tiny landing zones in the woods and swamps, much like those we would encounter in the mountains and jungles of Vietnam. The training was so realistic that during a night mission in early 1968, I even received a preview of what would face us in Vietnam.

We had headed out over the woods and passed the ranges where new Marines, going through infantry training at Camp Geiger, were practicing night-firing. It was dark all around us, with only a glow on the horizon where Jacksonville nightlife was heating up.

Suddenly a mock battle erupted, and the night was filled with the red glow of tracer rounds. They could be seen almost as soon as they were fired, first going fast, in a straight line toward an imaginary enemy, then slowing, seeming to float as they hit a rock and ricocheted off into the night.

The cockpit was bathed in a red glow from covered instrument lights so the pilots could keep their night vision intact. The rear cabin area was dark.

"Looks like the real thing, doesn't it?" I heard one of the pilots say on the intercom.

In fact, it was the real thing. Real Marines were firing real ammunition, and the only thing lacking was a real enemy firing back. I kept watching as long as the exercise on the ground continued, marveling at how many thousands of rounds were being fired, at the enormous energy being expended, and wondering how anyone could survive through something like that.

We would see that scene again, many more times, in the near future. Except it would be multiplied by the number of enemy rounds being fired at the Marines, and sometimes we would be targets, too.

I could feel it that night, flying above the mock battlegrounds south of Jacksonville. The training was nearly over. We had racked up some impressive accomplishments with our Stateside mission. It was almost time for Vietnam.

Chapter 12

From a distance the Huey looked like a mosquito compared to the huge CH-53. Even up close, the Marine Corps' smallest cargo helicopter was dwarfed by the newest and largest addition to its arsenal.

But like an angry bee, the Huey lifted off the runway and headed straight into the underside of the giant. Its rotors cut into the '53's control cables, and inside, the thirty combat-ready Marines heard a sickening *thump* as the two collided.

The troops couldn't see the Huey as they started spiraling downward, much too fast for control. But they felt a sinking sensation in their midsections and a growing sense of panic as they raced toward the warm, green forest waiting silently below.

I have said that flying Stateside was somewhat less stressful than flying in combat, and that's true. Another truth is that life in the Marine Corps can switch immediately from hard work, to fun and laughter, to tragedy, even in the supposedly peaceful atmosphere of a Stateside base.

It happens because of the nature of the Marine Corps, "First to fight" and all, and because constantly training for combat puts the troops in a continually high state of risk.

This risk factor became part of our lives throughout 1967 as a series of events combined to make flying at New River nearly as lethal as it was in combat.

The CH-46 helicopter was new to the service, and a series of fatal flaws caused crashes and loss of crew members' lives several times in 1967. As a result of one crash in another unit, our entire squadron was "grounded" on July 2, 1967, and stayed that way throughout the month so rotor blades could be tested for flaws. We went to work on a nearly round-the-clock basis, removing and replacing the blades, rotor heads, engines, and both transmissions.

Technical representatives from the Boeing Vertol factory in Pennsylvania, which manufactured the aircraft, also came to New River to assist. Since the work had to be completed in the shortest possible time, the night crew became an active part of the squadron. During that period I began a pattern that stayed with me most of my time in the squadron—working at night whenever I could rather than during the day.

One of the reasons I liked working the night shift had to do with a staff sergeant who joined us in 1967. His name was William Scoggins and he looked like a drill instructor. He was lean, had tattooed arms, kept his hair short, and was a career Marine. Working for Scoggins was great. He expected his crew to come to work sober, take their assignments, and go to town on them.

But occasionally, while everyone was busy, Scoggins would slip out to the commissary, a short walk from our hangar, and buy two six-packs of beer. He'd bring them back to the hangar and keep them behind his desk until all the work was finished. Aside from the time we were tearing the whole squadron apart, our worknight usually ended around 10 p.m.

Then Scoggins would break out a beer for everyone. It was a little unorthodox, but virtually everyone I knew liked Scoggins. He let you know exactly where you stood with him, and while he was tough, he was fair, and rewarded good work.

When the '46s were downed, that routine became impossible. Our workdays, which started at 4:00 p.m., more often than not lasted until well after midnight. The base mess hall was ordered to open for mid-rats—midnight rations—to feed the night crews. Many nights we'd break at 11:30 p.m., go to the mess hall for coffee and eggs, then go back and work a few more hours.

In the fall, when another crash caused the '46s to be downed again, and we tore the squadron apart again, Niesen's legend began to grow in 161. Word began circulating that Niesen would be on the hangar deck or patrolling the flight line late at night, sometimes forgoing his uniform for a pair of farmer-type bib overalls, lending a hand if he could, keeping an eye on things, and offering encouragement.

The legend got a big boost from a first mechanic named K. B. Johnson, who was kind of a wild guy, in a decent way, with an offbeat sense of humor. The story that circulated said KB was working alone, somewhere around midnight, inside the aft section of a '46, a hollow area that rose sixteen feet from ground level. Just inside the tail section, attached to the transmission, were generators, electrical wiring, and other equipment that had to be removed before the transmission could come out.

Johnson was working in the dark, standing on a ladder, preparing the transmission for removal, when he realized he needed another wrench. A figure entered below him, and Johnson, thinking it was one of the other mechanics, yelled down, "Hey, can you hand me that wrench?"

There was some rumbling around in the toolbox, and then the proper wrench was handed up. "Thanks, man," KB said.

"That's all right," came the answer, and KB froze.

It was the colonel!

KB came scrambling down the ladder, expecting to be royally reamed for not using proper military etiquette. But the colonel was gone, a shadowy figure in a darker night, heading out to another helicopter to check on another Marine.

That story spread throughout the squadron, and while it surprised some people, it also gave us a sense of teamwork with our officers. Johnson was working alone, his hands full, a flashlight tucked underneath his chin giving the only light, and it was reasonable to expect someone to lend a hand when needed, even if that someone was a lieutenant colonel who just happened to be in charge of the whole squadron.

I don't think there was a man in that unit who would have deliberately breached military etiquette or been insulting or caused embarrassment to the colonel. Yet we got the distinct impression from him that there was a time and a place for everything, and standing on top of a ladder at midnight with your hands full just wasn't the place for drill-field correctness.

That approach to command kept morale high at 161. After a round of inspections when the '46s were first downed, X-rays of the rotor blades revealed flaws that were making them come apart under stress. Later we also were told that an improperly manufactured gear in the aft transmission was the culprit in some crashes.

We continued with the job, reassembling all twenty-four of our helicopters, and the training resumed.

In September 1967 our squadron logged one thousand flight hours while training pilots. That meant that all of our aircraft, or birds as they were called—never choppers—had flown nearly fifty hours each for that month, a remarkable amount of flying in Stateside conditions.

It didn't actually happen that way. The squadron usually fluctuated around 75 percent readiness, depending on what maintenance was required on what number of aircraft. Our helicopters were regularly scheduled for major system reviews on a rotating basis, which kept them out of flight status for several days, and others could also be "down" waiting for parts if a major repair was required.

That meant the squadron had kept an extremely high readiness percentage, and those aircraft in "up" status had done a tremendous amount of flying.

The crash that caused the second round of inspections for the '46 occurred on October 6, 1967, just minutes before I was to leave on a ninety-six-hour pass. That amounted to a four-day weekend, and I had hitched a ride to an airfield in South Weymouth, Massachusetts, on one of our helicopters. From there I planned on taking a bus to Albany. The helicopter ride would shorten the trip by several hours.

But as we taxied out to the runway, a radio message to the pilots ordered us to return and shut down immediately. One of our birds, piloted by Maj. C. D. Riordan, had crash-landed in a field south of Jacksonville. The pilots had felt a vibration and landed just in the nick of time, because the entire aft pylon, which contained the rotor head and blades, had separated from the rest of the aircraft just as it touched down.

Later we were told that something had caused the synchronization shaft to snap, allowing the blades to freewheel, but the pilots got on the ground and everyone escaped before the aircraft was chewed up.

This time the squadron was back in the air on October 11. But on December 2, 1967, another fatal accident again brought all the '46s back down. So we started all over again, tearing them apart, removing blades, rotor heads, fore and aft transmissions, and both engines. It was after Christmas before the order was given to start flying again.

This time, however, in addition to searching for the problem, our aircraft also were modified for combat readiness. The frames were buttressed and strengthened, new rotor blades with greater strength and lifting abilities were installed, as were new, more powerful, General Electric jet engines.

Armored seats were installed for the pilots as well as armor for the engines and mounts for the machine guns. The port, or left, machine gun was mounted directly behind the cockpit. The starboard, or right, machine gun was mounted a bit farther aft, behind the side entrance door.

Eventually the investigation exposed the problem that had caused the crash, and it was corrected. Again we began rebuilding our squadron. Even before the December accident, however, we had been showing what the '46 was capable of if its flaws were corrected.

On September 29, 1967, we took part in a NATO exercise off the coast. Colonel Niesen was proud of our accomplishments and wanted to do something to show our participation and level of readiness. So on the day the U.S. secretary of the navy was reviewing the exercises, a total of twenty-one aircraft, nearly the entire squadron, flew over the dignitaries on the beach, writing 161 in the air with the helicopters.

That got their attention!

It's obvious that all of this activity was hard and serious work. People's lives were on the line, and the way we did our jobs had an impact on everyone around us. Most of the enlisted men in the squadron were in their late teens or early twenties, and while our civilian counterparts were generally thinking about how much money they were making, we were dealing with far more serious matters.

That is not to say, however, that we were a humorless bunch. There always seemed to be some zaniness going on, and I guess it was a testament to our mental strength that we still could keep a sense of humor.

Mike Elliot was a great one for giving us an unexpected laugh. Mike came from the Blue Ridge Mountain area of Tennessee and spoke with a fantastic drawl. He had originally enlisted in 1965 under a program that allowed promising recruits with some college, but not a four-year degree, to shoot for pilot training. If they made it and spent a tour as a pilot, the Marine Corps then sent them to finish college, requiring that they spend another tour on active duty upon graduation.

But this program had been canceled by presidential directive after Mike had already enlisted. So he was given the option of doing two years in the Marines, with no guarantee of what job he'd be assigned to, or changing to a four-year enlistment with an aviation guarantee.

Mike, intelligently I thought, opted for the four-year aviation guarantee. But after his two years had ended, and he still had two to go, Mike went out and had more than a few beers. He returned to the barracks and stretched out on his bunk moaning, "Oooooohhhh, I coulda been out today. Daaaaaaaamn, I coulda been oooooouuuuuut today" until he went to sleep, with the rest of us breaking up over his discomfort.

Another night he showed up at the hangar when I was working for Scoggins on the night crew. Mike had been out in town and "acquired" a navy chief's hat somewhere. He was wearing it along with his civilian clothes when he walked in.

Mike grabbed a portable radio that was used to communicate with work crews far out on the flight line. The sergeants used the radios to direct the crews to aircraft that needed repairs rather than have them waste time walking a quarter mile back and forth to the hangar.

There were very strict rules about conduct and language over the airwaves, and FCC regulations were strictly enforced. We used codes, such as "Avionics 1 to Avionics 3, over," to call from one place to another.

But Elliot pushed the transmit button and called, "Jockstrap 1, this is Jockstrap 69, over!"

He did that twice. Then the door to the Avionics area burst open and in walked M.Sgt. Robert Coryn. Master Sergeant Coryn was the senior enlisted man in charge of maintenance, very knowledgeable about his job, and generally a good guy, but you didn't want to rile him.

Elliot saw him coming and tried to hide in a cabinet, but Coryn had been around a bit himself and wasn't about to be fooled.

"Get out of that cabinet," he ordered. "Give me that cover!" referring to the chief's hat. "Where'd you get this anyway?"

There was camaraderie between navy chiefs and Marines of the same rank, so even though Elliot had gotten a navy cover, odds were that Coryn would see it got back to its owner.

"Go back to the barracks and sleep it off!" Coryn ordered.

Meanwhile, I was sitting over in a corner, holding my sides and my breath, about to explode from holding in the laughter. I thought the whole scene was pretty funny, but I didn't dare piss Coryn off.

I respected him, and since I was still on duty I figured I didn't need any extra assignments. But I was nearly turning purple and my sides hurt like hell. Coryn glanced over in my direction, gave me a real disgusted look, and left.

Probably because of his sense of humor, Mike and Scoggins got along very well, especially after Mike indicated an interest in sport parachute jumping, which was Scoggins' favorite recreation. Mike went to Scoggins' house one Saturday afternoon and learned how to roll when landing by jumping off a table.

The next Saturday, Mike went up and made his first parachute jump. I was really interested in this because, for all the flying I was doing, I never once had the urge to jump out of a helicopter, with or without a parachute.

In the late afternoon Mike came back, a little under the weather, and just jumped up onto his bunk.

I walked over and asked, "So, how'd it go?"

"It . . . was . . . great," Mike said, slowly. "It felt like a covey of quail fluttering out my asshole! *Ppppprrrrrr.* It was almost as good as sex!"

Mike went to sleep soon after that, and I went back to my bunk, trying to figure how you'd get a covey of quail in that part of your anatomy in the first place.

Mike wasn't the only guy who could give you a surprise laugh.

Sometimes it seemed that the guys were competing for who was the wildest, and one Saturday evening in 1967 three of them joined forces to give the squadron a lesson in zaniness.

It was about 3:00 a.m. when I woke to maniacal laughter from their area of the squad bay. Our barracks in New River was divided into cubicles, with four Marines bunking in each cube. The partitions were open to a center aisle and also near the outer wall. It wasn't an expensive hotel room, but still there was a semblance of privacy.

Two of the guys in question shared a cube about four bunks down from me, and on this particular Saturday night they were sitting there with one other, lighting farts and laughing their asses off after every one cut loose.

They were coming out with some classic lines like, "Holy shit, did you see that one? It was green!"

Or, "Wow, that blue one scorched my ass!"

Real class.

The whole barracks was cracking up. Except for Gary Parmenter. Parmenter, a rather short guy from the Boston area with a distinctive Massachusetts inflection in his voice, decided he'd had enough of it. He dropped down from his bunk and stormed over to the cube.

"Don't you know people here are trying to sleep? What's the matter with you anyway, sitting here at 3:00 a.m., lighting fahts?"

For a moment there was a stunned silence. Then a guy named Johnson erupted.

"Fahts?"

"Fahts."

"What the hell are fahts?"

"We ain't lighting fahts! We're lighting *farts!*"

At which point the whole barracks was laughing like madmen, and Parmenter stormed back to his bunk.

Years later, after one of the participants had become a successful financier, he told me they had primed for that night by drinking beer all day and loading up on chili and tacos.

"I think we set some records [for distance] that night," was his final word on the matter.

As crazy as it may seem, that kind of comic relief was

necessary to offset the serious side of Marine life. We had been aware of CH-46 crashes in Vietnam and of close calls to our own squadron already, but on June 23, 1967, life at New River went from serious to deadly.

It happened as a CH-53 was taking off loaded with thirty Marines. They were wearing packs, helmets, cartridge belts with ammo magazines, and canteens, and carrying rifles. They were taking part in what was called General Military Subjects, or GMS school.

Its primary purpose was to reacquaint those of us in the aviation part of the Marine Corps with our basic responsibilities as infantrymen. Each month, every squadron and support unit on the base would assign one or two people to the school.

I had attended it in the previous class. We had gone through the usual rituals of standing inspections and listening to lectures, but the school also had focused intensively on guerrilla warfare and counterinsurgency training. We had spent several days in the woods and swamps, defending fortified positions, attacking a mock Vietnamese village, relearning camouflage techniques, and honing our basic reconnaissance and surveillance skills. War was in our future, and they were training us to survive if we got shot down.

Mike Vicknus, a metalsmith from HMM-161 and a good friend with whom I had "swooped" north to Doug Braman's home a few months earlier, was in the next class. In his class the tactic known as vertical envelopment—dropping right down on the enemy using helicopters—was added to the course roster.

That day the CH-53 was loaded with Marines who would attack from the air. It took off from the pickup point and headed for the landing zone (LZ), but midway there the occupants felt a hard *thump* from below.

Those inside didn't know what had happened, but somehow a UH-1 Huey, doing touch-and-go maneuvers on the flight line, had been given clearance to take off and had flown directly into the underside of the '53.

The Huey exploded and crashed into a burning heap of wreckage. The '53's control cables, which ran along the underside of the aircraft, had been severed, but the pilot immediately attempted to autorotate—a technique that brings the craft straight down. At the last moment the pilot pulls up on the collective stick, which controls up and down movement, creating an air cushion with the rotor blades and allowing a relatively gentle landing.

It almost worked. But the '53 hit hard and bounced, and its tail section, including the tail rotor, broke off upon impact. Because the tail rotor was gone there was no countertorque to the huge blades on the top rotor, and the aircraft started spinning. Some Marines inside were thrown out, including the crew chief.

The craft came down again, hard, this time to rest. But the impact had broken fuel lines that ran up to the engines alongside the main rotor head on top. And the spinning had caused numerous broken bones among those inside.

I was still working on the night crew when the crash occurred, so I was asleep in my bunk. My first indication that something was wrong was the sound of sirens all over the base. I ran to the window near my bunk and saw a plume of black and white smoke rising from the spot where the Huey had crashed.

That night, long after the fires had been extinguished and the bodies taken to sick bay for identification, a Marine entered our barracks looking for some friends. He had been in the '53 and survived the crash. We gathered around him, asking questions.

"I was sitting right next to the tail section when it broke apart," he said. "I had my safety belt on, and I didn't get tossed around like some of the others. Then when it hit the second time I was thrown clear. I landed on my pack and passed out for a few seconds. When I came to, I ran over and started pulling some of the others out. I carried three to safety."

And then he stopped, his throat constricting and his voice cracking just a bit. "But they were piled up near the exits, with broken legs and arms. They couldn't get out the escape hatches and the fuel was spraying over them. And then it exploded. I couldn't get near it. For twenty seconds all I could hear was screaming. Then nothing. I'll never forget those screams as long as I live."

He never told us his name, and no one wanted to intrude at that point. Many years later I encountered him again when it was all over, and HMM-161's survivors were reunited. We still stay in touch. But that night he went on his way, taking his memories and leaving us with ours.

Mike Vicknus was a friend. We'd had fun that weekend we swooped to Connecticut. He had a Plymouth Cyclone, with a big engine and four on the floor, and I remember him blasting through Richmond on I-95 at something over ninety miles per hour.

I remembered telling him that the sign on the side of the road was the route number, not the speed limit, but he laughed and kept on going. His generator brushes had started going bad in Brooklyn later that night, and we made it as far as the Berlin Turnpike in Connecticut, about a half hour from Doug's house in Hebron, when we finally had to stop. Doug was out for the night, so we started walking and then got picked up by a guy who dropped us off at a local motel for the night. We called Doug the next morning, got Mike's car fixed, and had a good weekend.

There are no memorials for the twenty-two Marines who died in that crash. In fact, nineteen years later, when another helicopter crash claimed the lives of seventeen Marines, it was erroneously labeled the worst aviation disaster in Marine Corps history.

It wasn't, not that the seventeen Marines who died in the 1986 crash shouldn't also be remembered. But June 23,

1967, will always be remembered by those of us who were there as the day when twenty-two of our friends died a horrible death.

But perhaps the cruelest twist to an already tragic event came the night of the crash, just after the survivor had told his story. A sergeant who was on overnight duty at the barracks, taking phone calls, issuing liberty cards, making sure everything went smoothly during the evening, came out into the barracks from his office, his face ashen. He had just received a call from Mike's family. They had seen the news of the disaster on national television and wanted to make sure he was safe.

The identification process at sick bay had been slow because of the fire, and several of the victims were identified only through their dental records. Mike's parents hadn't yet received official notification of his death.

"I just switched them over to the squadron duty officer," the sergeant said. "I just didn't know what to say."

Chapter 13

Then it was time to go.

On April 20, 1968, the officers and men of HMM-161 gathered on the flight line at New River one last time. Family members came to see us off, and there were some intense emotions, with quite a few wives and girlfriends crying as all twenty-four of our '46s started cranking up.

We were going to Vietnam in style. Rather than boarding ship on the East Coast and sailing through the Panama Canal, we were flying our entire squadron to the West Coast en masse and would board ship in San Diego.

No one had ever done that before, so we were told. We not only intended to do it, we were going to do it in three flight days.

I had been fortunate enough to be selected as a crew member for YR-39, which was the designation for one of our helicopters. All HMM-161 aircraft had YR painted on them, signifying our Yankee Romeo call sign.

Individual aircraft were numbered 26 through 49. All the helicopters were fitted with two huge internal fuel tanks to extend our range, and the crew included three pilots so they could switch flight duties among them.

Each crew chief flew in the aircraft he was assigned to and was allowed one assistant. The squadron officers and noncoms selected a contingent of electricians, radiomen, mechanics, metalsmiths, and hydraulics technicians to make the flight so someone would be available to fix any potential breakdowns.

We took as much of the squadron gear as could fit inside the aircraft, and the remainder, along with the rest of the squadron personnel, flew to the Marine Corps air station at El Toro, California, by jet.

Everything that could be done had been. The metal shop had painted over all the white numbers and letters on the helicopters, blacking them out so they didn't make such easy targets.

We had trained on the .50-caliber machine guns, first on the range at Camp Lejeune, and then on a coastal range, firing at targets from inside the helicopters as we flew by.

Most of the squadron had gone on leave in early March, but I delayed my last leave until April 1. Because of that I was assigned to twenty days of mess duty at the New River mess hall, to replace one of the guys in my unit who was going on leave before me.

Our noncommissioned officer in charge of the avionics section, or NCOIC in Marine terminology, a master sergeant named Smidley, had given me the assignment but said it would be to my benefit in the long run. Smidley told me that if I took the detail then, I wouldn't get assigned to another one for the whole next year. And since I was scheduled for leave on April 1, I would have to do only twenty days instead of the usual thirty. Remember that because it comes up again later.

At any rate I did my twenty days, which sucked beyond belief, and then went on leave. Of course, no one told the mess hall about that arrangement, and as I was standing in the duty officer's office at the squadron hangar at 5:00 a.m. waiting for him to sign my leave papers, the mess hall called wanting to know why I hadn't reported for my shift.

A lieutenant, who knew how badly we hated mess duty, was on duty and had my leave papers right in front of him.

"Winter?" he said to the voice on the other end of the phone. "Just a minute. I'll check."

Then he signed his name authorizing me to leave, picked up the phone with what we called a "shit-eating grin" on his face, and said, "Sorry, he just went on leave."

I spent ten days at home, had some fun, said my good-byes, which were a bit emotional, especially when my family, minus Dad, accompanied me to the Albany Airport, and I returned to New River ready to go.

Our squadron had stabilized in February, meaning that anyone who wanted to could ask for a transfer and go to Vietnam early. Replacements were brought in, mostly from HMM-162, which shared part of the same hangar we were assigned to in New River. Many of them had gone through basic aviation schools with guys from 161. Then there were no more changes.

Mike Elliot was one of those who left early, along with Bill Ferrabee, a crew chief from Elyria, Ohio, who had been one of my closest friends in the squadron. Bill's real name was Orvis, but everyone called him Bill.

When we had first formed in 1966 we also had some veterans assigned to us who had returned from duty in jet squadrons in Vietnam. These included Ernie Swenson from Philadelphia and Tony LaPolla from Elizabeth, New Jersey. Tony and Ernie both had cars, both were electricians, and I made many swoops in their company.

They would drop me off at the Port Authority in New York, where I could catch a bus to Albany, and pick me up there on Sunday afternoons. But their enlistments had expired in 1967, along with those of several other veterans who had been assigned to our unit, and none of them reenlisted.

I felt badly about losing so many friends from the outfit. Elliot had been a constant source of inspiration and good humor.

In late 1967, Ferrabee had met a girl from a North Carolina farming community while on a weekend at the beach.

She had a sister and for a few months we double-dated nearly every weekend. It was great to have somewhere to go and someone who cared waiting for me, and those were some of my best times in the Marines. But it all came to an end around December.

Bill and Elliot both said they felt it was better to move on, and they did. That was the way of the Marine Corps, and something you just had to accept.

Friendships were made, but then friends moved on. It didn't change how you felt about people; you just didn't see them as much. One nice thing about being involved in Marine helicopters, though, was that it was a select group of people. If you stayed around long enough, you eventually started seeing people you knew from somewhere else. Friendships were put on hold, but they were never broken.

I had volunteered to go to Vietnam several times in 1967, strangely enough because I felt the war was passing me by. It seemed like we were kicking ass over there, and I didn't want it to end before I got there. But each time I applied for a transfer to a squadron in Vietnam, I was turned down, and stayed in New River continuing my training.

When they finally approved transfers in January 1968, I couldn't see much point in transferring to a new unit and starting all over, when the really exciting things were happening right there in 161.

So we solidified as a unit, made all the final preparations, and on the morning of April 20 said good-bye to the place that had been my home for eighteen months. We took off from New River in flights of four, heading southwest toward Louisiana. I spent most of the flight lying on top of, or alongside, tanks of jet fuel.

The North Carolina woods gave way to the red clay of South Carolina and Georgia, then Alabama, and a continuing pattern of woods, fields, and occasional towns. We generally stayed away from large cities and made it to a Strategic Air Command base in Mississippi before we needed fuel.

I got my first look at B-52 bombers there, the air force gave us box lunches, and we took off again, for Shreveport, Louisiana. I took a picture of the Mississippi River when we flew over it, and then it was on toward our next stop.

We arrived in the late afternoon, and since there wasn't enough room on the base to house us, we stayed overnight in a Best Western motel nearby. The officer-in-charge of 161's avionics section, the man I reported to, was a career warrant officer named William Bolena, and Niesen had given him the job of arranging housing for us while we went cross-country.

It was a hard job, but Bolena (known formally as Sir, Mister, or Gunner to signify his rank), who had been in the Marines since World War II, took it on, completed it, and we had housing at every overnight stop without a hitch.

The motel had a bar where most of the squadron gathered, and we were ordered not to go anywhere else that night. Our commanders didn't put a curfew on us, but they may as well have, and our movements were severely restricted. So, being good Marines, and doing our best to uphold the highest traditions of the Corps, we ducked out and hit a honky-tonk across the street as soon as all the officers went to their rooms.

We had a good time there, got into an argument with the locals, and got back to our rooms after midnight.

Reveille was at 0400, or 4:00 a.m. to the uninitiated, and I couldn't resist whistling "The Marine Hymn" loudly as we shouldered our seabags and headed down the deserted halls with civilians still sleeping soundly behind every door.

Outside, where dawn was just a thought and wouldn't be a reality for an hour or more yet, the air was heavy with the smell of magnolia blossoms. It was a beautiful perfume, and while I spent less than one day in Shreveport, the smell of that morning air remains a pleasant memory.

For the first time since I entered the military, I ate breakfast at an air force mess hall that day, and I was in for a dose of culture shock.

The air force offered us a choice of juice, eggs to order, rolls, muffins, crisp bacon, fresh fruit, fruit cups, pastries, and several types of cereal. I think I went into a daze, because I had never seen anything like that in the Marines.

Marine mess halls of that time were exactly as I described them, clean and functional, but there were no frills. There generally was one type of juice for breakfast, one type of eggs, usually scrambled or a runny version of over easy, greasy bacon that often sat soggy on slices of bread where the grease was sopped up, and shit-on-a-shingle was standard fare.

Shit-on-a-shingle is really creamed chipped beef on toast, but it looks like shit-on-a-shingle, and while I don't know what shit tastes like, or even if it has a taste, I bet if it does taste like something, it tastes like creamed chipped beef on toast.

I honestly think Marine mess halls are run the way they are for specific reasons. Nobody gets fat, and everyone stays mean. That's what Marines are supposed to be, lean and mean, and if you think about it, the best place for civilian cooking is back home, and that's not what we were all about.

While I was surprised at the air force mess hall, I also thought it was pretty decent of them to feed us like that. I had an extra cup of coffee and a warm feeling inside when we went to the flight line to take off.

Sometime during the previous night I had gotten separated from Bill Frantz and Roger Gangi, both electricians and both good friends. When I got to the flight line they were standing next to one of the helicopters with a sign and some flowers.

When I got close enough to read the sign, I started laughing because it read FUNERAL, NO PARKING.

I have no idea where they got it, although I'm sure that since we were Marines it had been "procured" with the best of intentions and certainly not stolen. We gagged it up with that sign and took turns having our pictures taken lying on top of the external fuel cell with flowers in our hands and the sign in front of us.

We couldn't possibly know it then, but that sign was going to come all too true, and in the not-too-distant future. I still have a picture of us posing with it next to a CH-46.

We continued our flight then, heading toward Texas, where we would refuel, and Arizona, where we would again stay overnight.

There is an interesting aspect to the air currents that flow through an open helicopter such as the '46 when it is in flight. Crew members learn and understand these currents quickly, because they spend all their time in the aft section. Pilots generally aren't aware of them because they spend all their time in the cockpit.

But we had three pilots for that flight, so one of them was always in the aft section. And like all human beings, pilots occasionally have to relieve themselves.

That is no problem when they are sitting in the cockpit, because underneath both seats are tubes, with funnel-like devices attached to them, officially called "relief tubes" for obvious reasons, but known informally as "piss tubes." If a pilot has to take a piss in flight, he simply reaches down for the tube, takes care of business, the urine goes out below, harmlessly, and that's that—unless, of course, you're hovering at ten feet and the pilot pisses directly on someone's head.

In the rear section it's a different story. There are no relief tubes. Crew members learn early that if you have to go, you do it when you are refueling. Fuel pits are always placed well away from everything else, whether in Vietnam or Stateside, simply because if an accident happens, only the fuel will be lost, not everything else in the area.

This is convenient because there is no one to get offended

if a crew member attaches the fuel hose to the aircraft and then takes out his own hose for a little instant relief.

A CH-46 has what is called tricycle landing gear, with one wheel in front and two in the rear. The rear landing gears are underneath the external fuel cells, and this configuration gives the '46 the appearance of a giant frog sitting on its haunches when it is on the ground. Thus '46 pilots ultimately became known as Phrog Flyers—kind of like the French spelling Phydeaux for Fido.

The fuel cells jutting away from the sides also gave crew members a convenient little retreat to stand in when they had to go. Of course, all of this meant nothing when you were on an extended flight with internal fuel cells and weren't scheduled to land for a while.

Inside the '46 a series of factors determines which way the wind blows. First is the entrance hatchway on the starboard side. It has two sections. The top opens inside the aircraft by sliding up on tracks along the ceiling. The bottom section is on hinges and opens outside the aircraft, upside down. There are steps built into the lower section so that when it is open, it provides access to the interior.

In the rear of a '46 is a large hatchway and ramp, both operated hydraulically. The hatchway opens up and inside the aircraft, flattening itself just below the aft transmission. The ramp is lowered to the outside, and like the rest of the cabin section, has cargo rollers to facilitate moving heavy gear and equipment.

Now, in flight, especially when it is hot, the crew chiefs generally open the top section of the starboard entranceway and the rear hatchway so a breeze blows through. As I said, this makes for some interesting air currents.

Not only does a breeze come in the side and go out the back, but the movement of the helicopter through the air creates a vacuum just behind the hatchway, and a major air current also comes in from the rear, moving forward with quite a bit of velocity.

Crew members know this. They know that if you have to take a piss in flight, you let it go out the side entranceway, where the air currents blow it away harmlessly.

However, a young lieutenant who was in the rear with us that day did not know this. He was one of our three pilots and he was in the aft section with us the second day of the flight, on reserve, because he had flown the first day. The lieutenant must have liked that air force mess hall as much as I did, and probably had a second cup of coffee, because somewhere over Texas he had to go.

We were going to touch down along the way for refueling, but anyone who has ever looked at a map of the United States can easily see it's a long way across Texas from Shreveport. The lieutenant couldn't wait.

After thinking about it for a bit, he went to the rear, standing just forward of the ramp, and took care of business in a paper cup. I thought he was back there because he wanted some privacy. Ever since Parris Island there had been no privacy for enlisted men, even during the most basic bodily functions, because, as in flying, you never knew when you were going to get caught short, and you just had to make do with whatever was at hand.

If we, meaning Cpl. D. W. Heath, the crew chief, or myself had any idea what was coming next, we would have warned him. No, I mean it, we would have told him rather than let the lieutenant take the consequences.

Because, he took the cup full of piss and threw it out the rear hatchway, where it was instantly caught by the air current, not the one going out, the one coming back in, and it blew piss all over his trouser legs and shoes. Which is what he had been trying to avoid in the first place.

Heath and I just about exploded laughing, partly because the lieutenant had an incredibly bewildered look on his face. But thank God he had a good sense of humor, because he started laughing, too.

"Why didn't you guys tell me that would happen?" he said.

"Because we're not in the habit of watching another guy take a piss, and we thought you knew better," was all we could tell him.

From then on the lieutenant used the side entranceway and chalked the whole matter up to experience.

The incident also served to point out a key feature of the relationship between 161's officers and enlisted men.

We knew proper military courtesy, and used it. But our lives were absolutely intertwined with our officers. We worked on those helicopters and fixed the problems, and then we all flew in them. The pilot was boss, and no one questioned that, but he relied on us to be his eyes and ears in the rear. Doing our job properly meant that the safety factor, for the pilots and everyone else, increased substantially.

Back in New River, Ernie Swenson, who had worked in an F-4 Phantom jet squadron in Vietnam, told me of a jet pilot who rode the enlisted men unmercifully. But enlisted men in jet squadrons don't fly in the aircraft they work on, only the pilots do.

Swenson said this particular pilot was taxiing out to the runway in Da Nang, made a turn, and his nosewheel fell off. An inspection showed that a pin, which was necessary to keep the wheel in place, just wasn't there.

Swenson said the pilot got the message and became much nicer to deal with after that. After all, the next time, maybe his engine would flame out over enemy territory, and maybe his parachute wouldn't work.

In HMM-161, 99 percent of the officers treated the enlisted men in a straightforward, professional manner, and there were no instances of sabotage. We were a multifaceted unit, but we worked together, and all of those facets depended on each other. It was a system that worked well and resulted in tremendous pride.

It also resulted in a sense of camaraderie that was evident

from the easy conversations we had with the pilots when they flew in the rear with us.

We had some good laughs about the lieutenant's escapade, but after that the trip was fairly routine, with the exception of the incredible scenery. Over Texas, I saw vast expanses of open spaces followed by miles upon miles of pumping oil wells. Then we entered the arid section with mostly desert below.

Over New Mexico, I saw endless sand, glowing white-hot below us, broken suddenly by a farm in the middle of nowhere, and a huge swath of green, existing only because of irrigation and looking strangely out of place.

In the distance I once saw what appeared to be a huge blue lake, but realized that it was only a mirage. I tried taking a picture of it, but when it was developed only white sand showed.

We stopped for refueling and flew on to Tucson. When I stood in the passageway to the cockpit, Tucson looked like it rested in the bottom of a huge bowl, miles across, with mountains forming the sides all around it.

The sun glared off a huge shiny spot to the south, which the pilots said was the air force graveyard for old planes. It seemed as though a million mirrors had been placed out in the desert and were almost blinding in their intensity.

Tucson was a nice place to stop. It was cool, even though it was in the desert, and we stayed through the next day and night. Since we had taken off from New River and Shreveport in flights of four, our squadron was spread out somewhat over the Southwest. One flight had been delayed when a hydraulic line burst over South Carolina, and a portion of the squadron pulled up near El Paso, Texas, to regroup and make repairs while we waited in Tucson.

Nonetheless, we were still on schedule. We were due in El Toro on April 23 at 3:00 p.m., and the colonel said that is exactly when we would be there. We spent most of our time in Tucson sightseeing and hanging around our motel. An electrician named Dave Allen was the only one of my friends who was old enough to rent a car, so he did, and we drove around checking out the terrain.

On the morning of the twenty-third we headed on to Yuma, where we stopped long enough for the remainder of the squadron to catch up. Once we were a complete unit again, the crews had a chance to swap tales while Niesen and the other officers discussed our approach to California. The base where the other flights stayed in Texas was very close to the Mexican border, so those who cared to went over to Juarez for their entertainment. From the stories, I judged they had somewhat of a wilder time than we did in Tucson.

Finally the details of the last flight of the journey were ironed out and we took off into California. We flew over the lower reaches of the Rocky Mountains during the trip and, while they weren't the highest part of the range, those mountains were the highest I had ever seen and were absolutely awe-inspiring. It was cloudy for most of that part of the trip, but the clouds were high and didn't obscure our view.

I saw old mine shafts deep in the mountains, which it must have taken days if not weeks to reach on foot. I saw ranches tucked away in hidden valleys and wondered who those people were, so far from the hustle and bustle outside. I envied them, too.

We were flying so high that oxygen was rare, and when I attempted to light a cigarette, I had to strike my lighter several times to get a flame. Even then it burned very low, with a strange cast to it from lack of oxygen.

At one point the pilots called to us to look at the cockpit instruments. The barometric altimeter, which registered how high we were above sea level, said nearly 11,000 feet. The radar altimeter, which registered how high we were above the ground immediately below us, said 50 feet!

The terrain was harsh and there was virtually no civilization. If we had developed problems, the only places to land would have been precarious at best.

But we flew over the mountains without a hitch. The '46s that had caused so much work a year earlier were now functioning exactly as the designers had intended. We broke out of the mountains into the bright sun of California and headed for El Toro.

We did that in style, too.

The Marine Corps Air Station at El Toro is south of Los Angeles, north of San Diego. There are numerous smaller communities in the area including Anaheim, Santa Ana, and Oceanside.

We came in low and slow, at one point writing 161 in helicopters again, and then shaking the citizenry of the towns below as the roar and thunder of assembled war machines swept over them. We spread that roar to the runway at El Toro and stopped the base personnel in their tracks as we came in for a landing exactly on time!

The rest of the squadron was waiting for us on the ground, cheering, and Boeing Vertol personnel were there, too, capturing it all on videotape to add to the tapes made during the flight. Videos of that cross-country flight still exist.

Niesen had said we could do it. We agreed and put everything we had into it. He was right!

Now we had exactly one week to check out every helicopter, fix any problems that had developed along the way, and board ship.

Weeks before, President Lyndon Johnson had ordered a major increase in troop strength in Vietnam as a result of the Tet Offensive in January and February. Our due date had been pushed up, and there was to be no time for pleasantries. I wasn't going to miss the war after all, and we were ordered to get there posthaste.

Chapter 14

I stood on the dock at San Diego, staring at the aircraft carrier designated LPH-5, more in wonderment than awe. The letters stood for Landing Platform, Helicopter, and the numeral 5 designated it as the fifth such ship in the navy. It was large, more than a football field long, gray, and loomed several stories above sea level.

But it wasn't the size of the ship that would take us to Vietnam that caused me to stand there transfixed, and it wasn't the roar and thunder of our helicopters landing on the flight deck.

It was the name.

I was going to war on the *USS Princeton,* the ship of the same name that my father had served on in World War II!

It wasn't the same ship, since his *Princeton* is still at the bottom of Leyte Gulf. This was a newer version, built to replace the one Dad had served on, but the similarities between his military service and mine were too close and too many to ignore. Earlier we had been told which ship we would be sailing on, so it wasn't surprise that held me spellbound as much as it was history.

I had called Dad and told him, and for a minute there had been only silence on the line. Both of us were thinking about those three hours he had spent in the ocean, and while I couldn't relate to that part of his life, I think Dad was probably remembering the sharks below and the Japanese Zeros above.

We shrugged it off and went on to discuss less weighty matters. But later, after we had finished our work at El Toro, after the trucks that would transport us to the ships had arrived, and after we had assembled in formation on the dock, I still felt a curious sense of being pulled into something I couldn't control, as though it was all planned out already and nothing I could do would change it.

Work on board the ship was feverish, since our whole schedule had been revised. Initially we weren't supposed to be heading out to Vietnam until the summer, and we were supposed to stop first at Hawaii for a few days, then Okinawa for a few more. All of our personal gear and extra uniforms, which weren't deemed essential for Vietnam, were supposed to be stored at Okinawa, where they would be returned thirteen months later when we were scheduled to come home.

But, in accordance with President Johnson's order to increase troop strength in Vietnam, all of the dates had been moved up. We boarded ship May 1 and left for Pearl Harbor, Hawaii, the next day, after a short trip up the coast to Long Beach, where we took on some extra aircraft destined for other squadrons already in Vietnam.

Our stay in Hawaii was for six hours, and we never hit Okinawa at all. We did get a few hours of liberty in Honolulu and spent most of it holed up in a cozy bar where the owner treated us well, and mixed drinks sold for fifty cents each. I called home one last time from there, and the first thing my father said when I told him where we were was "Stay off Hotel Street, it's full of hookers and muggers."

"Uh, Dad," I said, "I'm calling you from Hotel Street."

"Well, stay out of the hotels then!"

I took that part of his advice and told him I was with quite a few friends, so he felt a bit better. I must have given Dad one heck of a telephone bill that month because I always called from phone booths—collect of course—but he always agreed to accept the charges.

I was already thousands of miles away, but I just couldn't

pass up that one last chance to talk to him again. A lot had changed between Dad and me in the two years just past. After I finished, I went back to the bar until it was time to leave. We had to take liberty boats back to the ship because it was docked in a remote section of Pearl Harbor. We were in good spirits when we got back, properly saluted the flag and the officer of the deck when we came up the ladderway, and stepped on board.

But at the top of the ladderway, where it emptied onto the hangar deck, two lines of our squadron's officers and sergeants formed a corridor that we had to pass through to go belowdecks to our compartment. I couldn't figure out why they were there, and especially why we were being hustled along the way we were.

Just before I went belowdecks, another boatful of Marines arrived, and as I looked back at them I got quite a shock. Behind the rows of Marines, where the guys coming on board couldn't see them, were at least fifty sailors wearing black Shore Patrol armbands and carrying billy clubs!

I couldn't believe that! Somebody in charge actually thought it was necessary to guard against violence from us, just because we'd been out on a few hours' liberty!

Someone grabbed hold of me and hustled me belowdecks, but I'd already seen enough. Putting those sailors out there, as though they'd be needed, didn't make sense to us.

The Marines in HMM-161 were professional, and while they were pretty tough, they also were intelligent, and we were all volunteers. We had some people who weren't all that keen on the war in Vietnam, but most preferred to make their statements within the system, not by opposing it or creating discord.

I guess there will always be people who have a negative opinion of Marines that nothing will change, regardless of how uninformed it is. Despite the negative tones of that incident, we did get a good send-off when the ship was ready to depart. On the dock below, a rock 'n' roll band was assembled, and several Hawaiian girls in grass skirts put on a dance for us.

It was a lot better than our send-off from San Diego nearly a week earlier. We had been driven through the streets in vehicles called "cattle cars," long trailers with wire mesh over the windows and the two entrance doors. There were benches and poles to hang onto, but no individual seats. The Marine Corps used them to move a lot of people when there was no real regard for comfort.

Along the way, the citizenry of San Diego cursed and jeered us, making us feel really good about going to war.

It wasn't college kids or war protesters, either, but middle-aged people who shook their fists at us and shouted obscenities. One old man on a street corner yelled, "They should be taking you to jail. You're criminals!"

A crew chief named Al Morrow, who lived in upstate New York, responded by hanging off an overhead pipe with one hand and imitating an ape with the other, along with sound effects.

There was more than one "Fuck you!" and "Up yours!" directed back at the streets until we pulled through the gates of the navy base.

Hawaii, therefore, was a lot nicer to leave. We even got a bit of humor out of the situation when a taxicab came screeching up to the ship just as the sailors were about to raise the gangplank. Out jumped Jeff Sass, who apparently had stayed a bit too long in Honolulu and missed the last liberty boat. He hastily ran up the gangplank to the accompaniment of our cheers and laughter.

We were allowed to stand outside on the walkways below the flight deck for that part of our departure. But we were ordered belowdecks when the ship passed the Arizona Memorial and especially the officers club near the channel leading from the harbor.

That attitude toward the enlisted men in our squadron was exactly opposite of the way we were treated by our own officers, and we never did get used to it. Of equal importance was that many of our pilots didn't like the way the navy was treating us, either.

To get back at them, some of the younger lieutenants composed a song about the *Princeton* that was included in a repertoire of off-color music that became part of our tour. We had a few good guitar players in the squadron, including electricians Chuck Basinski from Florida and Don Smith from California, and we often got together in a group to do a few ballads.

In response to the *Princeton*'s cold treatment, a song was composed that contained the lyrics "LPH-5 is a hell of a place, the ship's company is a fucking disgrace . . ." It ended with the words, "For all they are doing they might as well be, shoveling shit on the South China Sea."

It wasn't a bad little song, but it certainly didn't earn us a place in the captain's heart. In fact, after a few days on ship, Marine enlisted men were banned from the fantail, where officers and enlisted alike had gathered after the end of each workday to relax and watch the sun go down.

That pretty much left us hanging out in our compartments after working hours, or sitting on catwalks above the foc'sle, which is navy talk for forecastle. On the *Princeton,* the foc'sle was an open section of the ship's bow below the flight deck.

Among other things, the *Princeton*'s anchors were stored on it when sailing. Our compartment, directly below the flight deck, had two hatchways that overlooked the foc'sle, with ladders leading down to it. From there we still could watch the ocean sliding by and catch some rays.

It was from the foc'sle that one of the three great dramas of our voyage to Vietnam got its start.

About 250 miles out from Hawaii, on a windy, mixed-bag kind of a day, a sailor was ordered to the foc'sle to paint the anchors. According to scuttlebutt—rumors—making the rounds in the squadron, he had been found guilty of possessing and using marijuana and was about to be thrown out of the navy. Before that, however, he had been sentenced to the ship's brig.

A lean, nasty-looking Marine gunnery sergeant, who was part of the ship's company, not our squadron, was in charge of the sailor while he was in the brig, and the gunny was making life hell for that guy. On the mess deck the sailor was treated like a recruit at Parris Island, and if he rattled his silverware, he didn't eat.

All this must have been too much for him, because on the day he was out on the foc'sle scraping paint off the anchors, he dived off the side of the ship!

Dad had told me that he was very lucky when his ship was sunk. The twin propellers under the stern pull tremendous volumes of water into them and can chew up anything or anyone in the vicinity, he'd said. Entering the ocean while those propellers were churning away just wasn't considered a good thing to do, Dad said.

In his case, Dad was lucky because the explosion that shot him into the water was powerful enough to send him out of the propellers' range. Dad said the explosion literally blew him right out of his shoes, although he doesn't remember exactly how it happened, and he entered the water barefoot.

This sailor also managed to escape the propellers' pull and ended up swimming in the ocean.

As soon as he went over, the sailor in charge of the detail radioed "Man overboard" to the bridge, and the ship instantly came alive. A gong started sounding, orders blared over the intercom—known as the "one M-C" because it operated on a 1-megacycle frequency—and the ship made a sharp turn to port.

All that was unnecessary, however, because on the flight deck, in his helicopter, with engines running and blades turning, was none other than Lt. Col. Paul W. Niesen.

Niesen took off immediately, located the floundering sailor, and since the waves were too rough for a rescue by hoist, landed his CH-46 right in the Pacific Ocean!

Pete Despard was crew chief for the colonel that day and later said that whatever his motivations were when he went over the side, "That sailor was damn happy to get pulled out."

Niesen flew back to the ship, the voyage continued, and the colonel's legend continued to grow.

One other matter of legendary proportions became part of our ocean crossing, and it had to do with my father and the fate of the USS *Princeton* he had served on.

The history of my family and ships named *Princeton* had circulated rather quickly through my squadron, and one night in our compartment it became a matter of intense discussion. Our living quarters consisted of three connecting compartments, and a half dozen of us were sitting in the most remote of the three, where there was no direct access from the rest of thc ship. We were sitting there because we had all smuggled booze on board and were having a drink.

Dad had told me how the bosun's mates on his ship would smash a billy club across the seabag of anyone boarding, to break any bottles they may have been trying to smuggle. Dad had his ways of getting booze on board and I figured out a few myself.

I had a fifth of Johnny Walker Red scotch, which I had wrapped very carefully in several layers of towels and several more layers of utility trousers and shirts. I figured it was well insulated, although no one smashed a billy club across my seabag or for that matter even searched us.

Up until a year previously I wouldn't have been drinking scotch because I hadn't liked it. But back in New River a Marine from Arizona, Bob Gill, another electrician and close friend, had spent an evening showing me how to "develop a taste" for Chivas Regal. I did, and those two brands are still among my favorites, although as time went by Glenmorangie took and maintains the all-time lead.

Included in the group that night on the *Princeton* was a Sergeant Thomas from the hydraulics section, who was on his second enlistment and going to Vietnam for a second tour. Also there was a crew chief, a lance corporal from Washington State named J. D. Cross.

Cross was considered the most irreverent individual in the squadron—and for good reason. In New River the pilots had been setting an altitude record in the '46 he crewed, and somewhere around 14,000 feet above sea level Cross had clicked onto the intercom from his station in the rear and said simply, "God sucks!"

Naturally that left everyone a bit edgy until they got back on the ground.

Cross also had a drink of some kind, and we were just shooting the breeze until Thomas asked, "What's this about your father serving on the *Princeton* and it getting sunk?"

Before I could answer, Cross piped up, "God doesn't have the balls to sink this ship!"

Everyone just kind of looked at him for exactly the count of two seconds. And then before anyone could say anything to him—*kaaaboooom!*—all hell broke loose.

A tremendous explosion rocked the ship, it shuddered, and then, just like the old *Navy Log* television shows, the ship's bell started going *bong, bong, bong* followed by, "General quarters, general quarters. All hands man your battle stations. This is not a drill. This is not a drill!"

No one in the Marines' compartment had the slightest idea what was happening, but it sounded bad. Sergeant Thomas looked like he was going to kill Cross, but Cross had taken off and was nowhere to be found. I think Thomas would have thrown him overboard if he had found him. We later learned that exactly two seconds after Cross' pronouncement, a boiler had exploded down in the engine area. It had completely disabled one engine and either severely injured or killed a sailor.

You can draw your own conclusions about the timing of

that incident. I have thought about it for many years, and I still don't have any definite answers. As a result of the explosion, however, the *Princeton* couldn't keep pace with the other ships in our task force, and we were forced to drop behind, crossing the remaining distance to Vietnam unescorted, except by a Russian spy ship.

Also as a result of that explosion, we sailed right into the middle of a Pacific typhoon.

That was one part of the voyage when our movements were restricted even further, and the navy didn't want us even on the foc'sle. But in this case I could understand the reasoning. We were about two-thirds of the way to Vietnam out in the middle of the Pacific Ocean with the closest land straight down. We were hit full force by that typhoon and its effects lasted for two days.

Our compartment, which housed roughly two hundred of us, was the most forward compartment in the ship above the waterline and therefore did a lot of moving around during the storm.

Like a number of ships in the fleet, the *Princeton* hadn't been built as a helicopter carrier. It was a World War II–era ship, intended to carry a squadron of navy fighter aircraft, and originally designated as a CVS.

But when aviation made the jump from propeller-driven aircraft to jets, there no longer was room or the capabilities needed on board to maintain the new squadrons of fighters. Therefore, such ships were given LPH designations and began carrying helicopter squadrons.

The ship had room for the crew, plus the pilots and squadron personnel. When on station off the coast of Vietnam, however, it carried an additional battalion of Marine infantry, for which it wasn't intended and didn't have sufficient room. Although there were no Marine infantry battalions on board, we still were berthed in that forward compartment, right where you'd feel every movement the ship made.

I had never been on board a ship before San Diego, but

luckily I got my sea legs almost immediately. Not everyone was quite so fortunate. Some guys, for instance, could handle the everyday motion, but when things started getting strange, they'd get a bit nauseous.

On a supposedly normal day, however, when one of our electricians was working on the flight deck, a sergeant named Bill Evans decided to play a trick on him. We were in a compartment designated for avionics personnel. It was located amidships, above the hangar deck level, and was relatively steady. But Evans, who had a great sense of humor, convinced us to start swaying back and forth, or side to side, depending on where we were standing, just as long as we all moved in the same direction in unison.

We tried it a few times, got it down perfectly, and started up just as our target returned from the flight deck. When he entered the compartment, which was about twenty feet by twenty feet, and saw a dozen or so of us swaying in the same direction, he didn't say much at first.

Then you could see the realization coming over his face that while we were all swaying, he wasn't feeling anything from the ship!

"All right you guys, come on. Knock it off!"

"Knock what off?" we asked him.

We kept it up, and he kept asking us to stop, and then suddenly, looking somewhat green, he made a beeline for the flight deck and some fresh air.

But that was nothing compared to the typhoon!

When it was hammering us full force, it would lift the bow of the ship right out of the water, giving the sensation of going up in an elevator very fast.

Then it would come crashing down, as though the elevator had gone out of control. But it didn't come straight down! It would shift first to the left, and then just as you'd adjust yourself to brace for that movement, it would slip right and then straight down again. Then the next wave would catch it, and it would begin to lift, and the cycle would repeat itself.

The ship was closed up tight as a drum, and we had been ordered to stay in the compartment. But at one point several of us opened the hatchway overlooking the foc'sle and went down the ladders for a look at the storm.

It was incredible. The foc'sle was a couple of stories above water level, but the waves were crashing up onto it, and we were later told that a few even made it as high as the flight deck.

The water was brown, and boiling, as though something had pissed it off and we were the objects of its anger.

I watched for about a half hour, and some of those waves, which came at us from at least three directions simultaneously, looked as big as a two-story house.

Then a detail of sailors, all dressed up in foul-weather gear and roped together, came out on the foc'sle to check on the anchors. When they saw us they became somewhat perturbed!

A bosun's mate, wearing a master-at-arms badge, signifying that he was in charge, looked like he was seeing things, and then yelled, "What the fuck are you guys doing out here?"

"Watching the ocean!" we yelled back.

"No one's supposed to be abovedecks! Get the fuck back in your compartment! These waves could wash you away and no one would even know you were gone! Are you guys fucking nuts?"

"No, we're Marines!"

He didn't have an answer for that. He just stood there looking disgusted while we went back up the ladder and into the compartment. I guess he was sorry he couldn't be a Marine.

Being restricted as we were, there wasn't much else to do, so I holed up in that remote area of the compartment, had a few belts of scotch, and watched people getting sick. It was pretty funny, especially when I'd walk across the compartment to the head, because you had to reset your course with every step to keep from falling down. I must've looked, well, like a drunken sailor, except for the uniform.

To the chagrin of anyone who wasn't weathering it too well, I went down to the mess deck twice for something to eat, although they weren't serving regular meals due to the storm.

It was two days from the time the wind started picking up and we had been given the order to get our helicopters belowdecks until the storm blew itself past us. By the morning of the second day the sky was blue and the wind was diminishing, although the ocean was still full of whitecaps.

At chow time the compartment emptied out, everyone finally heading for the mess deck, with most people using the outside catwalks instead of the internal passageways. I was determined to eat two eggs sunny side up, a little runny, just for the hell of it.

I was greeted by dazzling sunlight, a bright blue ocean, a fair wind, and at least a dozen guys leaning over the railing puking their guts out.

K. B. Johnson was right behind me, feeling absolutely chipper. He took one look at the situation and launched into a slightly off-key version of a then-popular Rascals song, "It's a beautiful morning. Think I'll go outside a while."

Behind me, along the rail, all I could hear was groans. As I turned to look, one Marine let loose with a trail of puke that got caught by the wind and was whipped along the side of the ship.

K. B. just kept strolling along, smiling and singing. We went belowdecks and ate our eggs sunny side up.

Chapter 15

"Fire in the zone! We're taking hits!"

I heard the urgent message over the headset in my helmet and tried to see where the shots were coming from. I was the starboard gunner on the third aircraft in a flight of four. We were making the initial assault, and we were the first wave. Three more flights of four helicopters each were behind us, and each helicopter carried a squad of infantrymen from the 4th Marine Regiment.

It was August 1968 and we were over rolling, heavily grassed and jungled terrain, south of Khe Sanh and just east of the Laotian border. The LZ was a grassy knoll, with heavy tree lines and ravines to the north. We were coming in from the east and that meant the fire was on my side!

I had been locked and loaded since we had cleared the concertina wire back at Quang Tri that morning, and now it was just a matter of finding out where the Vietnamese were and firing back.

"We've got muzzle flashes. In a gully fifty meters north of the zone."

At least now we knew where to look for them. Another message from the lead bird said more muzzle flashes had been seen coming from a hill about two hundred yards away.

I leaned out the window, got a glimpse of the area ahead, and swung my .50-caliber as far ahead as it would go. The machine guns were mounted on swivels that were bolted into the side of the helicopter. They had mechanical stops to limit their movement forward and back, up and down. We had excellent mobility as it was, but the stops were there for a purpose.

If the gun was swung too far forward, the bullets would go right through the pilot's head; too far back or downward and the external fuel cells could be ruptured. If the gun was pointed too high, it could chop off sections of the rotor blades.

We were coming in low and very fast, somewhere above 60 knots, to avoid as much fire as possible, so all of this was happening quickly. I glimpsed the area the lead bird had warned of, and as soon as it came into my line of fire, I opened up.

Three rounds, four rounds, three rounds, again four. I kept up the bursts, slamming the heavy bullets into any likely spots I could see. I kept waiting for the by-now-familiar *bwaaang,* the sharp metallic sound you hear when the enemy's bullets start finding the target.

As our tour had progressed, many crews had encountered small-arms fire, machine-gun fire, and occasional shots from 37mm antiaircraft guns. When the North Vietnamese found their mark—*bwaaang! bwaaang!*—the bullets slammed through the metal skin of our aircraft with an intensity that filled the inside with shrapnel and played havoc with people and flight systems.

As we closed on the Vietnamese positions, I upped my rate of fire to five rounds, six, seven, eight rounds to a burst. It was getting more frantic with each second! So far no one had been injured. The enemy bullets were going too high and passing harmlessly by.

But it was a donnybrook and a half! Out of the corner of my eye I saw J. D. Cross, the crew chief, also shooting out of the starboard hatchway with his M-14 rifle on full automatic. Cross was shorter and weighed even less than I, and the recoil from his rifle kept knocking him backward several steps. But each time he'd recover and come right back firing again.

He had full magazines taped together in twos, each upside down from the other, so when one ran out he could eject it, turn it upside down, and insert the other. It kept reloading time to a minimum.

Just then I ran out of the fifty rounds in the ammo box strapped to the side of my machine gun and had to reload, immediately! I flipped up the cover over the .50's chamber, threw the empty ammo box to the side, and grabbed for another. A grunt sitting next to my gun, looking helpless and scared half to death, jumped up to help me reload. He yanked the top off the box, passed it to me in one swift motion, and I reloaded and resumed firing.

As brave as they were, a lot of grunts hated being in the helicopters when we started taking hits, because they generally couldn't fire back and there was no place to go for cover. I always felt safer inside than outside, but being more familiar with ground activities, they felt just the opposite.

I imagine the guy helping me was happy just to have something to do until he could get the hell out of there.

Eight rounds. Nine rounds. I was putting out longer bursts. Aircraft farther back reported taking hits, and they were opening up, too. Still, no one in our bird was hit, but my adrenaline was flowing and I felt as if all my senses were on overdrive. I placed the thumb of my right hand over the butterfly trigger, wrapped my fingers around the handle near the trigger, and leaned right out the window.

Partly I was doing it to get a better view, but I also did it because I didn't want to succumb to fear, so in reaction, I went nuts. I screamed at the Vietnamese out there, wherever they were.

"You want a piece of this? Come on! Here it is, take a shot!"

All the time I kept firing, watching the tracers, yelling, swearing, even spitting at someone I couldn't see, but who was trying to kill me! And suddenly I felt the flare of the rotor blades as we settled into the LZ. I saw other grunts on the ground forming defensive positions.

Our ramp went down, the squad headed out, and the grunt who'd helped me reload made a beeline for the ground and his idea of safety. At the end of the ramp he stood for a split second, shot me back a "thumbs-up," and headed out to do battle. The whole engagement had lasted only about a minute. But it was a minute of total insanity, which is what war is anyway.

I never planned to act the way I did, but when the shooting started, something came over me and I acted on instinct. If you had asked me back then if I was ever scared in battle, I honestly could have answered "No!" Whether I knew it was coming or it just happened, my reaction was always the same. I felt the only way to survive was to use the adrenaline flowing in my blood to go far, far beyond fear.

"Staying on the offensive is 90 percent of winning a fight," Starbuck had told us. If it was crazy, fine! At least it kept you alive. Combat isn't a quiet chess game or a gentlemanly sports match. The punishment for losing is death. I had no intention of dying, and none of the others in the squadron acted as though they were opting for suicide, either.

Sometimes you just had to push yourself to a point of insanity. You could go outwardly crazy or appear calm as hell. But inside you were boiling, and if you could channel that energy into direct and accurate action, you had much better chances for survival.

We'd been in Vietnam for only three months in August, but I already was closing in on one hundred missions. Many of the crew chiefs, including Doug Braman and Al Munoz, had already surpassed that milestone.

We had arrived off the coast of Vietnam on May 16 and off-loaded on May 17. We had one day of indoctrination and then started flying combat missions. For the first couple of days we flew with HMM-262 aircraft as escorts until our pilots and crews were familiar with the terrain. Then we were on our own, and HMM-161 went to work.

I had to cool my heels for a week and a half because my primary job was aircraft electrician, not door gunner, and only a limited number of people from each job assignment could fly each month. Those days until the end of May passed very slowly, it seemed, until I was authorized to fly gunner.

I really wanted to be part of the battle. I wanted to fly. I wanted to fly all the time, and I wanted to be where the action was.

Luckily for me, not everyone in the squadron felt that way. There were a few guys with wives and children back home, for instance, who didn't want to stick their necks out any more than necessary, unless they absolutely had to, and flew just enough to earn their gunners' wings and a couple of Air Medals.

Gunners' wings were silver, with a gold center and three stars across the top. The stars were for each of your first three battles, but in addition, crewmen had to fly a total of twenty missions before qualifying for the wings.

A mission was counted when an aircraft went into a hot zone, whether it was on a resupply, medevac, or extracting or landing troops. After twenty missions, crews were awarded their wings, if they had actually engaged the enemy three times, and were awarded their first Air Medal.

For some guys, that was enough to show their bravery. Then they opted for ground assignments, which was fine by me, because it opened up more opportunities for me to fly. I found out what war was really about, almost immediately.

Khe Sanh was still an active little place in early June, even though the siege had been over for two months, and it still took shellings from the North Vietnamese. The hills surrounding the base, which were manned by our infantry and artillery, were regularly probed, usually at night.

We worked incredibly long days, resupplying the hills,

medevacing wounded Marines, carrying troops on assaults, and dropping Reconnaissance Marines into remote locations where they could monitor enemy movements.

On June 3, my third day of flying, we launched an assault into the same area near the Laotian border where, two months later, I would get into the firefight described earlier. I was flying as starboard gunner, Chuck Palmer was crew chief, and Bob Thompson, another electrician, was port gunner. That area hadn't been probed much in recent months, mainly because of the Tet Offensive and the siege at Khe Sanh.

I was in the first flight of four, but we didn't draw fire. We landed safely, and the grunts jumped out to form a perimeter. I was leaning out the window, watching closely, to be sure where our troops were.

One thing I never wanted to do in Vietnam, and never did, was to shoot our own people because of uncertainty over their location versus the North Vietnamese.

We lifted off, flew low over the forming perimeter, and suddenly I saw what appeared to be a garden. For a second I couldn't believe what I was seeing! What the hell was a garden doing out here in the middle of the jungle? Obviously, I thought later, the VC and NVA regulars were growing food out there. But those thoughts were rudely interrupted by a sound that would soon become familiar.

Bwaaang!

We had taken a hit!

It was the first time I had been shot at, and every nerve in my body seemed to explode. I couldn't tell whether I had been hit or not, and remembered being told by people who had been wounded that the first thing they felt was numb.

And as those thoughts were going through my mind, I saw, just past the garden, a black-pajama-clad figure wearing a conical-shaped straw hat running like hell for an opening in the jungle. And without thinking, I opened up with my .50. It all seemed like slow motion, that figure running, tracers from my barrel following him, and then both disappearing into the dark greenness.

I felt a tap on my shoulder and looked up. It was Palmer, and he was pointing down at my feet, where an inch from the heel of my right boot a bullet had plowed a furrow into the deck. When we landed for fuel, Chuck and I looked the exterior over and found that the bullet had entered the bottom of the helicopter, by a rotating beacon light that is used as a warning device for aircraft flying at a lower altitude. We had disconnected all those lights on our aircraft, but the VC still used them as aiming points.

The bullet had torn through the skin, slammed into a cargo roller, started it spinning, and ricocheted into the deck at my feet. Later I regretted that I didn't dig that bullet out of the deck and keep it as a souvenir.

I never knew for sure whether the VC who shot at us died. Thompson said he later heard that the grunts found a body in that location, but I didn't press the issue.

Combat had quickly become a constant for our squadron. HMM-161 had come to Vietnam as a well-trained, highly motivated group of people with the best of equipment, and we wasted no time in establishing ourselves.

In June we set an all-time flight record for a squadron of CH-46 helicopters, logging 2,400 flight hours. By the end of July the squadron had flown 5,524 hours, 3,968 missions, 22,814 sorties, and 2,954 medical evacuations, and had carried 4,257 tons of cargo.

For all of that, though, we often had to go to extremes to find the NVA and VC. Back home the media had made the Tet Offensive appear as a major defeat for the U.S. It apparently didn't occur to the armchair experts back at the briefing centers in Da Nang and Saigon that soldiers who had been fighting for more than thirty years in some cases could mount a coordinated offensive, especially when it was on a familiar battleground.

But in doing so the North Vietnamese had taken a terrible

beating. Our airstrip at Quang Tri was the northernmost helicopter base in South Vietnam, only about fifteen miles south of the DMZ. Yet, throughout the summer of 1968, rocket attacks and attempts to penetrate our perimeter were sharply reduced.

So the Marine infantry was hounding those remnants of the army that had attacked in January, rooting it out wherever northern soldiers or southern guerrillas could be found. Often that meant making major forays into the DMZ or conducting operations along the infiltration routes from Laos.

Wherever the grunts went, we went. We'd start on an initial assault, tearing into a landing zone in some remote section of jungle, dropping in hundreds of Marines within an hour or so. If the action was intense we'd sometimes divert to do gun runs, strafing enemy positions as the infantry prepared to assault from the ground.

We often were accompanied by Huey gunships from VMO-6, also stationed at Quang Tri, which had compiled a formidable record of thirteen hundred confirmed enemy kills from September 1965 to April 1968. If we encountered mortars or antiaircraft positions, the Hueys or jet aircraft would unleash their rockets.

When a firebase was established and the infantry started making patrols or conducting search-and-destroy missions, we'd resupply them with everything from food, water, and ammunition to mail, and occasionally beer.

When engagements with the North Vietnamese produced casualties, we were there to medevac them to aid stations or hospital ships off the coast if the injuries were severe. We regularly worked with the 1st, 3d, 4th, 5th, 7th, 9th, and 26th Marine Regiments. It often was dangerous, since most LZs were hostile. It also could be grueling.

As a rule, the pilots, numbering roughly three for each aircraft, were split into two shifts. One shift would take off between dawn and 7 a.m., depending on the morning's missions, returning to Quang Tri in the afternoon when another set of pilots would take over and fly all afternoon and into the evening. The crews, meanwhile, remained on board.

If a crew was assigned to an aircraft with an early mission, such as resupplying a firebase that had been under attack all night, it could lift off at 5:00 a.m. and fly nearly continuously until 8:00 p.m. or so. Two or three helicopters also were placed on standby for emergency resupply and medevacs all night.

Those gunners not assigned to night flights still had to remove the machine guns from the helicopters, take them to a shack that housed cleaning equipment, dismantle them, give them a good scrubbing, and reassemble them. The machine guns were stored in the squadron armory, which actually was a makeshift room on one side of a tin hangar.

When that was done, we returned to our hooches—twelve-by-twenty-foot buildings made with two-by-four frames and plywood floors and walls, with screens comprising the upper half of the walls for ventilation, and corrugated tin roofs—to collapse and try to get some sleep. Then at about 4:30 a.m. it started all over.

The pace was exhausting but necessary, and few complained about it with any conviction. We had waited more than two years for the chance to join the war, and we weren't going to do things halfheartedly.

Early in the war years U.S. troops faced much more activity from local Viet Cong than from North Vietnamese regulars. Death often was dealt from concealed booby traps or snipers, while engagements with full-force units were still a rarity.

By 1968, however, our fighting was against well-trained, well-equipped regular troops. They had rockets, artillery, machine guns, mortars, and RPGs (for either rifle- or rocket-propelled grenades) that were very effective against helicopters, along with Russian-made AK-47 assault rifles, and SKS rifles, both of which were accurate and sturdy. Our most dangerous encounters usually came either on initial assaults, where the flight might drop right into a concentration of enemy troops, or during insertions and extractions of Reconnaissance Marines.

Recons represented the cream of Marine Corps ground operations. They were trained in surveillance, camouflage, guerrilla warfare, counterinsurgency, scuba diving, parachute jumping, infiltration, and virtually every form of unconventional warfare that existed. They considered themselves a cut above every other form of Marine, refused to acknowledge the existence of the U.S. Army, Green Berets, or navy SEALs, and were absolutely convinced that one Recon was the equivalent of at least ten enemy soldiers.

Judging from what I saw during my tour in Vietnam, I have to agree with them.

An insertion was the term for picking up a team of Recons either at Quang Tri, where some of them were stationed, at Dong Ha, a supply base five miles farther north, or at LZ Stud, a staging area ten miles west of Dong Ha, and then taking them out to enemy territory, where they were dropped off.

An extraction meant picking up that team, either at a predesignated place and time, usually a week or so later, or yanking them out in a hurry if they ran into a real problem.

Going out with the Recons was always an experience. They always went to some off-the-wall location in the middle of what was called "Indian country," where encounters with infiltrating North Vietnamese troops were a likelihood rather than a possibility.

Sometimes five to eight Recons would go out for ten days to two weeks, just to keep an eye on things and call artillery strikes on top of infiltrating troops. Sometimes as many as twelve to fifteen would go together, for the express purpose of killing Vietnamese. Sometimes they'd barely get out of the helicopter before they would be "compromised," meaning seen by the enemy, and would have to call for an emergency extraction.

That happened on one of my first flights as gunner during a day of Recon work. We went to the headquarters at Quang Tri, where a briefing was held. I felt privileged to be there, as Recon officers discussed sensitive information including the locations of enemy infiltration movements and the missions of the teams we would insert that day. We started taking teams out, mostly near the Laotian border, and it went well for the first two insertions.

Then, on the third mission that day, we dropped a team off in a grassy area fifteen miles or so southeast of Khe Sanh, where the flat plain turned to rolling hills. We weren't out of the zone two minutes before the team leader radioed us.

"Sir, we are compromised!"

We turned back toward the insertion point immediately, and the pilot asked the team leader where they had moved since we dropped them off. But the team leader said the enemy troops were so close that he didn't want to give specific directions, since they may have been monitoring our radio transmissions.

There was no questioning his sincerity. As we listened to his conversation with the pilot, we realized that every word spoken from the ground was being whispered!

To overcome the problem of the Vietnamese listening in, the pilot and team leader discussed the winning team in the previous year's North-South football game, and which direction the Recons had taken relative to the designation of the winner or loser.

Ultimately it was decided that the team was about one hundred yards north of the zone where we had dropped them off.

The pilot radioed the situation to the ground, and then recommended, "Pop a smoke, and then tell us which color it is."

Suddenly a green smoke cloud appeared, along with a radio transmission that the team had indeed popped a green smoke. We headed for it while the team leader, still whispering, told us they could hear the Vietnamese moving toward their position. From the air it looked as though less than one hundred yards separated the good guys from the bad guys.

We dropped down for the extraction into an area of tall elephant grass. It appeared to be fifteen feet high or so and was a great cover for everyone, the Recons and the Vietnamese. The pilot didn't like that one bit and gave me the most all-encompassing order I ever received as a Marine. This was not unusual and may well have been standard for Marine helicopter pilots in Vietnam, as I have heard similar stories related by other gunners and air crewmen in the years since Vietnam.

"If you see something move, kill it!"

"Yes, sir!"

"If you think you see something move, kill it!"

"Yes, sir!"

"If you think you see something thinking about moving, kill it!"

"Yes, sir!"

"If someone lights a cigarette, kill him. If you think you see someone light a cigarette, kill him! Kill every rock, tree, and blade of grass out there. I don't want anything left alive when we leave!"

We landed, the Recons ran on board, and as soon as the ramp lifted, ensuring that the whole team was inside, we tore up that place!

If the NVA was coming, it ran into a solid wall of bullets. The Recons were firing with everything they had, and as far as I know, nothing was left alive in that LZ when we left. I'd bet that if I went back to that little part of Vietnam today, there would still be a pile of dead rocks and barren ground there.

For all our efforts, and our successes, however, there was bound to be a time when we also took our losses. That time came on June 19, one month to the day after we started combat operations in Vietnam. It was at Khe Sanh, not surprisingly, but didn't involve a direct engagement with enemy troops.

Our helicopters were picking up troops at the north end of the runway as part of an assault at another location. An old village, once quiet and unmolested, had stood slightly north of Khe Sanh. The thatched-roof hooches were there along with several trees that had survived both the incredible bombardment that had gone on from January to April and the occasional flurries of activity that had continued even after the siege ended.

When the siege was in full swing, the base was being resupplied by C-130 Hercules airplanes and other cargo aircraft capable of dropping supplies out of rear cargo hatches. The cargo pallets were attached to parachutes, which brought them to earth intact. But many of those parachutes were cut loose, only to end up getting caught in the trees at the north end of the base.

On June 19, 1968, helicopters from HMM-161 landed at the north end of Khe Sanh in a place called LZ Turkey, where Marine infantrymen were gathered, waiting to move out.

A CH-46 piloted by Capt. Lufkin S. Sharp, with 1st Lt. Michael D. Helmstetler as copilot, landed and lowered its ramp. As a squad of infantrymen ran on board, the rotor wash began whipping a parachute out of a nearby tree. Suddenly it was freed, blowing wildly in the wind, and then was drawn straight into the rotor blades.

The huge sheet caught in the blades, throwing them out of synchronization. The aft rotor head tilted and then went completely out of control. Miraculously, the infantrymen and crew were not injured. But the blades smashed through the cockpit, killing Sharp and Helmstetler.

Later the squadron sent technicians and mechanics to recover salvageable parts of the destroyed aircraft. The bodies had already been recovered and sent home for burial. They were good people, good pilots, and good Marines. They were liked and respected, and they were missed. The squadron cruise book, a yearbook detailing a unit's achievements, was dedicated to them, and a memorial service was held in their honor in a hangar at Quang Tri.

It was the first memorial service for a member of HMM-161 who died in combat during its 1968–69 tour. It would prove to be far, far from the last.

Chapter 16

The call to divert from our mission came just after we had left a load of supplies at a hilltop firebase southeast of Khe Sanh. It was still early in the morning, the first week of June, when I heard the transmission to our pilots ordering us to head to Khe Sanh for a major medevac.

That base was still a favorite target for North Vietnamese gunners. They sometimes would go days without firing a shot, and then unleash a fierce barrage of artillery fire, hoping to find Marines out in the open.

That was exactly what had happened, and as we landed, I saw a line of stretchers being carried toward us. I was stunned as the wounded came on board. I guess I expected clean bandages and gritty smiles, kind of like in the movies I'd seen as a kid.

But this was reality. The wounds had been covered only with quick battlefield dressings, with blood and body parts showing through. Every one of the wounded Marines had a plasma bag attached to his arm through a tube, and all of the wounds were serious.

Some had open stomach wounds with intestines exposed, some had what were called "sucking chest wounds," indicating that a lung had been punctured, chunks of flesh were torn from arms, legs, and trunks, and blood was everywhere.

I was flying as starboard gunner, and two Marines placed a stretcher at my feet. A corpsman thrust a plasma bag into my hand and yelled, "Start squeezing!"

I was momentarily shocked by what I was seeing, but automatically started squeezing the plasma into the Marine's veins. I was thinking that my first responsibility was to stay at my post, which was the machine gun, but if I did I felt sure that a Marine would die.

I looked out at the hills surrounding Khe Sanh as we took off and came to the realization that since the siege had been broken, any enemy units remaining in the vicinity would not be close enough to direct accurate fire at the helicopter, especially since we were picking up speed quickly. Also, if they had been close enough to shoot us down, they would have done so.

There were eight wounded Marines on the deck, and only two corpsmen had accompanied them. I saw the crew chief and the port gunner squeezing plasma into other Marines and turned my full attention to the man at my feet.

He was a large blond-haired guy, looking to be in his mid-twenties. A chunk of flesh about the size of a softball had been torn out of his right thigh by a piece of shrapnel, and blood was oozing through his bandages. He started talking to me, shouting above the noise of the wind and engines.

"I gotta talk," he yelled. "They shot me full of morphine for the pain, but I can still feel it."

I let him talk, and looked around to see how everyone else was doing. It didn't look good. Every face was etched in pain, the deck was awash with blood, and I felt a queasy sensation in the pit of my stomach.

Aside from getting shot at, there was no more intense introduction to the destruction of war than medical-evacuation, or medevac, missions. They could come at any time, since our area of operation was spread out from the coast to the Laotian border and from the DMZ down to Phu Bai, about thirty miles south of Quang Tri. Occasionally we would operate in the Da Nang area or even farther south. Attacks at outposts or firebases could erupt without warning, and casualties were an inevitable result.

It wasn't that we hadn't been prepared. I could still remember Starbuck's first-aid lectures on Parris Island, and I could hear him repeating, "Apply direct pressure to a bleeding wound. Put a clean bandage, damp if possible, lightly over exposed intestines. If you don't have anything else, put the cellophane from your cigarette pack over a sucking chest wound to seal it."

I remembered follow-up courses back in Camp Geiger and New River, as older, more experienced Marines did everything they could to prepare us for the realities of battle. But this was the first time I had seen it for real, and it was a feeling unlike any I had ever encountered. I realized then that it wasn't the blood that was causing my uneasiness. It was the feeling of helplessness. I felt that I should be doing more, much, much more, but didn't know what.

Later I realized there was no more I could have done. Keeping that one Marine alive for a fifteen-minute flight out to one of the hospital ships, either the USS *Repose* or USS *Sanctuary,* was all I could hope to do. Any further care would have to be given by people with far more experience and equipment than was found on the average helicopter.

The wounded Marine was still talking and suddenly yelled to me, "What's your MOS?" That stood for military occupational specialty, or job assignment. "Are you a gunner all the time?"

"No," I answered. "I'm a 6242—helicopter electrician. I volunteer to fly gunner. I do it about half the time."

"I knew some electricians, down in Da Nang a few years ago," he said.

"What outfit?" I asked.

He mentioned a jet squadron, and I recognized it as being the one Swenson and LaPolla had belonged to. It was a jet attack squadron that used Phantom aircraft.

"I knew guys from there," I said. "They came to our outfit after their tour ended in 1966."

"What were their names?"

"Ernie Swenson and Tony LaPolla."

I thought briefly of all those swoops home we had made the previous year. It seemed like a decade had passed since then.

"I knew them," he said. That kind of set me back. What was this grunt doing on my helicopter, with a chunk of his leg missing, if he had been in a jet squadron three years earlier?

"How did you know Swenson?"

"Everybody knew Ernie Swenson!"

That was absolutely correct. Cpl. Ernie Swenson had done two things in his four-year Marine career that set him apart from all the rest and gave him a place in Marine Corps folklore, if not its official history.

Swenson told me in New River that he had worked his way up to plane captain status in his jet squadron. That meant he could sit in the cockpit, start the engines, and bring them up to idle speed for testing purposes. He also could taxi the aircraft from a parking spot on the flight line to a hangar, or vice versa.

He did that one day in Da Nang—start the engines, that is. And then, Ernie told me this himself, the electronic fuel programmers malfunctioned and the engines went to 100 percent throttle. That's usually what a pilot does when he wants to take off!

Ernie said the Phantom jumped its chocks, blocks designed to keep the tires from rolling when it is parked, and headed off across the flight line.

"I jumped out of the cockpit, ran across the wing, and jumped down to the flight deck. I hit hard on my heels, fell, and the wheel rolled right over my hair. It just missed my skull."

The aircraft rolled across the flight line and buried itself in the sand at the edge of the runway. No one was seriously injured, although Ernie said he had hairline fractures in both of his heels.

The wounded Marine remembered that incident. He also remembered one other—as did nearly everyone who was anywhere near the Da Nang flight line in 1965.

Ernie once again was in the cockpit, and all the electrical systems were energized. The aircraft was armed with rockets and bullets. Somehow a switch was thrown. Maybe it was jostled, or bumped, or elbowed. It doesn't matter how it happened; what does matter is the fact that a rocket was fired from that aircraft!

At the time, the 9th Marines were still stationed in the Da Nang area and were bivouacked on the other side of the flight line.

"The rocket took off right for the 9th Marines area," Ernie told me.

It entered a tent, but miraculously there was no explosion. Perhaps it was armed to fire but not explode. I wasn't there so I don't know.

However, Ernie said, "A Marine came out of his tent, carrying the rocket in his arms, and asked, 'Did anyone lose this?' He said it landed on an empty cot. Some shot, huh?"

The wounded Marine said he remembered that incident, too.

As the conversation progressed, we were nearing the hospital ships and I asked, "So how did you know those guys?"

"This is my second enlistment," he answered. "I was in hydraulics. Then I finished college and went to Officer Candidate School. That's where I got these," he said, reaching up to flip over his collar.

The wind had been blowing his collar lapels back toward his shoulder and I hadn't been looking at them, but then I got another shock. There were gold bars on his collar. This guy was a lieutenant!

"Sorry, sir!" I said, as I tried to make amends. Here I had been gabbing with him, not realizing he was an officer.

"No sweat," he said.

Gesturing at the gold bars, he said, "I got these at Quan-

HMM-161 crew chief Jeff Sorenson, right, puts the finishing touches on a logo for fellow crew chief Mike Galvin's aircraft at the Marine Corps Air Facility in New River, North Carolina, in April 1968.
USMC PHOTO.

A snappy salute from the guard on duty greets a visitor to the New River Air Facility in early 1968.
USMC PHOTO.

PROVISIONAL MARINE AIRCRAFT GROUP 39
SHEPHERD OF THE [illegible]
QUANG TRI, RVN
21 October 1968

IN MEMORIUM

\+ + +

CAPTAIN JOSEPH L. POWELL JR., USMC
Born: 5 November 1942 Died: 17 October 1968
Age: 25 years 11 months, 12 days
Husband of: Karen West Powell
Father of: Sean Michael Powell
Son of: Mr. and Mrs. Joseph L. Powell Sr.

\+

FIRST LIEUTENANT JAMES N. SWEET, USMCR
Born: 8 September 1945 Died: 17 October 1968
Age: 23 years, 1 month, 11 days
Son of: Mr. and Mrs. Newton R. Sweet

\+

CORPORAL JOHN R. FARRAZZANO, USMC
Born: 17 February 1946 Died: 17 October 1968
Age: 22 years 8 months
Son of: Mr. and Mrs. Frank Farrazzano

\+

LANCE CORPORAL ROBERT M. CHEEK, USMC
Born: 21 June 1948 Died: 17 October 1968
Age: 20 years, 5 months, 25 days
Son of: Mr. Haskell Cheek and Mrs. May Stapleton
Husband of: Evelyn Jane Cheek

\+

LANCE CORPORAL WILLIAM D. FRANTZ, USMC
Born: 2 June 1948 Died: 17 October 1968
Age: 20 years, 5 months, 15 days
Son of: Mr. and Mrs. Herbert W. Frantz

\+

HM2 DAYNE Y. SCOTT, USN
Born 28 September 1933 Died: 17 October 1968
Age: 35 years, 19 days
Husband of: Lynne Scott
Father of: Ledayna Rose Scott and Brenda Lee Scott

\+ Earth Has No Sorrow That Heaven Can Not Heal +

CROSS / USN 0120 ©1967 N00140-67-C-0212

Oct. 21, 1968 was a sad day for HMM-161 at the Quang Tri, RVN, airstrip as a memorial service was held for six members of the squadron who died during combat operations four days earlier on Oct. 17.
AUTHOR'S COLLECTION.

Troops file aboard HMM-161 Sea Knight helicopters prior to launching a monsoon season assault in the DMZ/Laotian border area. USMC PHOTO.

A CH-46 Sea Knight passes over a firebase that has been sprayed from above with Agent Orange, hence the skeleton-like tree trunks. Marine infantrymen are visible in the lower right corner. USMC PHOTO.

A Huey gunship provides close cover for a downed CH-46 in the rugged terrain of I Corps as recovery crews work to fix it during Operation Mameluke Thrust in late May 1968.
USMC PHOTO.

The walking wounded make for a waiting CH-46 A-Model Sea Knight helicopter which will take them to aid stations in the rear. The action took place in the spring of 1968 southwest of Da Nang.
USMC PHOTO.

A heavily laden squad of infantry makes for a waiting CH-46 helicopter from HMM-161 in the rugged country south of the Demilitarized Zone separating North and South Vietnam.
USMC PHOTO.

Marines of the Second Battalion, Fifth Regiment charge from CH-46 helicopters into muddy rice paddies during Operation Colorado in August 1966. USMC PHOTO.

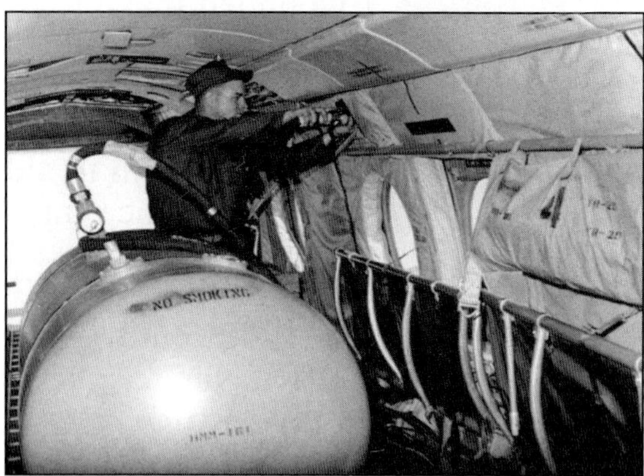

An HMM-161 crewmember attaches a line to an internal fuel tank that extended the CH-46's range and reduced the number of stops the squadron made to refuel during its cross country flight from North Carolina to California in April 1968.
USMC PHOTO.

Heavily camouflaged Marine Recons move into the high grasslands of northern I Corps after a drop zone insertion by HMM-161.
USMC PHOTO.

CH-46 Sea Knight helicopters from HMM-161 embark on a massive airlift from Vandergrift Combat Base, southeast of Khe Sanh in mid-1968. USMC PHOTO.

A captured North Vietnamese anti-aircraft weapon rests on the sands at the Quang Tri air strip next to the HMM-161 flight line. DON "OOGA" SMITH.

Two views of the author, left, at his gunner station prior to takeoff in June 1968, and inside a "hooch" at Phu Bai in early 1969.
AUTHOR'S COLLECTION.

A Navy Seabee holds the remains of a rocket that slammed into the base at Quang Tri during an attack in 1968.
DON "OOGA" SMITH.

The Rockpile, a sharp outcropping that gave the Marines a clear view of infiltration routes across the Demilitarized Zone into South Vietnam. The landing pad was so small that helicopters could land only their rear wheels to drop off or take on passengers and cargo.
DON "OOGA" SMITH.

The shattered remains of a CH-46 that crashed and burned lie near the perimeter fence at Quang Tri. Recovery crews brought as much of the aircraft as possible back to the airstrip to salvage any usable parts. DON "OOGA" SMITH.

Peering out the starboard hatchway as a flight of CH-46 helicopters approach the Quang Tri airstrip from the north. To the left of the lead helicopter, the river that formed the base perimeter on the east can be viewed, and Highway 1, the western perimeter, is on the right. DON "OOGA" SMITH.

The Quang Tri River separates the perimeter of the Marine airstrip from a village. The bucolic daytime scene often changed drastically at night when gunfire from the tree line behind the Vietnamese farmer would target the base. A sampan flying the South Vietnamese flag is visible just beyond the concertina wire. AUTHOR'S COLLECTION.

A view of the HMM-161 squadron area from the southeast. The perimeter is visible at the bottom of the photo.
DON "OOGA" SMITH.

Lt. Col. Paul W. Niesen.
USMC PHOTO.

Drill Instructor Sgt. Robert F. Starbuck on duty at Parris Island, January 1966.
USMC PHOTO.

tico. Then they put me in artillery. That's how I got this!" he added, pointing to his wound. It had been his gun emplacement the North Vietnamese had shelled that day.

"Some deal!" he said.

I had been pumping the plasma the whole time we had been talking. This was a man who knew friends of mine. I wouldn't have wanted him to die under any circumstances, but now it was as though a friend's life was in my hands.

I kept pumping, and he kept talking. Then we arrived at the *Sanctuary.*

Attendants ran on board to carry the wounded to operating rooms and someone grabbed the plasma bag from my hands. They picked him up in a hurry and I watched as they carried him away. Only then, I realized, I'd never asked his name. I watched as they went down the ramp. He waved once and was gone. I hope he made it.

While carrying wounded Marines from the battlefields was a major part of medevac duties, not all our missions resulted from bombs or bullets. There were other dangers out there that could put a Marine in an equally precarious position.

One such mission out in the boonies involved a PFC who somehow or other got hit by a jeep. When we got that call, in September, everyone on the crew just kind of looked at each other with a "You've got to be kidding me" expression.

The 4th Marines were conducting operations in a relatively flat area about twenty miles south of the DMZ, just east of the rolling hills that led to higher ground and the Laotian border. Somehow the Marine had been struck, just as if he'd been crossing a street against the light back home. He was alive and had no broken bones, but he did have a head injury and was acting somewhat erratically. His commanders asked for a helicopter to take him to the ship, where they could examine him.

But first we had to get him there, and that Marine wasn't very cooperative. A telephone connected directly to the crew was concealed behind a flap on the outside of the helicopter, midway between the pilot and the starboard entranceway. An infantry lieutenant ran up, took out the phone, and told the pilot, "Watch him, he's acting pretty strange!"

We got him on board and started to strap him onto one of the cloth bench seats that ran along the walls of the interior. Then the guy went crazy on us. We had already taken off and were about 200 feet in the air when he started screaming, kicking, flailing about with his fists, and strenuously resisting attempts to strap him down.

As Marine infantrymen went, he was pretty small, looking to be about five-feet-five-inches or so and maybe 130 pounds. But he was going wild and was hard to control. In addition, he was trying to jump out the entranceway!

We all dived on him. I got one leg, the port gunner got the other, and the crew chief held him around the middle. Since we had been designated to fly medevacs all day, we had a corpsman with us, who gave the guy a shot of something, and that quieted him down. But we didn't rest easy or take our eyes off of him until we got to the ship.

Getting hit by a jeep wasn't the typical type of injury we saw in Vietnam, but it also wasn't the only type of accident that could happen. And the everyday kind of accident, that barely rates a shrug back home, could escalate into a major situation when it happened in remote jungles.

A case in point occurred in October, in the northwest corner of South Vietnam near the border with North Vietnam and Laos. The terrain was heavily forested, hilly, and rocky—a perfect place for someone to break a bone. Again I was flying gunner during a day consisting solely of medevac missions.

A Marine had taken a fall while out on patrol and had broken his leg. He was miles from his base camp, and the terrain was too rough to try moving him. Fortunately, we were carrying an assortment of special equipment that made it easier to get the injured and wounded on board.

There was no open space nearby, so we had to take him out of the jungle by hoist. We could penetrate down as far as 250 feet with our hoist cables, and in the triple-canopy jungle south of Khe Sanh we sometimes used all the cable. In this case, however, we could maintain a hover at about 80 feet.

We sent down a special strap-in stretcher, which was used for people with broken backs, necks, or other injuries that required immobilizing them. The injured person could be placed in the basket-type stretcher, strapped in, and hoisted up without causing further injury. This took time, however, and called for considerable skill on the part of our pilots, who had to maintain a perfect hover while the work proceeded on the ground.

It also became a bit hectic because a sniper opened up on us right in the middle of the extraction!

I could see down to the ground from my post and watched as the infantrymen strapped in the injured man. It was nice country down there, with trees, waist-high grass, a small, fast-running stream nearby, and quite a few rocks. It was pretty to look at, but also provided perfect cover for the sniper.

The grunts had a good idea where the firing was coming from, so I hammered out some bursts in that direction to keep the Vietnamese off balance, and their heads down, while the stretcher came up. In a few minutes we had the man inside, placed the stretcher gently down on the deck, and headed for an aid station.

Just before we left, a platoon commander on the ground radioed up a "Thank you, and well done to the crew."

I was pretty proud of that. I had a lot of respect for the people on the ground. They were doing an unbelievably difficult job, and they were doing it very well. I was happy to be helping any way I could, and when they felt good enough to say "well done," it made me feel that our efforts were worthwhile.

The area where that Marine broke his leg was familiar territory to us, and in November it was there that I participated in the most bizarre medevac of my tour.

In the hills northwest of Khe Sanh a Marine patrol had been wading through a swampy area and become infested with leeches. But only one extremely unlucky Marine had one of those leeches crawl into his penis and attach itself there!

Two days later that guy couldn't piss to save his life, and in fact that's what it was coming down to. Not only was he in extreme pain, but the poisons that the kidneys normally clean out of the human body were backing up inside him.

To make matters much, much worse, it was the rainy season, and flying in the monsoons, with thick cloud cover, was very dangerous. The Marine was stranded at an outpost on the edge of a cliff. Normally it wouldn't have been difficult to extract him, but in this case heavy clouds covered the entire area.

While the terrain dropped dramatically on the cliff side of the outpost, the other side consisted of a gently sloping hill that descended several hundred feet over a half mile or so. The clouds and wind direction that day combined to set up a continual flow from the sloping side, over the tops of the trees, and then sharply down on the cliff side. It gave the appearance of a waterfall, with the clouds flowing to the brink of the cliff and then dropping away.

It also prevented us from getting down to take the Marine out of there, because we couldn't see the LZ. Our pilots kept up a running dialogue with the ground commander, trying to figure if there was enough space for us to get in, with directions coming from the ground based on the sound of our rotors. The pilots finally decided the zone was too small for precise maneuvering, so we began circling, waiting for a break in the weather.

We finally had to head back to refuel, and another helicopter came on station while we were gone. The clouds broke for a minute as we were on our way back, so the other helicopter dropped in and pulled the Marine out of there.

At least a half dozen helicopters in the vicinity had been monitoring the situation, and everyone was cheering for that poor guy when he got out. As usual, I have no idea how that Marine made out. It was very rare for the crews to get feedback on the results of our actions; we just did our jobs and hoped for the best.

Our jobs occasionally consisted of handling those strange situations, but they still amounted to only a break in the overall mission of extracting the wounded. Since battles weren't fought on preset schedules, medevac calls came at all hours of the day and night. While it was difficult enough to get the wounded out of a hot zone in the daytime, it could be absolutely terrible in the dark.

We rotated the job of flying night medevac, and I caught it once every few weeks. In the fall, well after dark, we received a call to head to a firebase near the DMZ where a battle was in progress and wounded Marines needed help immediately.

We headed out over darkened villages, watching illumination flares pop up at the perimeters of bases and outposts. It was a surrealistic scene, with the darkness being broken by streams of tracers racing back and forth from the opposing sides. Depending on what the North Vietnamese were using for ammunition, the tracers were red or green.

It was a pretty eerie sight down there and reminded me of that night back in New River when we flew over the mock battle at the night-firing range. But this time the picture was complete, with a real enemy firing real bullets back at the Marines.

Vietnam seemed to be inordinately dark at night, and it took a full moon to give any kind of decent illumination. But I had developed excellent night vision, so I still could make out details on the ground, and whenever we neared battle scenes the fierce exchange of tracers was unmistakable.

The tracers accounted for one bullet out of every five that were fired, and they usually ran horizontally until the sound of helicopter blades reached the ground. Then one side would shift skyward. Crews developed a straightforward method for determining the level of danger—if the enemy bullets were missing by a wide margin, they appeared to float, but if they were close, they zipped right past.

Performing night medevacs posed quite a dilemma for the pilots, because they wanted to get to the wounded Marines, but you can't do that if your helicopter is being shot down. It was an education for gunners to be firing back with a .50-caliber machine gun and realize that its one stream of tracers seemed ineffectual against so many.

But there was help out there on those dark nights, in the form of one radio call that was heard frequently and carried the simultaneous effects of welcome relief and raising the hair on the back of our necks.

"This is The Spook!"

Hearing those words meant we had been joined by a C-130 Spectre gunship, also called "Spooky." They were specially outfitted air force gunships, and were considered an advancement over the original "Puff the Magic Dragon" C-47 gunships. They carried electrically controlled Gatling guns that could fire thirty-six hundred rounds per minute, and put a bullet in every square inch of a football field in that time, as well as huge flares that could turn a nighttime battlefield into day.

The methodology followed by the Spooky pilots included quick instructions to the helicopter pilots, amounting to "stay out of our flight path and get set for some fun," then a dialogue with the ground commander making sure they knew the exact coordinates of everyone on the ground, Marines and the North Vietnamese, right down to the inch.

Then they'd make a pass, tossing out huge illumination flares that lit the place up like Times Square on New Year's Eve, turn, and come back with the Gatling guns blazing.

Tracers coming up from the ground would train momentarily on the sound of the aircraft engines, but what a sight going back down!

It was a red waterfall, and the sound was unbelievable! It wasn't a bang or a boom; it was a mechanical roar that shook the night. One pass, turn, another, turn, another. Then the Spook would pull back and give the go-ahead to pick up the wounded.

Where there had been enemy automatic weapons and machine guns a few minutes earlier, there was only silence. Even if any NVA soldiers were left alive after that, they weren't stupid enough to advertise their positions and ask for more.

Helicopter crews often reported encountering the Spook in those dark Vietnam nights. I saw it on several occasions and each time I was in awe of what that machine could do.

Help from the Spook meant that a much-needed mission would be completed with far less difficulty and some badly shot-up marines would have a faster ride to aid stations and hospitals. Nonetheless, flying medevacs left me with mixed feelings of satisfaction and depression.

I was happy when we could get those guys to hospitals in time to save them. But the extent of the wounds I saw always left me with the feeling that I had first encountered at Khe Sanh. I just wished I could do more.

It was on that first medevac when I really came to grips with what war was all about. It seemed like a scene from a movie. But in all the John Wayne movies we'd ever watched, the good guys survived. Even if the hero was killed, there'd be a director somewhere yelling "Cut," and then the actors could get up and go on living.

But this was no movie, and celluloid heroes aren't real. This was war. There was no director, and no one to yell "Cut" when things didn't go right.

When the heroes died, it was for real, and forever.

Chapter 17

There was something about Bill Frantz, standing in front of the avionics hooch with a rake in his hand, raking the sand, that just didn't fit into my picture of what we were supposed to be doing in Vietnam.

So what if the sand had footprints in it? Even when he raked it and put nice, neat lines in it, the wind and constant traffic messed it up again in an hour.

I decided right then that I had to make my mark in Vietnam. I had to launch myself into the situation and take a stand. So I put down my helmet, pistol, flight jacket, and flak jacket, let out a rebel yell, and did a running broad jump right into the raked area. But the results weren't what I had expected.

It wasn't as though I hadn't warned Bill of my intentions, and it wasn't as though he hadn't warned me of the risks. I wasn't even the only person who put footprints into that raked section.

Our squadron area on the flight line ended with the avionics hooch, which was right next to a tent that served as a dispatch center for the motor transport section. Every morning at 7:00 a.m., all the truck drivers would walk across the gleaming, white sand to the edge of the flight line, stand in formation, go through roll call, and get their assignments. Then they would trudge back across the sand and go about their business.

Unfortunately, on June 1, the day I started flying gunner,

M.Sgt. R. R. Smidley gave Bill the assignment of coming to the avionics hooch every day at 6:30 a.m., taking a rake that somebody had dug up somewhere, and raking that sand into neat lines. Then, usually before anyone else got there to appreciate his job, the truck drivers walked across the sand going to and from their formation, obliterating all of Bill's nice, neat lines.

Bill didn't like that job, but he was the kind of Marine who could chalk it up to experience. Bill was one of the classiest people I had ever met and could whistle the entire "William Tell Overture"—and not just the familiar *Lone Ranger* part either.

He stood about five-feet-nine-inches tall, weighed about 150 or so, with short dark hair and glasses. He was very serious about being a Marine. Bill once told me he had been in the Marines for two years before he relaxed enough to nod to people he knew when he passed them on a sidewalk, rather than looking straight ahead, as we had been taught in boot camp.

Bill came from Florida and talked a lot about a girl back there, who worked for an airline, saying he wanted to marry her when he went home. Since I was flying gunner, I was coming in early every day to prepare for our flights, and most days was there to watch Bill rake those lines, always marveling at the complete waste of talent. Raking the sand wasn't accomplishing anything, but in return for coming in early every morning, Smidley was letting Bill off an hour early each afternoon, just when the day's flights were returning and his talents as an electrician were needed most.

Quang Tri wasn't exactly the Monte Carlo of Vietnam. There were no clubs, no recreational facilities, and no leisure-time activities.

What you had at Quang Tri was sand, heat, work, and fighting, surrounded by bunkers and barbed wire. Snipers often fired at us from the village across the river to the east. To the north was another village, where snipers would fire into the bellies of our helicopters when we took off. To the west was Highway 1, across which were some infantry installations and Recon headquarters, then miles of flat plains with nothing out there but war.

To the south was the village of Quang Tri, but it was off-limits because we were too close to North Vietnam and the place was full of infiltrators. So when you had time off you did nothing, except maybe write a letter or wait for the end of the workday so you could talk to someone.

On June 13, I was scheduled for a 7:00 a.m. launch, and the duty sergeant woke me up at 5:30. I went to the flight line, checked the schedule, checked the machine guns out of the armory, loaded up on ammunition, and went to the avionics hooch to see if there was any hot water to make a cup of C-ration coffee. Bill was just finishing his raking as I approached.

"You know this is a waste of time," I said to Bill.

"I know," Bill answered.

"I don't know why he has you doing this," I said.

"I don't, either," Bill answered.

"Today I think I'd like to be first," I said.

"First at what?" Bill asked.

"First at putting my footprints in that sand," I said.

"I don't care," Bill said.

That's when I put my gear down on the sand. Bill looked up from his raking and said, "Uh, Ron, I don't think you'd better."

"I have to, Bill. It's just something I've got to do!"

"Ron, I really don't think you should."

Let's face it. I should have been tipped off that something was wrong. At first Bill said he didn't care, then the next thing I knew, he was saying the exact opposite. That's when I made my jump.

"Whattya think?" I asked Bill.

"I think you're in deep shit," he said.

"Why?" I asked.

"Look behind you," Bill muttered while he reraked the area where I'd landed.

I did, and there, standing next to my jackets, helmet, and pistol, was none other than Master Sergeant Smidley. He didn't say anything, he just kind of looked at me with a tight little smile and walked into the avionics hooch.

"Oh, shit. Why didn't you tell me he was back there?" I asked Bill.

"I tried to," Bill answered.

You'd have thought, with all the flying, fighting, and working we were doing, that there wouldn't have been any time for the run-of-the-mill, back-in-the-States make-work details that some career Marines thought was necessary to maintain discipline and order.

That's what I thought, but I was dead wrong. Because even with all we were doing, there were a few, generally in administrative positions that didn't involve flying or fighting, who had plenty of time to think up things for us to do.

Many of these resulted from conditions inside the concertina wire that surrounded the Quang Tri airstrip. It was a hot, dusty environment, especially for the first six months or so we lived there. The dry season started in late April and had been going strong for about a month when we landed on May 17.

The first night I slept in Vietnam it was so hot that I lay on top of my cot wearing nothing but my skivvies. When I woke up at 6:00 a.m., it still was around 90 degrees or so. I hate waking up cold, and my first awakening "in-country" was beautiful.

"I can't believe this," I remember thinking. "It's really nice."

Unfortunately, it couldn't last. What I didn't realize immediately, but soon found out, was that the price you pay for 90-degree nights is extremely hot days.

The temperature often reached 120 or more in the daytime. In a place where there is little shade and the wind feels like the breath of a blast furnace, the heat soon becomes a continually aggravating presence. It's there all the time and has to be dealt with all the time. The metal sides of the helicopters, which we had to climb over when working on them, were so hot they would burn our hands and arms. The windshield of the '46 had an outside air temperature gauge attached to it, with a display in degrees Celsius.

Even in the shade those gauges routinely would be pegged above 50 degrees Celsius in the dry season. You couldn't write letters home without them being smeared with sweat and dirt.

But the human body is adaptable. After a while, 120-degree heat seemed normal, because our bodies adapted to it. Therefore, if the temperature dropped 20 degrees or so overnight, into the eighties or nineties, for instance, it had the same effect as if we had been home with a daytime temperature of 75 degrees and overnight lows in the fifties or forties. By the time the rainy season started in October, I already was sleeping under a quilted poncho liner at night.

As if the heat weren't enough, Quang Tri was also turned into a dust storm by noon every day. When constructing the airstrip at Quang Tri, the Seabees had trucked in tons upon tons of white sand to make the base level, which was required for the flight line and runway.

The runway was about a half mile long, enough for helicopters and C-130 cargo aircraft, but not for jets. Highway 1, known as the Street Without Joy, ran alongside the runway on the west, and the Quang Tri River formed the boundary on the east. The sand was level under the flight line, but it dipped down a couple of feet between the edge of the line and the row of maintenance hooches. Somewhere toward the end of August, somebody got the idea that we should prepare for the wet season by digging a ditch between the flight line and the maintenance hooches, apparently so the flight line wouldn't be flooded when it rained.

Things were a bit slow for a few days and Sergeant Scoggins had just given me the afternoon off, the first I'd had since arriving in May. I had no real plans, but I had the misfortune of walking past a sergeant named Barlow at just this time, and he snagged me.

I spent the next three hours digging a ditch the length of the squadron area.

That was a pain, but the futility of the detail wasn't apparent until a few weeks later when we got hit with a storm off the South China Sea. Then the ditch filled up with water and everyone had to make a long detour to get from the flight line to the maintenance area.

Since that wasn't such a good idea, someone figured the ditch should be filled back up. I happened to be walking past Barlow at just this time, and—yeah, you guessed it. He snagged me again, and I spent the next few hours filling up the same ditch I had dug previously.

While the wet season had its own problems, it was the dry season that seemed to provide the most opportunities for Mickey Mouse nonsense. The wind did a good job of blowing the dry sand around, which bothered most people, but especially aggravated Master Sergeant Smidley. Smidley, as you may remember from New River, was our noncommissioned officer in charge of the avionics section.

Besides being in charge of about thirty electrical and electronics technicians, he had some interesting ideas about neatness, especially for a place like Quang Tri. He also didn't like anyone messing up his sand.

On June 13, the day of my Great Leap into History, I went out flying as usual and came back that night, hoping Smidley had just figured it wasn't worth getting all upset about. I mean, after all, what had I done? I put a set of footprints in sand that momentarily would be riddled with sets of footprints. Right?

Yeah, well, Smidley didn't see it that way. I was walking into the avionics hooch later that afternoon after completing the day's missions, and Chuck Muth, a radioman, was walking out.

"Hey, Ron, I hear you're going on mess duty."

"No way, Chuck. I had mess duty in New River just before we left."

"Well, you better check inside. Smidley's got you down to start on the fifteenth."

I walked inside, checked out the status board that said who was working where, and there I was, listed as starting mess duty on the fifteenth, just like Chuck had said.

Smidley had a bit of a cubbyhole that was his office, so I went in and asked him about the assignment. I had been hoping to fly the remainder of the month, and he'd said when I took mess duty in New River that I was good for a whole year before I had to do it again.

He'd also said that I had to take only twenty days of mess duty at New River, instead of the usual thirty, as a bonus for helping out when nearly everyone else was on leave. Remember I said that? Remember I said to remember that because it would come up again?

Well, when I brought it up to Smidley, about not having the detail for the next year, he said, "I meant for the fiscal year. And since the fiscal year ends in two weeks, I figured you could get a start on next year's assignments."

What a crock! I'd never even heard of a fiscal year having anything to do with extra duty assignments before that.

"Besides," he said, "you spent only twenty days on mess duty at New River. The normal period is thirty days."

I was royally unhappy about that, but Smidley was adamant. I was going on mess duty and that was that.

I sent a letter home to the folks mentioning what had happened, and Dad thought that was pretty funny. He'd been put on mess duty when he was on the *Princeton,* because of a discussion he had with an ensign. Dad was a highly skilled machinist, which was his job in the navy, and had made a special part for an aircraft. But the ensign said he had done it wrong.

It turned out Dad was right, so the reward he got for knowing his job so well was thirty days' mess duty. But that was like throwing the proverbial rabbit into the briar patch for him.

They'd put Dad on midnights, with a Marine cook. The cook required that Dad put a bunch of potatoes into an automatic potato peeler each night, and then left him alone. On top of that, the Marine would fix Dad whatever he wanted for a meal.

Dad said he ate a lot of steak and french fries that month.

"It was the best duty I ever had," Dad said.

That is not the way it was for me in Quang Tri! The alleged mess hall at Quang Tri was a hellhole. It was a long, low building located at the southeast corner of the compound. It had slatted wood sides for ventilation, a corrugated metal roof, and screens all the way around from roof to deck.

The main entrance door faced west, with an enclosed area for officers on the left of it, and another enclosed area for staff NCOs on the right. Both had separate entrances. Prior to each meal, enlisted men lined up in front of that center door, waiting for permission to enter. Often we would get a show from jets making air strikes across the river or to the south of us.

When a jet came in and dropped its bombs or napalm, the line would erupt with shouts of "Get some!" Then everyone would turn back to what they were doing and wait for the door to open.

Inside, the main section was a low, dark room with tables and benches on the left and right, and a chow line in the middle against the far wall. The back of the building had a wing for the cooking stoves and sinks.

Lower-ranking enlisted men, starting with sergeants on down to privates, didn't have dishes, so we ate out of our mess kits. We'd walk through the chow line, take whatever was available, and eat what we could of it. Then we'd leave by a door on the north side of the building, where we found two rows of garbage cans, four to a row.

The first can in each row was for garbage. The remaining three were filled with water, and each had a submersible burner that heated the water until it was boiling. One contained detergent for washing and the last two were for rinsing.

I guess that method killed any germs on the mess kits, but it didn't take care of the grease, and within a week or so a lot of us came down with diarrhea. When we started wiping off the mess kits after the final rinse, our bodies returned somewhat to normal.

That is the way it was when I wasn't on mess duty.

When I was *on* mess duty, I had the task of waiting on the staff NCOs in their little section of the mess hall, where they had a mini–chow line so they wouldn't have to stand in the same line as the rest of us. It should have been relatively decent duty, as opposed to working on the main chow line or back in the galley scrubbing pots, but it wasn't.

Most of the sergeants from HMM-161 treated me well, but it seemed as though every other outfit in Quang Tri had a perpetual supply of first-class pains coming through that door three times a day. Whatever gripe they had, whether it was the heat, the dust, a bad letter from home, things not going right in their squadron, you name it, they took it out on the three of us working in the staff NCO section.

I've never heard so many irrelevant complaints in my life, nor had so many people try to make it seem as though I was personally responsible for everything that had gone wrong in their world in the past six months. It was hot, dusty, dirty duty, but it also was humiliating and frustrating. I came to hate some of those sergeants, and every day when I awoke at 4:00 a.m. to face more of their harassment, my stomach was twisted into a knot. It seemed as though that detail would never end.

Being an NCO waiter wasn't quite the same as being a DI waiter on Parris Island. Mostly we were responsible for making sure the mini–chow line was stocked with whatever was being offered for food, that the tables were cleared as soon as a space was empty, and that the place was clean.

I have to admit that the cooks at Quang Tri did their best to make a decent meal despite the severe restrictions they were under. There was very little fresh food, and most of what we ate was dehydrated or canned. Fresh milk was virtually unheard-of, and I was receiving a regular supply of presweetened Kool-Aid from home to mix with our drinking water.

Sometimes a supply shipment would come up from Da Nang and they'd have fresh eggs. But a large supply of fresh food couldn't be kept at Quang Tri because the storage facilities were pretty small and it would spoil quickly in the heat.

But they did try, and when they had something fresh, such as eggs, they went all out to make them special, at least in the staff NCO mess. Out on the regular chow line the troops generally got a coagulated mess of scrambled eggs, but the staff NCOs got omelets!

Omelets were just about unheard-of for everyone else, but each morning a cook stood at a small grill just inside the door with a ready supply of eggs, cheese, onions, peppers, and mushrooms, and made omelets to order!

What surprised me even more was that some of those sergeants still complained, when they should have been glad as could be that they had fresh eggs at all.

As bad as they were at morning chow, though, it was noon chow—lunch—that really brought out the asshole in most of them.

Noon chow was special because it was terribly hot by then, usually up around 100 degrees, getting even hotter, and the wind had been blowing down from the hills twenty miles to the west for about four hours.

For all of the time I lived in Center Brunswick at my

grandfather's farm, and for about three years when I lived in Wynantskill, the houses were heated by coal stoves, and one of my chores was fetching coal and stoking the fire. When a fire was going really hot and you opened the door to put on some more coal, the heat would hit you full in the face, causing you to catch your breath and making your eyes tear up.

That's the way the wind felt at Quang Tri. That wind could really get flying, and there was nothing between the hills and us but dust and sand. By noon the dust was steadily blowing through the screens, landing on everything, including exposed food, and adding a bit of crunch to lunch.

That's when some of the complaints really got out of hand. We would be hustling to keep the chow line supplied and at the same time keep the ever-accumulating sand off the tables. Sweat and sand would be running into our eyes and down the backs and fronts of our T-shirts, and we'd itch all over and generally be feeling miserable.

Nonetheless, we'd hear a constant stream of "Hey, Marine, there's no potatoes" (or meat, or carrots, or whatever was missing), or "Hey, Marine, there's grit in this food"—as though we were supposed to order the wind to stop blowing—or, best of all, while we were trying to take care of four demands simultaneously, "Hey, Marine, there's dust all over this fucking table!" To which I had to physically restrain myself from replying, "No shit, Sherlock, there's fucking dust all over everything!"

Evening chow—dinner—was just as bad, but here I figured out a way to fool them. It came upon me accidentally at the end of my first week of mess duty. After the mess from noon chow had been cleared away, we usually were given an hour or two to do whatever we wanted, with the requirement that we be back by 3:30 p.m.—or 1530 in military time—to prepare for evening chow.

But one day I was ordered to get my flak jacket, helmet, and rifle, and ride shotgun with a supply truck—called a six-by—that was headed to Dong Ha, a huge supply base five miles north of us. I discovered that the truck went up there every afternoon to get the next day's supplies.

I really didn't mind riding shotgun because I was getting away from the airstrip for a few hours, and I hadn't seen any of the countryside up close.

That ride, and many like it that I took later, was great. We rode in the back, standing up, keeping an eye on the terrain as we passed little hamlets where people would wave and call to us. Pretty girls along the way would try to get us to stop, yelling, "Hey GI. You number one. I love you too much!"

Sometimes they'd be especially pretty and I'd tell the guys riding with me, "Hold on to me or I'm jumping off here!"

I wouldn't have, of course, because we'd been warned about a rare and deadly strain of VD called the black syph, infecting every woman in the area. If a Marine caught the black syph, we were told, he would be shipped to a remote island in the South China Sea, where his penis would rot off and he would die.

I didn't believe that any more than I believed a similar story about the women having razor blades inserted in their vaginas to cut horny little Marines' penises to pieces. But I did know that the area was dangerous, and I wouldn't have wanted to be out there alone.

The only part of the trip I didn't like came on a day when we passed a truckload of garbage that was headed to the dump south of the airstrip. A bus loaded with Vietnamese civilians was right in front of us, and just before we passed the truck a garbage can fell out.

The bus screeched to a halt and a beautiful girl, with long, straight black hair, wearing an *ao dai* with white pants and a turquoise top, jumped out and grabbed the can, pulling it back to the bus. A half dozen people jumped out to help her, and some even started fighting over it.

I remember thinking that a woman as beautiful as she was would have no problem becoming a model in the States, or anything else she wanted to be for that matter. And here she was going through our garbage! It didn't make me feel any better about our sergeants and the way they complained about their food. Dehydrated roast beef or shrimp might not make it in a big-time restaurant back home, but it sure must have beat whatever the Vietnamese were eating.

When we arrived at Dong Ha, we drove through the supply area, loading boxes of canned goods as they were selected by one of the senior cooks.

It took about an hour there, and about a half hour each way. When we got back to Quang Tri, we took another hour to unload the truck. The great thing about the detail was that it was sweaty, dirty work. By the time we were finished, we were filthy.

No staff NCO in the world wants his food handled by a dirty lance corporal. Since evening chow was ready to start when we got back, and since the showers didn't come on for an hour, I was told to take off for the day.

I volunteered to make the supply run nearly every day after that. The cooks rotated a day on and a day off so I didn't work for the same person more than once a week, and therefore no one figured out how often I was missing the evening meal.

For once I fooled them, and for the evening meals at least, I was spared the constant abuse from the sergeants. As much as I resented that, though, the icing on the cake came not from one of our Marines, but from a visiting air force sergeant who showed up just toward the end of noon chow one day.

We had no problem with feeding the guy. Lots of transients came through Quang Tri on their way to one place or another. But this guy was something else. It was right around the end of June, just before the combat base at Khe Sanh was closed forever.

The sergeant had gone there for some reason or other the day before and was forced to remain overnight before he could hitch a helicopter ride out. It wasn't considered a big deal to most Marines in the area because at the moment it was no more dangerous than spending a night anywhere else in northern I Corps.

Also, there was a very strict pecking order among Marines regarding their length of service in Vietnam. The longer you had been in-country, the higher your place. The job you had also had a direct bearing on status. Recons and frontline infantrymen shared the top rung, while others who lived, worked, and fought in the general area were spread out below.

Rear-echelon clerks and such—who went to work in dress uniforms with ties, shined shoes, and brass, got to take a hot shower every day with filtered water, and lived in air-conditioned barracks back in Da Nang—were at the absolute bottom.

Your role in the history of Khe Sanh also had a bearing on your status. If you were part of the battalions that initially established the base and remained there throughout the siege, you were golden. If you were part of the aircrews that did resupply runs through the enemy guns, you also had quite a bit of prestige.

If you flew there later on, while there was still plenty of war to be involved in, you had at least paid your dues, even if the price wasn't as steep as it had been a few months earlier. But by the end of June, Khe Sanh was on its way to oblivion.

The infantry battalions were moving out, engineers were destroying the bunkers, and what action was left had shifted out to the hilltop firebases.

An element of the Marine Band was even scheduled to go there in a few days to play taps for the Marines who had died during the siege, and there was no way a band would have been allowed there if anyone thought it would be in danger.

So in walks an air force sergeant, accompanied by another air force sergeant, who immediately begins ordering us to wait on him hand and foot because "this man's been to Khe Sanh!"

I was working with a guy named Mike, and we gave each other a "So?" kind of look and pointed to the plates (staff NCOs and officers did get to have plates) and chow line.

"You get your food there."

That didn't satisfy them, though, and it was obvious they didn't realize how stupid they sounded.

"Get this man some coffee. Get this man some more meat. Get this man this, get this man that. This man spent the night at Khe Sanh!"

I once read an account of the battle for Khe Sanh by a journalist who went to great lengths to make it appear that he had been there for the entire siege. Only at the end of his article did he admit he'd been there for one night before hopping into a helicopter and getting out.

This same journalist claimed he was routinely ferried around Vietnam by Marines flying Chinook helicopters, apparently not knowing that while there were some similarities between Chinooks and CH-46s, they were two entirely different types of helicopter. Chinooks were flown by army pilots, not Marines, so either he'd been flying in CH-46s or he didn't know the difference between a Marine and a soldier, which is something you don't want to mess up, from either point of view, if you value your front teeth!

There is no way a person who can hop in and out of a battle can ever fully understand the feelings of a person who has to stay there until it is over, so I wasn't impressed with that account of Khe Sanh. And if a guy can't figure out what type of helicopter he is in, or who is flying it, I don't have much faith in the rest of what he writes, either. I figured the guy was just trying to make a name for himself.

We had pretty much the same outlook on the air force sergeant. Especially since Mike *had* spent the entire siege at Khe Sanh. He was a member of the crash crew, which meant he had to go out during artillery barrages if a helicopter or cargo aircraft was hit, attempt to put out the fire, and help rescue crew members, often while artillery, mortars, rockets, and small-arms fire was coming at them from all directions.

That was one courageous group of people, and Mike wasn't happy with what he was hearing from that sergeant.

"Get this man some bread. He's hungry! He's been to Khe Sanh!"

Mike walked over to the chow line, grabbed five slices of bread, walked to the table where the two sergeants were sitting, and slammed the bread down.

"There's your fucking bread!" Mike yelled and walked away out to the main mess hall.

"What the fuck's his problem?" Big Mouth asked.

"Oh, don't mind him," I told the guy. "You see, he was at Khe Sanh, too, but for the whole siege. He was on the crash crew and he saw a lot of guys die up there. It bothers him sometimes when people start talking about it, especially somebody who just spent one night there when the place is nearly abandoned."

They started looking at each other a bit sheepishly and then I really let them have it.

"Yeah, they say Mike's not the same since Khe Sanh. He masturbates a lot now because of it!"

"He what?"

"He masturbates. He told me he used to do it up there at Khe Sanh when they still had showers. He did it in the officers' shower once and got caught by a major. But he just laughed at the major and told him 'Tell me you don't do it, too!' When the major started stammering, Mike just walked away laughing.

"Now he does it five or six times a day. We've tried to tell him to stop or he'll go blind, but he won't!"

By now they had strange looks on their faces, kind of a cross between disgust and dismay.

"Has he done that today?"

Talk about stupid questions. I felt like telling him, "Sure, that's all I've got to do. Run around and see who the hell is jerking off every day!"

Instead I told him, "Probably. And I think he's on his way to do it again, now that you've upset him!"

"Well, I hope to hell he washes his hands," the would-be hero proclaimed.

"I don't think so," I said. "That's the other thing we've been trying to get him to work on."

With that I turned on my heel, a little smile on my face, and busied myself cleaning sand off tables.

Within thirty seconds both of them were gone, their food unfinished, and the five slices of bread right where Mike had left them.

Chapter 18

My father used to tell me that there is only one way to explain the mysteries of life and death, and why some very good people die when some lesser forms of humanity go on living.

"When your number's up, it's up, and there's nothing you can do about it," he'd say.

That adage seemed to hold true for HMM-161 as it progressed through the summer and fall of 1968. Despite our training, despite our motivation, despite the best efforts of pilots and crews, there were times when someone was in the wrong place at the wrong time.

The American media had portrayed the war in Vietnam as a contest of American high technology against peasant farmers who used only their wits and obsolete weapons. It is true that initially the war was fought against the Viet Cong, and they often relied heavily on crude booby traps to inflict losses on us.

But in the years after 1966, when most American troops fought in Vietnam, much of the conflict was between U.S. troops and North Vietnamese regulars. They were very well armed, also with high-technology weapons.

They were motivated, believing they were fighting for their homeland, and while beaten in every single major battle with us, were still being sent south in huge numbers. Our crews and pilots encountered sophisticated weapons such as radar-controlled machine guns and 37mm antiaircraft emplacements. Many of these encounters came in the area of the Demiliarized Zone (DMZ) or the Laotian border, where the Vietnamese were attempting to protect infiltration routes.

In August, south of Khe Sanh, I was flying in a formation of twelve helicopters preparing to make an initial assault on a new LZ at the head of the A Shau Valley. We could see Phantom jets dropping napalm and bombs below us, "prepping the zone" as it was called.

We were circling at about 5,000 feet, waiting for the word to go in, when the air nearby exploded in a maelstrom of heat, sound, and smoke. Some of those big North Vietnamese guns, which had been focused on Khe Sanh a few months earlier, were still in place across the Laotian border, well within range of the area we were circling, and had homed in on our formation with timed shells that exploded in midair.

I think everyone was shocked by what was being thrown at us, but there was no time to dwell on it. I heard a quick command to break the formation, and the flight spiraled down toward the jungle out of sight of the ridges in Laos. We escaped their guns, but for a second there I had the feeling I was in an old World War II movie.

As the North Vietnamese recovered from their losses during Tet and started to send larger numbers of troops south, we began to see heavier engagements, and more dangerous flying. Despite our earlier losses from accidents, we had not lost anyone in combat, until the summer of 1968, when the war came home to 161 permanently.

It was during a troop insertion on a hill named 697, for its height in meters above sea level, in the area of Hills 881 North and South, two mounds of equal height a short distance north of Khe Sanh where major fighting had occurred in 1967 and again during the recent siege. Doug Braman was in that flight, and they were preparing to land troops. But the hills were pockmarked with old foxholes and bomb craters, and as Doug tells it, "The craters were filled with NVA soldiers. They started popping up, firing."

Ken Brandes, a New York City native, was the crew chief in the lead helicopter. Brandes had been in 161 from its earliest days back in New River and was one of the most competent crew chiefs in the squadron. He had lived off base with his wife and infant daughter, and pretty much stayed out of the shenanigans that went on among those of us who lived in the barracks.

Ken was my height, a little heavier, with dark hair and expressive brown eyes. He had a quiet sense of humor and an air of knowing what he was doing. Brandes had been one of the first mechanics back at New River to work his way up to crew chief status when 161 was in its forming stages. He was well liked and ran a tight ship when he was flying. You knew when you flew with Ken that everything in that helicopter was in order, and that you were expected to toe the line.

As the flight neared the LZ, the firing became intense. Brandes' helicopter was hit heavily, automatic weapon fire ripping through the metal skin as though it were tissue paper. Ken, hit five times in the chest, was killed instantly.

Word of Ken's death spread quickly through the squadron back at Quang Tri. Death was not new to us, and not unexpected. But if you had placed odds on who would have been considered most likely to be killed, Ken Brandes' name probably wouldn't have been on the list. Things were never really jovial at Quang Tri, although we did our best to find humor in our situation, as do all soldiers who are engaged in combat. But you could tell from the looks on the faces around the squadron that afternoon that Ken's death hit a lot of people hard.

It is a sad fact of war that when young men go to fight, and envision battlefield death, they rarely foresee their own or those of their more capable and competent comrades. Thus it comes as a shock, even among Marines who are prepared for battle, that a bullet can end the life of a well-liked friend just as easily as the life of someone you often may have wished was dead.

Dad also used to say, "The good die young." His words rang so true that day.

A memorial service was held in a hangar later that week. Everyone who was not flying went to it. A chaplain who had never known Ken tried to say some words of inspiration, but frankly I didn't feel very inspired by them.

His death did cause one major change in the way crew members approached flying, however. Many of us had been debating the use of flak jackets, semi-bulletproof vests that would stop some of the shrapnel. Since we could just as easily be fired at with heavy-caliber weapons, many people felt that the vests would just disintegrate and add to the amount of shrapnel we were exposed to if we were hit.

Like many of us, Ken wasn't wearing his flak jacket that day, and there is no reason to believe anything would have happened differently even if he had been fully outfitted. But after that, everyone started showing up with their flak jackets on, apparently believing that a little protection was better than none.

Most days I wore a flak jacket over a green T-shirt, utility trousers, and flight boots, with a gun belt strapped to my waist. Like many of my friends in the squadron, I preferred a more hardened, wilder look to the textbook battlefield image. I had seen a picture of a combat Marine in a newsmagazine back home the previous year with UNCLE SAM'S HIRED GUN printed across the back of his flak jacket. I identified with that photo, as did my friends I suppose, and in keeping with our gunslinger image, many of us also didn't wear the flight suits we were issued. But after Ken died, the flight suits came back on. They couldn't stop a bullet, but they were flame resistant, and we came to the realization that we needed every edge we could get.

In addition to our unorthodox dress, we also carried odd

assortments of weapons when we flew. Captured AK-47s or SKS rifles were favorites, along with M-14s or M-16s, pistols, and knives. I preferred my M-16, a double-edged commando knife, and a pistol. Many crew members, including Doug and Al Munoz, preferred regulation K-bar survival knives. Later on I would switch from an M-16 to an M-79 grenade launcher as a backup weapon. I thought it provided a very nice equalizing force.

Those days when bullets smashed through our helicopters with impunity and the airwaves were filled with the fury of battle brought not only death to our squadron, but many close calls as well. The first few times our helicopters returned to base with battle damage they were swarmed over by the curious, and the crews encountered a form of instant celebrity. But within a month of our arrival in Vietnam, it was no longer unusual for our helicopters to return to Quang Tri ripped by bullet holes.

All of our missions had the potential to be dangerous, even those that started out routinely, and it wasn't unheard-of to be shot at more than once in a day. In some cases being shot at got to be so commonplace that it wasn't even considered a big deal—unless you were hit.

Occasionally an escape from injury was just short of miraculous. During a flight in midsummer, Doug Braman was sitting on a box containing .50-caliber ammunition, apparently thinking he was high enough above the terrain to be relatively safe for a few minutes. But then there was the familiar *bwaaang,* and he felt a thud below him.

Doug moved the box and found a bullet hole in the deck beneath the spot where it had been sitting. Upending the box, he found the bullet had also gone through it into the ammunition inside. Somehow the bullet didn't penetrate all the way through, and equally important, didn't set off any of the ammunition!

Doug kept the bullet, put it on a chain, and wore it on his

camouflage rain cover for a long, long time as a reminder of just how close he came to being ripped apart that day.

It would seem that working as a helicopter technician, especially in the electronics fields, would be a safer-than-normal job. But our avionics shop had more than its share of injuries. Staff Sergeant Scoggins, for instance, came back from flying one day with a wound to the neck that had just missed the jugular vein.

But my vote for the all-time close call record goes to an electrician from New Jersey named Bob Shannon. He was a longtime friend whom I had accompanied on many of our weekend "swoops" the previous year, and he had a painful, unnerving experience almost beyond belief.

Shannon was tall and kind of thin, and walked with a bit of a ditty-bop stride. We nicknamed him Chesty, partly because of his middle name—Chester—partly for the great Marine general Chesty Puller, and partly because of the way Shannon's chest stuck out when he walked.

Shannon had a real laid-back attitude and was one of the most likable and funniest people I knew. It wasn't very funny, however, the day in late summer when Chesty was flying gunner during a firefight and a bullet came right under his machine gun and hit him in the crotch!

Shannon said it felt like a mule kicked him. He was bleeding, but when he got to the medical station the corpsmen found that only the skin of his scrotum had been broken. Nonetheless, the wound was painful in the extreme. Chesty spent about three weeks on light duty, and every time I saw him he was walking very slowly, the old ditty-bop replaced by a wide-legged stance. He usually was holding onto the sandbag blast walls we had built around our hooches as he moved along.

Toward the end of his convalescence period I had a brief talk with Shannon, especially about the long-term consequences of his wound. I was working the night crew for a few weeks and came back to my hooch around 2:00 a.m. Chesty was sitting on top of the adjacent bunker.

He had scrounged a bottle of whiskey and called to me to join him. We shot the breeze about inconsequential things for twenty minutes or so, passing the bottle back and forth, developing a pretty good buzz as we went. Eventually, I asked him if his wound was healing all right.

"Yeah, I'm just about ready to go back on normal duty," he said.

"Any permanent damage?" I asked, trying to be discreet. "I mean, can you still get it up?"

"I was pretty worried about that," he said. Then with a sly look, he added, "But I tried it out last night and everything works just fine." Considering where we were at the time, and how much whiskey we had just consumed, that struck me as really, really funny.

But while you could occasionally get a laugh out of the war, not everyone was as fortunate as Shannon and Braman.

Paul Bevil, a crew chief who also had been around the squadron since 1966, caught a round through the belly of his helicopter that continued right through his heel. Paul, like the other crew chiefs in 161, was known for his competence and thoroughness. He was an integral member of the squadron, and I liked flying with him.

The day he was wounded, Paul was medevaced out permanently. We never had a chance to find out how he was doing or even where he went. We had to rely on secondhand information about how he got hit and what happened afterward.

Paul's wound pointed up one of the stranger aspects of the war, and the difficulty we had in dealing with it. As with so many others in our squadron, his presence and abilities were considered an important part of our lives. Then, suddenly, he was gone, never to be heard from again.

That happened repeatedly as the roll of 161's dead and wounded grew. One moment they were there, friends and comrades, the next they simply were no longer part of our lives, leaving us only speculation and memories.

Even Colonel Niesen wasn't exempt from the danger at Quang Tri. His turn came in July as we participated in an operation dubbed Lancaster II. It was a full-force assault right into the Demilitarized Zone, intended to confront infiltrating Vietnamese head-on, kick their asses, capture equipment, and destroy their supplies.

In addition to the '46s, other aircraft ranging from observation and gunship helicopters right up to jet fighter-bombers participated to provide additional firepower for the advancing infantry.

HMM-161 maintenance crews had worked hard to get as many "down" aircrafts to an "up" status as possible and provided sixteen helicopters for the launch. The day had started with a Reconnaissance insertion, ended up with a full-fledged assault, and when it was done thirteen aircraft had taken hits.

When the flight for the assault left Quang Tri, it looked and sounded like a movie of those huge bombing runs over Europe some twenty years earlier. The operation involved a fast, low flight straight toward the DMZ, and it went like clockwork.

The NVA soldiers were dug in up in the DMZ, but they also were hit hard. The firing was intense on both sides, and in the middle of the assault a bullet ripped right through the cockpit of Niesen's aircraft, spraying shattered Plexiglas into his face. Another bullet from below caught his copilot, Lt. Charles Songer, in his leg.

The crew chief, S.Sgt. Eugene Lee, rushed forward and placed a tourniquet around Songer's leg, stemming the flow of blood until they reached an aid station. Niesen was the epitome of the professional Marine, flying back to Quang Tri only after Songer was safe.

I was on the flight line as he taxied in and saw nearly every high-ranking NCO and officer in the squadron heading out to meet him. Niesen got out, a somber look on his face. He answered the anxious queries from the officers who had gathered around him and started toward the Quang Tri sick bay.

But then, in a classic understatement, Niesen stopped, turned on his heel, looked at his helicopter, which closely resembled a piece of Swiss cheese, and said with a completely straight face, "By the way, gentlemen, the bird is down!"

There was a ripple of relieved laughter, and maintenance crews immediately swarmed over the aircraft to assess the damage.

It was one more story in Niesen's growing legend. Considering the intensity of the fighting in Lancaster II, we were pretty lucky that day, since no one was killed.

As the months passed, however, we continued to lose pilots and crewmen, either to death or to wounds that sent them permanently out of the war zone. On August 18 our squadron armorer, Sgt. Wayne A. Wild, was shot in one eye, the one wound he said he feared more than any other. He was permanently medevaced.

On September 2, mortar fire downed one helicopter and wounded the pilot, Capt. Gary Parker. A second 161 aircraft, piloted by Maj. Joseph Felter, landed nearby to help the stranded crew. Rodney Weiss, crew chief on Felter's aircraft, unhesitatingly ran to the downed helicopter under heavy fire, helping Parker and the rest of the crew into his aircraft.

Major Felter steadily remained in the zone despite the heavy fire until the wounded and other crew members made it to his aircraft, and then flew them to safety. The courage of people like Felter and Weiss in dire circumstances exemplified what I believe were common attributes of virtually all Marine airmen, pilots and crewmen alike, and by extension, the U.S. Marine Corps.

But sometimes it was the routine days, the flights that you made over and over, to the point where they all became a blur, that suddenly erupted in violence and death. October 17, 1968, was one of those days, with our squadron making steady runs to the Laotian border area, often for medevacs.

An experienced crew was flying medevac for 161 that day. The pilots were Capt. Joseph Powell and 1st Lt. James Sweet, both top-notch aviators and Marines. Bill Frantz was flying gunner, along with John Ferrazzano. Ferrazzano worked in the flight equipment shop with another good friend, Don Vaughn.

Ferrazzano was from New York City, stood about five-feet-five or so, had a constant grin, a flashing smile, and boundless energy. Since he worked with Vaughn, Ferrazzano also had to be incredibly tolerant because you never knew what Don was going to pull, or when.

Rounding out the crew were a corpsman, Dayne Scott, and Robert Cheek, the crew chief. Scott had been around the navy and Marine Corps for well over a decade and was a good man to have on medevacs. Cheek, like so many other crew chiefs, had been in the squadron since our days in New River and really knew his job. He was about my height, a bit stocky, and quietly competent.

They got a call for a medevac near the Laotian border and responded. They located the zone and were on the way to pick up the wounded Marine.

There were two stories about what happened next. One said they were still off the ground, coming down, when an NVA soldier equipped with rifle-propelled grenades fired straight toward the helicopter and blew it up. The official version, the one carried in the squadron daily log, said the aircraft flew into a ridge buried in cloud cover.

I still don't know which version is correct, but two facts remain. No one got to that aircraft until the next day, and regardless of how it happened, it had crashed and burned. Not one person in the crew survived.

When the word came back to Quang Tri, I was stunned, as were many of my comrades. We had been dealing with death on a large scale for five months now, but in one instant we lost six vital people. That night Staff Sergeant Scoggins came to my hooch, carrying a bottle of whiskey. Technically, lower-ranking enlisted Marines weren't allowed any liquor, except two cans of beer each day when it was available.

But Scoggins was known to bend the rules on occasion, and this was one of them. Scoggins was a Marine who cared deeply about the men under him. He never made a big deal about it, but that's the way he was. Bill Frantz had been so well liked by everyone in the avionics section that his death was a major shock.

It was obvious that Scoggins was terribly upset, and said he had come to drink "to the memory of Bill Frantz." Several of us sat with him taking hits off that bottle as long as it lasted.

On October 21 a memorial service was held in one of the hangars. Those services were getting all too frequent, and at first I didn't want to go, not because I didn't care about Bill and the others on the crew, but because I didn't need that kind of ceremony to honor their memory. But Scoggins changed my mind with a simple question.

"If it was you that had died, wouldn't you want to know that people cared enough to go to your service?"

I went, and listened to the chaplain talk about each of the men who had died. Cheek, always up on his helicopter, fixing something, making sure everything was in perfect condition. Ferrazzano, whom I'll always remember as smiling, with those white teeth of his flashing. I had flown with Powell and Sweet and knew them as consummate professionals, as was Scott. Powell, Scott, and Cheek had been married. Powell had a son, and Scott had two daughters.

I learned much later that the tragedy of that day extended far beyond the confines of our squadron. Somewhere back in the States—the World as we called it—six sets of families, most of whom probably didn't know each other and never would, had received six telegrams, telling them of the tragic end to six lives and of unalterable changes to theirs as well.

On October 17, Captain Powell was less than a month short of his twenty-sixth birthday. Lieutenant Sweet had turned twenty-three, one month and eleven days earlier. Scott turned thirty-five only nineteen days before he died. Ferrazzano was twenty-two, Cheek twenty. Bill Frantz was twenty years, five months, and fifteen days old.

In Quang Tri the hangar was jammed for the service. It had been a terrible week and, along with a chaplain, bandsmen had been flown in to play the hymns. They played a version of the "Navy Hymn," containing the words "O hear us when we lift our prayer, for those in peril in the air."

But it was the playing of taps that was so solemn. It was then that I was thinking of Bill Frantz—walking so erect, because that's the way Marines are supposed to walk; sharing a cake that an aunt had sent to him only a few weeks earlier, because Marines share things like that from home; whistling his "William Tell Overture" and trying to teach it to me. I wondered about that girl back in Florida, someone Bill had cared enough about to contemplate marriage.

I was remembering a morning four months earlier, when he was raking sand, and I couldn't wait to get my footprints into those nice, neat lines. I would have given anything then to put some lines in a patch of sand and let Bill do the jumping this time.

Suddenly that mental vault I had built back at Parris Island, a lifetime ago, with the strong walls to contain my emotions, didn't seem large enough or very strong at all.

Chapter 19

The body of the enemy soldier was dumped unceremoniously on the ramp of our helicopter and we took off. He was dead, his limbs sprawled every which way, his chest torn open from bullets.

His eyes were still open, and staring, but they were glassy and didn't see anymore. He was dressed in the uniform of the North Vietnamese Army, and his field pack was still on his back. A few minutes earlier he had been out there, in the jungle near Laos, shooting at us. I had been shooting back at him.

Serving in the air wing isn't the same as being in the infantry, but it is still war. This war in particular pointed up some of the basic concepts of the Marine Corps that make it different from any other branch of the service.

Whether Marines are trained to be clerks or cooks, pilots or truck drivers, computer programmers or Recons, there is one aspect of their backgrounds that is common. All Marines are first trained as infantrymen, and the only goal of the infantryman is to kill the enemy.

Sometimes a person can join the Marines and be given a job that is so far removed from the actual fighting that there is virtually no chance of that person ever registering a kill or even being directly involved in the fighting.

But compared to the other services, the Marine Corps is small, which is why it is an elite unit, and lacks large contingents of noncombatants who will never see action. Marine

Corps history is replete with instances of cooks and clerks being thrust into the heat of battle and suddenly having to call on that initial infantry training.

In a matter of minutes, Marines who have been deskbound most of their careers have found themselves in situations where they must make a conscious decision to kill other human beings. Sometimes that decision is an agonizing one, but the general rule of combat is simple. If you don't kill the enemy, the enemy will surely kill you.

Most infantrymen, Recons, artillerymen, and such know that rule before they ever enter the combat zone. There is no hesitation when the shooting starts, because to hesitate is to die. They know their job and they do it.

The life of a helicopter gunner was similar to that of the grunts, at least as far as making decisions on life and death. Most Marines who join helicopter squadrons do so because they don't want to be in the rear with the gear. They opted for aviation assignments either because they wanted training for related civilian jobs when their tours of duty ended, or, if they contemplated more than one enlistment, because they liked to fly.

It was commonly assumed among the Marines who went through basic aviation "A" schools in Florida or Memphis that those who chose assignments in jet squadrons probably would not see any direct action. Jet squadrons were stationed at large bases such as Da Nang or Chu Lai and usually had infantry regiments guarding their perimeters.

As the war progressed and the size of the jet bases increased, the squadron areas became farther from the perimeters and often were nearly outside the range of NVA rocket attacks—relatively safe as far as Vietnam went.

Those Marines who opted for helicopters, on the other hand, could pretty well assume that they would see action, either as crewmen or at the bases where they were stationed.

Helicopter bases in Vietnam generally were not in locations where you would consider going for vacation. Three primary bases were built for Marine helicopters, including Quang Tri; Phu Bai, about thirty miles south of Quang Tri; and Marble Mountain, which was part of the Da Nang complex, ninety miles or so south of the DMZ. The bases got smaller and living conditions more primitive moving north from Da Nang to Quang Tri.

The airstrip at Quang Tri was part of a row of American outposts, usually within artillery range of the DMZ, which stretched from the coast to Khe Sanh. Our helicopters and crews often stayed overnight at outposts with names like LZ Stud—later called Vandergrift Combat Base—Khe Sanh, or An Hoa, an outpost west of Da Nang on the southern end of the A Shau Valley near an especially hostile area called The Arizona.

Phu Bai was close to Hue City and had seen heavy action during the Tet Offensive. In fact, months after Tet was over, when we flew to the Hue/Phu Bai area, the stench of death from the thousands of civilians who had been slaughtered or buried alive in a mass grave by the North Vietnamese invaders still permeated the air.

Marble Mountain was the only one of the three bases that was considered in "the rear," yet its helicopter squadrons routinely flew the area including An Hoa, the lower A Shau Valley, and The Arizona, all of which was dangerous territory.

Of the three bases, Marble Mountain also was the last place you wanted to be in a rocket attack because Vietnamese civilians had been allowed to work there for several years. Thus, the Viet Cong among them had the living and work areas well marked off for their nighttime rice paddy rocket attacks.

In Quang Tri, many of 161's enlisted men flew as door gunners and also took rotations on perimeter guard and in reactionary platoons. Perimeter guard was a one-month tour of duty requiring living in a bunker on the section of the perimeter overlooking the river and the Vietnamese village across the river from us.

Those on perimeter guard saw a fair amount of action, either from sniper fire, infiltration attempts, or rocket attacks.

Reactionary platoon members had to stop whatever they were doing when an attack started, whether it was incoming rockets or probes along the perimeter, grab their helmets, rifles, flak jackets, and ammunition, run to the perimeter, and fill in gaps between the bunkers.

I regularly served on the reactionary platoon and spent many nights standing watch in shallow foxholes or in abandoned rice paddies at the edge of the airstrip. We had quite a few firefights with Vietnamese while serving on the perimeter. Often they were shooting at us from a school at the edge of the village across the river—a school the Americans had built for the village.

Still, for most of us, our primary contacts with enemy soldiers came out in the boonies, whether it was the grasslands of the DMZ or the jungles near Laos. It was during these engagements that the issue of kill or be killed was the most evident.

Sometimes the question of whether a gunner had killed enemy soldiers was never settled. Fire would come from tree lines, spider holes, or bunkers, and all you could do was fire back.

If the firing stopped it was either because the enemy had died, run away, or was keeping his head down. Often when you are flying, and the shooting is confined to a one-minute frenzy, there is no time or opportunity to determine confirmed kills. Sometimes, however, there was no question at all as to the fate of those on the other side.

Foremost among those who had no questions about the results of their actions was one of our crew chiefs, Bill Gruby, who was involved in two firefights in early June that resulted in numerous confirmed kills. Bullets first came from a Vietnamese hut during an initial assault, and Bill immediately returned fire. He aimed into the hut, which it turned out was filled with explosives and North Vietnamese soldiers. The hut exploded.

Two days later he was in another firefight, and when both days were tallied, Gruby was credited with fourteen confirmed kills. Bill drew little stick figures on his flak jacket, one for each confirmed kill, with the word *help* written below them.

I had barely begun flying gunner when Bill was involved in those actions, but seeing his reaction made a dramatic impact on how I felt about the whole concept of confirmed kills. When I was in the States, and even when we first got to Vietnam, I was anxious to show that I was a reliable combat Marine, and killing enemy soldiers was the surest way to receive that designation.

But after Bill's first encounter, I decided that I just wanted to be sure we all came back every time I flew gunner, and that I was well regarded by the crew chiefs and pilots. In a few short days my opinion on killing the enemy changed from something to brag about to something for which we all had to take responsibility.

There were times when it was pretty apparent that the NVA soldiers died as a result of fire from the helicopter, although their deaths were not necessarily confirmed. Such was the case on a day in November when we flew a squad of Recons to the Laotian border area, about four miles west of Khe Sanh. The abandoned base was behind us, but still visible. The entire area was a relatively flat plateau, with small scrub brush and elephant grass.

We were supposed to set the Recons down in an area that was nearly to the Laotian border. When we reached the zone, the elephant grass appeared to be six to eight feet high, with some trees about ten feet high. Normally it wouldn't have been a bad zone, and the trees, more like brush, wouldn't have damaged the rotor blades.

When our downblast started spreading the grass apart, however, the pilots realized that it was more like sixteen feet high, and those small scrub bushes actually were twenty-foot-high-trees, which would have caused serious damage to the blades.

The pilots stopped the descent and hovered for a few seconds to see if there was a better area to land.

Suddenly a Recon next to me fired out the window with an M-79 grenade launcher. He had spotted several North Vietnamese soldiers in the grass at the edge of the zone and didn't have to be told what to do about it. Usually only crew members were supposed to fire from the aircraft, due to the danger of hitting fuel cells or rotor blades.

But Recons were a pretty independent bunch and generally ignored that rule. In fact, it was a common practice throughout the squadron to remove the Plexiglas windows from the aft section of the helicopter if the day was to be spent inserting and extracting Recons.

Often they would play John Wayne and kick out the windows at the first sign of action. Most of the crew chiefs had removed the windows anyway to prevent injuries from shattered Plexiglas during firefights and provide some extra ventilation in the dry season.

But if they hadn't, the Recons would take care of it. That flight immediately erupted into a heavy firefight, with all the Recons shooting, as were the port gunner, an electrician named Jack Athey, and myself. The mission was aborted, and two Huey gunships that had been flying support for us raked the zone with rocket and machine gun fire.

Considering that we had ten people tearing the place up with two .50-caliber machine guns, two M-79 grenade launchers, and numerous M-16s, it really didn't seem necessary for the Hueys to get into the act.

But they did, and after their strafing run was over, the

Huey pilots radioed that they counted six bodies in the zone. They also said they were taking credit for the kills. For all I know they may have been killing people who already were dead when we aborted the mission. But to be honest, while some may have fought the issue, it was that body, the one that had been dumped on our ramp a few months earlier, that had cemented my attitude concerning confirmed kills.

It had been late summer and a series of new hilltop bases was being built south of Khe Sanh, heading toward the Laotian border. When we had first flown over that area in June, I spotted a hacked-out stretch of jungle where the North Vietnamese were trying to build a road—part of the Ho Chi Minh Trail.

It always was a dangerous place, and we generally took fire there. We were bringing supplies to one of the bases—they were named after birds, including LZ Robin and LZ Loon—and we were fired upon from my side.

I thought I had seen a muzzle flash and put several heavy bursts right into the area it had come from. The firing stopped. We were working in a flight of two helicopters, but no one else got into the act, except for some grunts on the ground who opened up when they heard we were taking fire and saw where my tracers were going.

We dropped off the supplies, went back for more, and returned. When we got there, the grunts said they had found a body and wanted it returned to LZ Loon, where officers from the intelligence section would go through the captured documents looking for information on the soldier's identity, his unit, and other pieces of the intel puzzle.

It was then that the body was dumped on our ramp. I was surprised at how young he looked. It was hard to tell for sure, but I figured him for eighteen or so. His midsection had been hit several times by what looked like very large bullets, perhaps from my .50-caliber, perhaps from something someone was shooting on the ground.

We weren't supposed to touch the body, but the crew chief

opened the pack and looked inside anyway. There were letters and other documents I couldn't read, and a picture that instantly drew my attention.

It was the man lying before us, taken back in North Vietnam somewhere, before he came south to do battle with me. He was dressed in a formal military uniform, looking very handsome and standing next to a beautiful Vietnamese girl who was wearing a formal gown. It apparently was taken at some kind of military ball or perhaps a graduation from a military school.

They looked very happy together, with wide smiles on their faces. I couldn't take my eyes off that picture, and I didn't want to look back at the body. Somehow it all seemed so wrong then.

I remember asking myself, "Is this what it's all about? I come thousands of miles to shoot at a person I've never met and have no grudge against?"

I kept wondering about him, thinking that he may even have been someone I would have liked if we had met under different circumstances. I also wondered a lot about that girl. I wasn't sure how they did it in North Vietnam, but pretty soon, I was sure, she would be notified that the handsome young man who had posed for that picture wasn't coming back to her.

He didn't fit the image I'd had of a sneering enemy soldier. I know his counterparts were guilty of major atrocities in the South—much worse than the massacre at My Lai, which wouldn't be exposed for more than a year. While I never could condone what American troops did in that village, the media never seemed too anxious to show what the North Vietnamese were doing on a much larger scale—in the name of national unity and communist policy.

Concepts and strategies are one thing. But this was person to person, and I kept looking at that dead soldier, man to man. He wasn't looking back, though, not with his eyes anyway.

Many years later I talked about that day, and that soldier, with Doug Braman. His reaction was simple.

"You did what you had to do, because if you didn't he'd have killed you."

That was pretty much the way I felt then, too. But down inside I had realized another truth about war, similar to the one I had learned on my first medevac at Khe Sanh.

War is fought by young men, many of whom are just trying to justify themselves in an adult world. They often are used by the older, wiser, more manipulative adults for purposes that are dubious at best. A good slogan, the lure of fame, the chance to stand out among your peers, all are good incentives for young men to go into battle.

If along the way the reasons become obscure, or the purposes are exposed as shallow, it is the young men, not the older, more manipulative adults, who will die.

In other wars the issues seemed more clear-cut, and the killing was easier to justify. In other wars they made heroes of the fighters. In Vietnam we just had young men shooting and dying, doing their best to survive, and in many cases acting with extraordinary bravery that was never reported back home. In many cases we had left, and would come back to, a country that criticized us for going in the first place, regardless of how we acted while there.

I never paid much attention to the people who protested the war from the safety of their college campuses, but I have to admit that I had some very real feelings about the purpose of war that day. Because I believe in freedom, because I hate communism, and because I met many Vietnamese who felt the same way, I never regretted going there or fighting.

Once there, my justification for being actively involved in the killing was a combination of belief in the cause, and self-preservation. I wasn't going to agonize over that young man, but I wasn't going to forget him, either.

Now, decades later, I can still remember those blank, unseeing eyes and that bloody body. Some nights, in my dreams, I see a picture of a dashing man in uniform and a pretty girl in a gown. They have smiling, happy faces.

But those smiles could last only on film. And reality was lying on the deck of a CH-46 helicopter, with limbs askew and a chest full of holes.

Chapter 20

I was sitting on a two-holer at the edge of the Quang Tri perimeter, reading a book and thinking about life in general, when the screen about two feet above my head suddenly buckled inward and I heard a *bwap* sound. Not a *bwaaang,* as in the helicopters, but *bwap.*

Regardless of the difference in the noise, the source was the same. I was getting shot at! I have noted that a river separated us from a Vietnamese village, and they sometimes sniped at us, which had just occurred and reminded me that the Viet Cong didn't even have respect for a guy going to the bathroom and trying to catch up on his reading.

I was pissed—no pun intended—but I also was unarmed. I partially hiked up my trousers, blasted out the door, mooned the other side of the river, and headed for safety. I didn't have time to buckle the belt or button the fly.

The command bunker for the perimeter guard was a short distance away, and several guys were near the entrance. They had heard the shot and were trying to figure where it came from when I came flying out of the two-holer.

They all started laughing, and I have to admit I must have made a bit of a comic figure. By the time I was safely inside the row of hooches, without being shot at again, I had settled down. Rather than making a big deal about it, I just went to another part of the enlisted hooch area, found another unoccupied head, out of sight of the perimeter this time, and finished what I had started.

One of the harder-to-believe aspects of life in Vietnam was the incredible difference in living conditions that could exist between bases that were only an hour or so away from each other.

Da Nang, for instance, had hot and cold running water, flush toilets, movies, clubs, and decent mess halls. The China Beach area on the coast, just east of downtown Da Nang, had been designated an in-country rest and recuperation area, where Marines could come in from the boonies for a few days. They had rock 'n' roll bands, beer, good food, slot machines, a beach, showers, and even beds with real mattresses, sheets, and pillowcases.

Quang Tri, however, while only ninety miles north, could just as well have been on some remote Pacific island. To say that living conditions at Quang Tri were primitive was an understatement. It never ceased to amaze me that so many technological advances had been made in the world and so many were in daily use only ninety miles away, but somehow they had bypassed us as though we were part of a different century.

Whether it was providing for the most basic biological functions or solving really difficult matters, such as building showers with clean water, the airstrip at Quang Tri was a place where you could count on finding only the rudiments of civilization, and forget about anything fancy.

Take the basic function of urinating, for instance. Everywhere else in the world the average man can find a bathroom either with a toilet or urinal, or, if caught in a difficult situation, he can slip behind a convenient tree or bush. In Quang Tri there were no bathrooms with toilets, and no bushes or trees.

What we did have were "piss tubes." Piss tubes were fifty-five-gallon drums that had their bottoms and tops taken off and then were sunk in the sand, on end, with about six inches protruding above ground level. A piece of wire mesh screen was placed over the top, and if you had to go, you just pissed into the barrel. They were placed around the hooch and work areas to provide a measure of convenience when someone had to go real bad. The theory behind this arrangement was based on the concept that no group could piss enough to fill the barrel before all the urine seeped into the ground.

Wrong!

For some reason it never did seem to seep into the ground, and instead the barrels filled up with a foul-smelling substance that reminded me of, well, stale urine I guess. God help you if you settled for a bunk in the corner of a hooch next to a piss tube. There was nothing like a hot steamy night, with a bit of a breeze wafting through the screen, after first passing lightly over the top of a piss tube, to really ruin a sound sleep.

They were nasty little devices in other ways, too, which is what one of our sergeants found out during a night rocket attack. I'll allow him to remain nameless, because it has been a long time since this happened, but when the rockets started falling, he jumped from his cot and ran outside as fast as he could, heading for the opening to an adjacent bunker.

But he forgot that a piss tube was directly in the path between the hooch door and the bunker opening. The screen over the piss tube wasn't strong, and the opening of a fifty-five-gallon drum is rather wide, so, *kerplunk,* as they say in the cartoons, in he went.

It was bad enough that the guy smelled like piss and had the shit scared out of him, too. But to really add to his discomfort, no one would allow him in the bunker during the rocket attack, and he couldn't even take a shower.

Which brings me to the matter of cleanliness. There were two kinds of showers at Quang Tri. One, which worked twenty-four hours a day and had clean, filtered water, was for officers. The other, which worked two hours a day and had dirty water, was for enlisted men.

The officers' shower was located in a section of the eastern part of the base where the officers lived. They had Quonset huts rather than hooches, and a huge water tower, holding somewhere in the vicinity of a thousand gallons, to provide water for the showers.

That water was filtered before it was pumped to the holding tank, so the officers always smelled clean. We were proud of and close to our officers, but that water tower was still a symbol of the adage "rank has its privileges."

The enlisted showers worked only twice a day, from 7:00 to 8:00 a.m. and 5:00 to 6:00 p.m. Water for the enlisted showers came from the river that formed our eastern perimeter and was about two hundred feet away. The river originated in the mountains northeast of us, passed by Khe Sanh, then circled south of Quang Tri City, then north again past us. Up in the mountains this water was probably clean, but it wasn't by the time it got to us. The water was not filtered, which made it unsuitable for drinking and brushing your teeth.

The building where we took showers was at the edge of the enlisted hooch area. It had two wide-open rooms, one with sinks for shaving and the other where the showerheads were located. Did I say showerheads? Excuse me. There was one pipe coming up from the river, and inside the building it was split into two pipes that ran above the room, six feet or so off the deck. Each pipe had about six outlets spaced along its length, making for a dozen shower locations. There was a control valve for each outlet that had two positions, off and on. When it was on, the one-inch pipe was wide open and the water spilled out.

The water pump operated during the worst possible hours for most people in the squadrons. Those on flight duty generally took off by 7:00 a.m. and weren't back until dark, so they missed both the early and late shower hours.

Those working on the ground also were usually at the flight line by 7:00 a.m., so they missed the early showers, but often could get back in time for the evening showers. That is not as great as it may sound, however.

Because upstream from the place where the water pipe entered the river, a bunch of Vietnamese farmers had a spot where they washed their water buffalo. They did this twice a day, once between 7:00 and 8:00 a.m., and once between 5:00 and 6:00 p.m.—the same exact time that the pump was turned on downstream to draw in water for the enlisted showers.

It should be noted that water buffalo don't have any manners or toilet training. They think a river is a good place to relieve themselves, and so what if a bunch of American Marines are downstream, pumping some of that now-fouled water into a pipe to spray over their bodies in a futile effort to get clean?

The result of the combination of Ivory soap and filthy water was a smell that was half clean, half dirty, and not at all very pleasant. However, I have maintained for several years that my full head of hair is at least partly the result of having my scalp fertilized by the water in the Quang Tri showers.

But as disgusting as those showers were, they were better than no showers at all. Those of us who were flying with any regularity were reminded of this often, since we often were in the company of grunts. They got to take showers only when they came in from the boonies, at places such as Vandergrift Combat Base.

That happened once every few weeks or so, and they generally developed an odor that was a combination of sweat, dirt, blood, piss, shit, gun smoke, and whatever else they had encountered. So even though we weren't always pleasant to be around, I was constantly reminded that others had it worse.

There were, of course, people who decided to circumvent the matter anyway. One of our electricians, John Zanercik, got to a point one night where he said he just had to have a shower. He had worked a long, hot, hard day, one of many in a row, had missed the later shower hour, and decided to do something about it.

John was just under six feet tall, in his mid-twenties, and looked older than most of the rest of us. He had shaved his head and grown a Fu Manchu mustache. John operated on the theory that when a Marine is naked, no one knows what rank he is if they don't know him personally.

So one night about 10:00 p.m. he strolled over to the officers' shower, walked in like he owned the place, took a shower, shaved, brushed his teeth, and strolled out. He said there were a few officers in there, but they didn't know him, he didn't know them, and while he got a few strange looks, no one challenged him.

I didn't think I looked old enough to pull off a stunt like that, but I did have one other way to occasionally get clean. We had large portable water tanks, also called "water buffaloes," which contained about 250 gallons and were parked in between the rows of hooches. The water inside was clean and used for brushing teeth and filling canteens.

This water was to be used sparingly, and we were told not to use it for cleansing purposes. That would have been difficult anyway, since the water tanks had four spigots on one end that were only about three feet off the ground, requiring the moves of a contortionist if you wanted to use them for showers.

But on occasion, when I got to the point where I couldn't stand myself any longer, I'd go out late at night, strip down, and squat under a spigot. I'd reach up, hold it open until I was completely wet, and then soap up. When I was soaped, I'd open the spigot again and rinse off. This was a stopgap measure and used only when things got really bad.

Oddly enough, after a while we developed a certain pride in not having any luxuries. If we went to Da Nang, for instance, where some sections of the base had clean, hot water and flush toilets, we treated the inhabitants with a measure of disdain. After all, who came to a war zone to sleep in real beds, with mattresses and sheets, take hot showers, eat regular meals, and smell like a French whore?

Of course, they looked at us with disdain also, as in, "Christ, when the hell was the last time you washed?" Chuck Muth once told me that on his first trip to Da Nang he sat on a real toilet and flushed it a bunch of times, just to remember. Flush toilets were unheard-of at Quang Tri.

We had "two-holers." A two-holer was a kind of outhouse, with two seats. Like most other buildings at Quang Tri, the two-holers were made from two-by-fours, plywood, and screen, with tin roofs. The plywood sides went up about five feet or so, with screen around the last two feet up to the roofs. They were just big enough for two people at one time, with bench-type seats that had two holes cut in them.

Although two-holers looked like old-fashioned outhouses, they had one basic difference, a testimony to modern ingenuity. Instead of sitting over a pit in the ground, the two-holers had a hinged flap on the backside, which opened underneath the holes. Inside, two buckets of diesel fuel were strategically placed to receive the offerings from above. Once every day a truck would make the rounds of the two-holers. The Marines it was carrying would remove the filled buckets, replace them, and take the fuel and shit to the edge of the base, where they were burned.

In the Marine Corps, every kind of detail that involved doing something other than your regular job, and that no one else wanted to do, was called a "shit detail." In this case, although riding around removing and burning shit really was a "shit" detail, the cans of fuel and shit were euphemistically called "honey buckets," so it was named the "honey bucket detail." I never did see any bees hanging around there, though.

After a while we got used to the two-holers, even though we had to bring C-ration toilet paper, since whoever ordered supplies always seemed to forget to order regular toilet paper. My favorite two-holer was about a hundred feet from my hooch, right next to the perimeter. You could go down there in the afternoon, take a book, and hope for a breeze from the river to cool things off a bit, which was why I had walked down there that afternoon in late July.

Since I had always enjoyed reading, and everyone from home had been sending me paperback books, I was carrying one in the back pocket of my jungle utilities. I would read anything they would send, westerns, mysteries, sex books, it didn't matter as long as I had something.

On this particular afternoon, however, I got to the two-holer and delayed my book-reading for a moment to study the new graffiti on the walls. The walls of the heads in Vietnam had some of the best graffiti, and some of the best observations on the state of the war, that you could find anywhere.

All those journalists running around, hopping rides in helicopters and interviewing complainers for their stories, really missed out on the best barometer of troop morale. It was on the walls of the two-holers, but it seemed that few journalists ever went in them. The best of the new stuff that day was memorable.

"There is no gravity—this place sucks!"

I had been contemplating that when the sniper cut loose and ended my reveries.

Sniping incidents such as that one were pretty common in Quang Tri. We took a lot of rounds on the perimeter, which were considered part of a day's work, but there were two times when the snipers made quite an impression. They both involved warrant officers in our squadron.

WO William Bolena, the officer-in-charge of avionics, had served in both World War II and Korea. He knew about combat and had taken extensive precautions to ensure that his men had an edge over the Vietnamese.

When we first arrived in Quang Tri, Gunner Bolena had ordered all the electricians and radiomen to build a sandbag blast wall around the avionics hooch. This involved a lot of work, since we also had to build walls around our hooches back in the enlisted living area, but we all pitched in.

Bolena had seen what artillery can do, and lectured us on the proper procedures for survival in case we were caught in the open during an attack. So at the front entrance to the avionics hooch, facing the flight line, we even built a secondary wall to give us some shelter if rockets were coming in near the helicopters.

A lot of guys from other squadrons laughed at that, and the avionics hooch was dubbed "Fort Bolena." But the gunner had been around, knew what he was doing, and we didn't question him.

Bolena was a quiet sort, until you riled him, liked to play chess, and had a good sense of humor. He didn't mind when we used a section of the Marsden matting from the flight line to build a bridge over that ditch I'd had to dig so we had direct access to the avionics hooch from the flight line. He even laughed when several of us lined up one night and marched across the bridge whistling the theme from *The Bridge on the River Kwai.*

So I was shocked one afternoon in August when Bolena came in the back door of the avionics hooch in a highly agitated state. He had just come from a Quonset hut next to the perimeter that the officers had designated an "officers club."

It wasn't much as such things go, and I don't know if they had any more beer in there than the enlisted men did. But it was someplace to go to get out of the sun at noon—until that afternoon. Bolena spent a lot of time outdoors and had a deep tan. But that day he looked as though he had seen a ghost.

"I just got shot at!" he exclaimed as he came through the door. Bolena said he had been opening the door to the hut when a bullet slammed into the doorjamb inches above his head. Bolena had been shot at before in his Marine career, but he'd survived, and he had every intention of leaving this war in one piece. That incident, however, served to remind us of just how vulnerable we were, even when we thought we were relatively safe.

A similar incident had such a surprise ending that it caught the attention of reporters from the *Navy Times*. It happened as CWO (Chief Warrant Officer) Donald E. Lambert, who was in charge of all maintenance on our helicopters, was walking on a road that ran between the living areas and the flight line. He was on a section that ran west to east and was visible from the perimeter and the village across the river.

A shot rang out and the bullet struck Lambert in the leg. But it didn't penetrate! Not only didn't it penetrate the skin, it didn't even go through his trousers. That shot prompted a tremendous amount of discussion, and it finally was decided that Lambert had been shot with an old bullet, from an old rifle, probably dating back to the days of the French involvement in Vietnam. Apparently the powder in the bullet had enough energy to fire, but not enough to keep the bullet going at a lethal speed. Gunner Lambert was an extremely lucky man that day.

If the sanitary facilities and incoming rounds from the Vietnamese weren't enough to make you miserable in Quang Tri, the food was sure to. Although I knew how hard the cooks worked to provide decent meals for us, the combination of tropical weather and remoteness made it preferable to eat C rations rather than go to the mess hall.

Which is what Doug Braman took into account when he decided we should be eating better. Just after I had finished my tour of mess duty, a new mess hall was completed. It was designed to keep the sand out and had larger storage facilities, but the food didn't get any better.

Since we were usually in the air or about to be in the air when the mess hall was open, we couldn't eat there often anyway. We also had discovered a way to maintain a good supply of the best C rations. A section of LZ Stud had been cordoned off to store thousands of cases of them, and flight crews would be issued a case per aircraft when we stopped there.

Someone discovered there was a hole in the concertina wire that surrounded the pallets of rations, and while one crewman would go to the gate to check out a case, two more would go behind the stacks and "liberate" a few more. There were several types of meals in a case of C rations, some distinctly better than others. For instance, franks and beans was a favorite, as was canned spaghetti along with meals that contained mixed fruits, or peaches, or jelly to spread on crackers.

On the other hand, two types of meals—ham and scrambled eggs, and ham and lima beans—were universally detested. The ham and scrambled eggs was a greasy coagulated mess that was only marginally palatable if heated. However, heating was done with small quarter-sized heat tablets that weren't always available, and even if they were, there wasn't always time to use them. The combination of ham and lima beans was just plain disgusting.

To avoid having confrontations with the lesser-liked meals took a lot of finagling. Often crews from several helicopters would assemble and trade their meals, depending on who liked what. A crew chief from Vermont, Mike Galvin, figured out that each case had a code on it. If you understood the code, you knew ahead of time which meals the case contained.

Mike absolutely loved a combination of peaches, which were the dessert in one meal, mixed with pound cake, which was the dessert in another meal. So Mike made a point of loading up on cases marked with the proper code for peaches and pound cake. He would go to great lengths to keep a supply of them on hand.

But it was Doug who finally hit on a way to spice up mealtime. It required combining food from two sources at once and the natural characteristics of a helicopter. Back in Quang Tri someone had come up with the idea of establishing a post exchange, or PX, which in Da Nang or the States amounted to a military department store.

The "PX" at Quang Tri was actually a tent that covered some makeshift shelves, with a Marine in attendance manning an old cash register. The only supplies on hand were shaving cream, razors, soap, and, strangely enough, a supply of canned Old El Paso tortillas and enchiladas. What we were supposed to do with those was anybody's guess. But I was there with Doug one day and he bought several cans of each.

I flew with nearly every crew chief in our squadron at one time or another, but if at all possible I flew with Doug or Al Munoz. Our encounters back in the States had resulted in a mutual trust and the knowledge that our backs were safe if we were with each other.

So it wasn't unusual a few days later when Doug stopped me on the flight line and told me he had requested that I fly as gunner with him the next day. It *was* unusual the next morning, however, when Doug asked me in the middle of a flight if I was hungry. We were on a daylong resupply mission that required us to make numerous trips to LZ Stud to pick up supplies, which were stacked in huge cargo nets that were attached to a hook in the belly of the '46.

We'd then fly the supplies to landing zones throughout the area and drop them off. At the beginning and end of each flight, the crew chief would be busy for a few minutes, but unless we were fired upon the rest of the mission was pretty boring.

I asked Doug what he had to eat, and he pulled out a few cans of C rations and some of the enchiladas. Remembering numerous encounters with cold C rations that went back to boot camp, there was no way I was looking forward to them. I didn't relish the idea of digging into a cold can of enchiladas, either, and told Doug so.

Without a word he went to the rear of the helicopter and stepped onto the ramp right underneath the engine compartment. The engines were separated from the interior by two fire doors that could easily be opened by twisting a series of locking screws.

The doors were on hinges and would swing down and away, providing access to the engines. On each side of the engine compartment, right next to the engines, was a recessed area that resembled a narrow shelf. The engines operated at about 600 degrees Fahrenheit, and the interior of the engine compartment was like an oven. So Doug put a few cans of C rations and a few cans of enchiladas onto the shelf, closed the access doors, and cooked dinner.

A minute later the pilot was keying his intercom button and looking back through the passageway.

“Crew chief. What’s that smell?”

“Just C rations, sir.” There was some muttering about C rations never smelling that good before, but we just clammed up. We liked our pilots, we liked them a lot, but they got hot showers and clean water, so it was only fair that we have a hot meal occasionally.

Five minutes later he took the cans down, opened them, and served my first ever in-flight meal. All things considered, it wasn’t bad.

Chapter 21

We were skimming the treetops at the head of the A Shau Valley, doing about 120 knots, coming in fast for a strafing run. As sometimes happened when the younger lieutenants were flying, a rock 'n' roll station was playing in my headset, and the Stones were blasting out, "Hey, hey, you, you, get off of my cloud."

It was mid-November and the war had established itself as "Rock 'n' roll—lock and load!" We had seen so much death and destruction, fighting, and dying in the past six months that my emotions had taken on an unreal quality, a hardness, necessary to protect me from the reality of war.

Sometimes I really wanted to be able to feel something, anything, other than anger. But I couldn't, and it didn't even bother me. Flying became an escape for me, and if I could mix the roar of battle with hard-driving rock, so much the better. I no longer cared if someone out there died; it was the luck of the draw.

Sometimes I didn't even care if I died, and figured if my time was up, it was up; otherwise there was no sense worrying about it. I looked at it with a "kill or be killed" attitude. Too many of my friends were getting killed there for me to have any sympathy for the North Vietnamese.

We approached the target area, I opened up, and the beat from the Stones was joined by the metallic thunder of my .50-caliber. I knew what was coming ahead of time, so I had dispensed with the 50-round box and had loaded a string of ammunition directly from a 500-round box.

Six- and eight-round bursts kept roaring out of the barrel, and I watched with a kind of detached satisfaction as the tracers went directly into the target. I kept firing until we had passed over the zone and the pilots radioed to cease.

I felt a sense of relief, sweating in the cool air, and reached for a cigarette. Strafing runs had become part of our routine now that the North Vietnamese were back in force, and aside from flying reconnaissance insertions, they were my favorite missions.

There was a sense of power in those actions that far exceeded anything I have ever felt since. I was twenty when I got there and had turned twenty-one in October. I had, at that point in my life, direct control over everything I saw outside that helicopter and its effect on my life. When the engines began their high-pitched scream and the rotors began turning, I'd feel a sharp sense of excitement and my blood began pounding. I'd lock and load as we flew over the perimeter at the north end of the base, and then hold back as long as was necessary, keeping the excitement level just below the surface.

Then we'd get a call for assistance, or take fire in a zone, and I'd explode with all that pent-up frustration, spewing bursts of destruction out the end of the .50. I solved every problem I had right there on the spot—at least until the next time.

Life was harsh, not only in Quang Tri, but throughout northern I Corps in November 1968, and there were three ways to deal with it. You could fly forever, immersing yourself in the work and the war to a point of exhaustion, leaving little time for reflecting on the heat, or the rain, or the death.

If nonstop work and fighting weren't your ways of dealing with unpleasantness, you could find a way to make music part of your life, and do your best to lose yourself in its rhythms as much as possible.

Or, you could turn into a booze scrounger, trying to drink yourself into oblivion each night and spending half the next day recovering before starting all over again. In reality, many of the Marines in HMM-161 took on portions of all three of those choices.

We worked nonstop because we had to, and, for the most part, because we believed in what we were doing. To keep all those helicopters flying as much as they did took monumental efforts by everyone in the squadron. I never saw the final statistics, but shortly after our sixth month in Quang Tri we were told that all the flight records set by other units in one-year tours in Vietnam had been broken by HMM-161 in our first six months.

When you consider that early in our tour, when the dry season was at its worst, we lost nearly half the engines in our squadron due to sand being sucked into the intakes, that accomplishment takes on even larger proportions. That loss of engines was solved when we installed barrier filters, similar to the filters used in home furnaces, over the intakes. Before that, however, crews of mechanics added a new job to their duties—carrying a good engine from an aircraft that was going to be down due to other difficulties to another aircraft that was otherwise in flying condition, but had lost one or both of its engines.

But our difficulties didn't stop us from flying, and it was the flying that I liked most. It was also the flying that kept me close to music. We had several types of radios in the helicopters, and some could pick up regular broadcasts as well as air and ground communications. Many of the pilots would turn the radios on when we were on routine flights, and some of the younger pilots would keep rock 'n' roll playing when we went into a hot zone.

At a place called Pleiku in the Central Highlands, the Armed Forces Radio Network had established a radio station that began broadcasting each day at 6:00 a.m. If you were flying and the pilot had turned the radio on, or if you were back in Quang Tri and someone had a transistor radio, the day would always start with the announcer calling "Gooooood moorrrning, Vietnam!"

As often as not the assembled voices would reply, "Shut the fuck up!"

His cheerfulness wasn't really unappreciated, and he did play good rock 'n' roll music, so I would go to great lengths to keep it playing.

When we'd swoop down from the sky on a gun run, with machine guns blazing, we usually could get some appropriate rock music for accompaniment. Sometimes, when the action had stalled for a bit, the music and the sheer beauty of seeing that country from the air would be soothing counterpoints to the heat and fighting on the ground. Flying in Vietnam was often beautiful, and when high in the air you could see villages, small cities, rivers, and mountains.

Sometimes, in the fresh coolness of the air rushing by, we would catch the smell of burning vegetation from napalm strikes. It wasn't an unpleasant smell at all and reminded me of leaf-burning time back home.

Other times the war would intrude on those scenes, as the eruptions from artillery, naval gunfire, or B-52 strikes would send smoke and dirt billowing upward. B-52 strikes, especially, were as awesome from the air as they were from the ground.

At night their rumble could be heard from miles away, seeming to last for eternity, and the flash from the explosions lit up the sky. We called it "Arc Lighting" and the power that was unleashed in those strikes provided a very real sense of human mortality. During the day, if we were flying near the target area, we would receive orders to move out of the way, and then watch as the bombs erupted in an endless stream.

When we were finished with a day's missions or were heading back to Quang Tri for a change of pilots, we'd often end up flying ten feet over the dirt highways at 140 knots.

Low, fast flights often were required to avoid enemy fire,

but those flights also were a kind of release for everyone in the crew. We'd stand at the starboard entranceway, watching the road and terrain flash past in an incredible blur. Norman Curl, an electronics technician in the avionics section, had brought a movie camera with him and got some excellent footage of one of those flights from the side entrance door. I watched it many years later and it showed quite clearly just how fast we were going and how close we were to the ground.

Sometimes we'd head down Highway 9, from LZ Stud to Dong Ha, and then take a right, heading south on Highway 1. We could have cut directly across, from LZ Stud to Quang Tri, a course that was something like using the hypotenuse on a right triangle, but it was more fun to go via the highways, especially if they were busy.

We'd buzz army truck drivers who would get nervous and flip us the bird. Sometimes Vietnamese civilians would be riding bicycles and we'd pass just over their heads, the downblast from our rotors sending them into a ditch. That probably didn't do much for international relations, but we did it anyway.

The only time I ever saw a Recon looking scared was on one of those flights, when we were taking five of them to Quang Tri to head out for R&R. We were very low that day, doing hop, skip, and jump maneuvers over rice paddy dikes and tree lines, and the Recons looked as though we were crazy as hell and bound to crash any minute.

In the meantime, the crew members—myself, the crew chief, and the port gunner—were standing at the starboard entranceway urging the pilots to go faster.

Some of our best younger pilots, including Lt. Al Doktor, known as Doc, Lt. Tom Martindale, known as Marty, and Lt. T. J. Sullivan, one of the pilots in the helicopter I flew in during our cross-country flight back in the States, could handle those helicopters as though they were jet fighters, and flying with them was a blast.

Martindale was one of the best-liked pilots in the squadron, especially among the enlisted men. Those who knew him well said Martindale had been a corporal before he went to officer's school and became a pilot, and he had a natural ability to handle his authority and inspire respect at the same time.

Doug Braman said one of his wildest flights with Martindale involved a high-speed, low-level pass along the Quang Tri River during which Marty dipped the aft section to see if he could spin the tires on the water. I wasn't on that flight, but I did ride with him often on Recon missions and initial assaults. During a flight to Dong Ha to pick up a Recon team one October morning, Marty flew so low over the villages along the way that he ordered me to check the bottom for damage when we arrived at Dong Ha.

An FM antenna, roughly ten feet long and used to communicate with ground troops, was attached to the bottom of a CH-46. It was on a motorized coupling that extended it straight down for greater range while in flight and retracted it flat against the bottom when landing.

Sometimes a pilot would forget to retract it, land on it, break it, and the radiomen back at the squadron would have to replace it. That morning, however, the FM antenna had been retracted during the whole flight and Martindale still told me to check it.

During a gun run out in the Laotian border area that month, as I was readying my .50-caliber, I heard Martindale turn the controls over to the copilot so he could fire his 9mm pistol out the cockpit window. Since we were making a straight pass over the target area, it really didn't matter who had the controls, but the crews got a kick out of Martindale's willingness to join the fight.

When we were finished with a day of flying, had returned to Quang Tri, and dismantled and cleaned the guns, most of us would head back to the hooches with hopes of scrounging some beer. When we first arrived, Quang Tri had been barren. The hooches were wide-open spaces with cots lined up inside, providing for only the basics of existence.

But our squadron personnel had a wide range of talents, those the Marine Corps had taught us and others picked up elsewhere. After bunkers were built to provide shelter in rocket attacks, some of the guys began to wire them for lights and sound, and they became hangouts where a half dozen or more guys would gather at night, shooting the breeze, drinking if they could get alcohol, and listening to tunes. Some guys even slept in the bunkers, and the only thing that interrupted their music was "incoming."

We listened to whatever we could get our hands on, the Stones, the Beatles, the Righteous Brothers, Roy Orbison, Janis Joplin with Big Brother and the Holding Company, Cream, the Doors. At first it all came from transistor radios, tuned in to the Armed Forces station. Later, as we began making occasional trips to Da Nang, tape recorders started showing up, with tapes reflecting the tastes of whoever did the buying.

Music was our line to the World. Sometimes disc jockeys back in the States would dedicate entire shows of the hottest hits to units in Vietnam, and then would send over the tapes. Those were the best tapes because they had the greatest selections of music.

Music by itself was fine, but music with a beer accompaniment was heaven—and a form of insulation against the war outside. Since we were authorized to have only two beers per day, and since there often was no beer to be had regardless of what we were authorized to have, we had to devise ways of getting it.

Sergeant Barlow, the same NCO who had me dig that ditch at the flight line, was in charge of providing beers for the flight crews. But even when he could get it, Barlow would put a case on the steps of the line shack, where flight assignments were posted, pop all the tops, and leave the beers sitting in the sun. He had been ordered not to create a situation where crews could horde beer and then drink a bunch all at once. The result was that crews returning just before dark found their beer sitting there hot as hell, with foam running down the sides. But that wasn't the only supply of booze in the world.

At first we started buying it from Vietnamese who ran little stands on the side of Highway 1. That was risky because they cut the bottoms out of the bottles and could do any number of things to the booze before reinserting the cut-out section. It could simply be cut with water, so they could make an even bigger profit, or, if they were Viet Cong, they could put anything from ground glass to gasoline to acid in it.

There were a number of ways to protect oneself against some of that, such as straining it through bread or trying to light it on fire to check for gasoline, but eventually everyone just drank it.

Trips to Da Nang also helped the booze supply because down there we could find a friendly airman or soldier to buy it for us from their monthly ration—for a price. That price was often steep, but pretty soon smuggled bottles of booze began showing up.

It obviously was difficult to bring back a couple cases of beer, but after a while, when someone was going to Da Nang, we could put in an order for booze, because even if it was unauthorized, it was easy to hide. Whenever someone was going down there, I ordered a couple bottles of Johnny Walker Red to keep on hand.

I'd be lying if I didn't point out here that marijuana also made the rounds at Quang Tri. It did, but it wasn't as popular as beer. Back in New River, perhaps only a half dozen guys had tried any form of drugs. That group not only smoked pot, they drank cough medicine, popped pills, and took anything else they could get their hands on.

But they were considered the oddballs. By the midpoint in our tour most of the lower-ranking enlisted men had at least tried marijuana, but trying it and being hooked on it were two different things. It was very easy to get because Vietnamese threw it over the wire, an ounce at a time, in exchange for menthol cigarettes. But even though most people tried it, drugs weren't used that extensively in our squadron.

I didn't try it because of John Messick, my friend from back home. When we had been reunited in New River, he had told me stories about the effect marijuana had on some of his friends when he was in Vietnam, and he told me that no matter what else I did, to stay away from drugs.

"I'll buy you a case of beer if you can come home in thirteen months, look me in the eye, and tell me truthfully that you didn't do drugs in Vietnam," he said. I promised him I wouldn't, and I made good on the promise.

In late summer two things happened in Quang Tri that opened up the beer supply. The old mess hall I had worked in was on its way out when I served mess duty, and the Seabees were building a new one that had better storage facilities, including two huge reefers—walk-in freezers—and that also would keep the sand out.

When the new mess hall was completed, the old mess hall was turned over to the enlisted men as a club of sorts. To help out, some of the pilots went down to Da Nang and scrounged two old Coca-Cola freezers, which barely worked but at least could cool off some beer.

One of the official supply routes for beer required a trip up the coast on barges from Da Nang to the Cua Viet River a few miles north of us and a short distance south of the DMZ. The barges were off-loaded, and the beer was stored at Dong Ha for distribution to the thousands of Marines in the area.

After the E club was established in Quang Tri, a barge full of beer was delivered to Dong Ha, and the airstrip sent a flatbed truck up to get as much as possible. They were allotted one pallet, or eighty-eight cases, for the whole base.

That may sound like a lot, until you realize that there were about one thousand Marines stationed at Quang Tri. That amounts to slightly more than two beers per person.

Okay, if you subtract all the officers and the senior NCOs, who had their own supplies, it probably amounted to a six-pack for everyone ranked sergeant and below. Perhaps 10 percent of all the rest didn't drink, so maybe you could add an extra beer per person to the rest of us. What that amounted to, under the regulation of two beers per person per day, was roughly a four-day supply of beer. And who knew when the next supply would come?

A group of us went to the "club" the night that beer came in, armed with two tickets each for two beers each. A line had gathered outside the entrance to the old mess hall, just as it had a month earlier when we ate there. The old coolers could accommodate about four or five cases at a time, and when that ran out, there was no way they could cool off another four or five cases in any reasonable amount of time.

Understand, I am not complaining! Drinking semi-warm beer was still better than drinking the brews left for us at the flight line. For a few days, at least, we had it. That was much better than the grunts were getting just a few miles north and west of us, so I really was grateful for what we had.

But we had to figure out a way to make it last. Enter Doug Braman. Doug took a stroll out back, where the remainder of that pallet was sitting. He came back with the information that not only were there probably seventy cases stacked up there, but they also had broken another half dozen cases down and the loose beer was sitting in three garbage cans.

The beer also was being guarded, Doug said. We drank our authorized beer and went back to our hooch area. Then we waited for dark. It came. We headed back to the club. But this time we went around to the back. We took a few other guys with us so there were two people for each garbage can of beer—these were clean, new garbage cans.

We hid behind some boxes and waited for our chance. Some latecomers were still in the club, and the guards temporarily wandered away. We moved. Doug and I grabbed one can, the four others grabbed the other two cans, and we took off. We almost made it undetected but one of the guards turned around, saw us, and yelled something incredibly intelligent like, "Hey, stop!"

We just started running. Between 161's area and us were four rows of hooches where HMM-262 and VMO-6, the Huey squadron, were quartered. In the Marine Corps you are not supposed to enter another unit's living area without permission. It is analogous to breaking a formation, which can get you beat all to hell.

But we had beer! And we had guards chasing us!

So we ran into hooches and out of hooches. We ran into bunkers and out of bunkers. A lot of guys looked up in surprise, but when they realized what was going on, they didn't even challenge us. It wouldn't have mattered because we were running so fast, we would have been out of there before anything could be done about it.

I think some of the guys figured there might be something in it for them anyway because the guards were finding everything from people to cots in their way when they ran into the hooches. We finally made it back to our hooches, eluding the guards in the process.

There were plenty of empty sandbags in Quang Tri because we were always building blast walls and bunkers, so we started dividing the loot and filling the sandbags with cans of beer for storage. We had only one problem with that portion of the operation, and it resulted from the discovery that one of the garbage cans was full of soda, not beer. We were a bit upset about that, but we figured we could always mix the soda with booze, so we divided that, too.

Each person involved took his share of beer, headed to a secret place, and buried it. For weeks after that the sands of Quang Tri would suddenly sprout a six-pack or two, on demand. It wasn't cold, but it was beer, our beer, and no one could say, "That's it. You've had your two. No more tonight." Some things in life are just worth fighting for.

The other addition to our booze supply line came from a

totally unexpected source—the United States Air Force. There had been reports for quite some time that Russian helicopters had been sighted just north of the DMZ. As part of the area's defenses and to help keep track of events in the North, a radar station had been built at Quang Tri, manned by air force operators.

They were joined by the crews of Jolly Green Giant helicopters, which were dispatched north of the DMZ to rescue downed pilots—one of the most dangerous jobs in Vietnam for anyone, in any service. The radar operators said they rotated in from Okinawa for sixty-day assignments and then went back.

Then they revealed that they had booze beyond belief! They were authorized beer, wine, and hard liquor by the case each month. Since the airmen had a surplus stored in a hooch built especially for them, and we had a shortage, they began selling it to us.

For about a week they were reasonable. A fifth of booze went for ten dollars, a six-pack of beer for five. Then they realized that we all had money on the books and nowhere to spend it, so the price went up. A fifth of I. W. Harper bourbon began selling for twenty dollars, probably four times its cost down in Da Nang. They made quite a profit off us for a while, and then upped the ante again.

However, we did have one bargaining chip, in the form of war souvenirs that some airmen coveted. They wanted to go back to Okinawa with evidence that they'd really been in a dangerous area, and dealing with us was a less-than-lethal way to prove it. They started demanding items that could be used to bolster their war stories, such as camouflaged jungle utilities and K-bar combat knives.

Then they wanted captured weapons, or weapons of any kind. There were quite a few SKS rifles and AK-47s floating around, so for a while that demand was easy, but then it even spread to M-16s and American pistols. It got to a point where

I figured the price wasn't worth it, but plenty of people still bartered for the stock of booze in their hooch.

Just the existence of that hooch was a constant reminder that there are vast differences between what the Marine Corps and air force consider proper living conditions. Obviously people don't join the air force to live under the same conditions as Marines. But that hooch was air-conditioned, painted blue—reminding me of a big robin's egg sitting in the sand—and they even planted special flowers around it. It wasn't exactly a morale booster for the Marines, living only a hundred yards away in comparative squalor.

Sometimes during rocket attacks I'd sit on top of my hooch and hope that one would go over and blow that hooch to hell—as long as no one was in it and we could salvage the booze. Until that hooch was built, we'd considered ourselves lucky if we didn't have to spend the night in a bunker or rice paddy.

To compensate, we reverted to a form of mental protection, taking pride in doing our jobs without all the frills, and shrugging off what they had as "soft." Regardless of how we viewed our situation, we were reminded through our daily missions to the boondocks that just a few miles away grunts were living in holes in the ground all the time, getting shot at all the time.

And we didn't really complain, because compared to the grunts, having a chance for a regular shower, a cot to sleep on, and a roof of any kind over our heads, was almost as good as a night in a Sheraton.

Chapter 22

In the middle of the second week of December 1968, with no warning and no fanfare, I was called to the avionics hooch and informed that I was being transferred to a new squadron, HMM-364, which at the moment was stationed at Phu Bai.

It came as a complete shock, and the fact that many others in the squadron also were being transferred to other units really didn't lessen the impact. After more than two years together, after seven months in combat, after all our successes and all our losses, HMM-161 was being broken up. Within the next few months nearly 75 percent of the original members of the squadron would leave.

The exodus was being led by Lieutenant Colonel Niesen, who was promoted to commanding officer of Provisional Marine Air Group 39, the top job at Quang Tri. We knew of Niesen's promotion and had been told that a new commanding officer would arrive to take over 161, but we hadn't expected so many of the rest of us to leave also.

There was a reason, of course. If we all stayed together until the following June and all decided to go home, we would be leaving all of our helicopters behind with no one to work on them. By breaking us up and bringing in new personnel, the squadron would have a roster of people with different rotation dates and wouldn't be left understaffed.

Nonetheless, the dismantling of 161 came at a time when we were hitting hard at the North Vietnamese and regularly being engaged in battles. In the first week of December, I had flown several times with Al Morrow, the crew chief from upstate New York, and we had seen fighting during nearly every flight.

Among the missions we flew that week was an emergency Recon extraction in the hills south of Khe Sanh, where a team had been compromised. The Recons were in heavy jungle where there was no chance of establishing a landing zone. We hauled them out one at a time through trees so high it required the use of nearly all of the 250 feet of hoist cable we carried.

As the Recons were coming up the hoist, the North Vietnamese were shooting at us from the ground. Midway through the operation, with a six-foot, 200-pound Recon halfway up to the helicopter, the cable on Morrow's hoist began to unravel. We got that Marine in but couldn't take a chance with the others. Doug Braman's helicopter, which was flying with us, came in to complete the extraction.

Later that week, again with Morrow, spotters on top of the Rockpile, a huge rock formation overlooking the DMZ, saw an entire North Vietnamese regiment infiltrating to the south through an area called Helicopter Valley. We had been transporting the 4th Marines from firebases south of Khe Sanh to LZ Stud, which had recently been renamed Vandergrift Combat Base, for showers and a hot meal.

Before everyone was back, however, we were diverted to the coastal area, where the 9th Marines were conducting an operation. We started taking them to zones ringing the southern end of Helicopter Valley to block the North Vietnamese.

When more infantrymen were needed to complete the operation, we returned to Vandergrift and started loading up the 4th Marines we had just brought there. These troops were flown to zones inside the valley, to push the Vietnamese toward the 9th Marines—and that is where things got bad.

The Vietnamese were strung out along the valley floor, and we began flying right over some of their positions. First we took sniper fire. We fired back. On the next trip in with another squad of Marines, we took automatic weapon fire. We fired back.

On the third trip to the same LZ, with another squad of infantry, we took no fire. But seconds after the squad ran from the helicopter to take defensive positions, mortars began landing in the zone. We were called back to medevac a half dozen Marines we had just brought in. And then the mortar rounds began falling around the helicopter, bracketing it, shaking it with their force. That was when a spotter pilot in a small fixed-wing plane above the valley saw a smoke ring from a mortar tube.

He called in an F-4 Phantom jet circling high above us. The Phantom came in with a load of napalm and dropped the canisters on a hill about seventy-five yards away. It went up with a searing explosion that turned everything red, orange, black, and smoky.

The mortars ceased, and I said a silent "Thank you" to the pilots of the spotter aircraft and the Phantom. The rest of the airlift went off quietly, but days like that one had become all too typical.

In addition to working with our own troops, we also brought elements of the Army of the Republic of Vietnam, South Vietnamese soldiers known as ARVNs, to the DMZ a few days later to join in that fight. It didn't go exactly as well as we would have liked. I was flying with Don Baker, a crew chief from Oklahoma, when the aircraft was ordered to Camp Carroll, an artillery base south of the Rockpile, to pick up the ARVN troops. When we got there we saw a battalion standing in formation, flags flying, and camera crews from American broadcasting organizations filming the operation for the evening news.

When we landed, the ARVNs ran toward the helicopters, banners flying bravely, making a good show for the TV crews. But as usual, no one from the networks got on board to film what happened when we got to the DMZ. As we approached the zone, we were receiving reports of other helicopters taking fire. When we landed, many of the ARVNs didn't want to get out. Baker had to physically shove some of them off the aircraft, and he ordered me to conduct a thorough sweep of the interior to make sure there were no hand grenades left behind by northern sympathizers.

That scene was repeated several times until the entire battalion had been lifted to the DMZ. It may seem from that incident that the ARVNs weren't very motivated. In some cases that was true. Other units, however, had established very good records in the war and were full of soldiers determined to keep South Vietnam free. The key was in figuring out which was which before your helicopter exploded.

We racked it up as just another day in Vietnam, where everything was abnormal and the only thing you could be sure of was that nothing would go as planned.

Even Thanksgiving Day hadn't been the kind of day it was intended to be. I spent the entire day flying gunner on a flight of helicopters delivering hot turkey dinners to virtually every firebase and outpost in the area.

It was a long day, flown in the cloudy grayness that comes with monsoon season. The grunts got turkey, mashed potatoes, vegetables, fresh fruits, and beer. They deserved every bit of it.

The only problem with that day was the way it almost ended. By the time we returned to Quang Tri and headed to the mess hall, whatever had been served for Thanksgiving dinner there was gone. There weren't even crumbs left. I hadn't eaten all day and was really looking forward to having a good meal for a change. But there I was, headed back to my hooch to see what I had left in the way of C rations.

But a new guy, Billy Bazemore, saved the day. Billy was a cheerful, stocky guy who had joined the squadron only a month or so earlier. He had a contagious, outgoing personality, and while most new people were referred to as FNGs, for fucking new guys, he was quickly accepted.

Bazemore had been assigned to the hooch I lived in and also had spent Thanksgiving Day flying. I was sitting on my cot feeling pretty disgusted about missing dinner when he came in, took one look at my face, and asked what was wrong.

I told him, and he quickly pulled a box out from under his bunk. In it he displayed a precooked canned turkey, canned potatoes, carrots, and cranberry sauce. Someone in his family had correctly figured that Thanksgiving dinner in Quang Tri might not be the same as it is in the States and sent some provisions to make up for it.

I came up with some additives from my box of Cs to help out with the meal. Also, I happily discovered that a package had arrived from home, containing a Sara Lee cake that somehow had survived and would become our dessert. Our meal wasn't bad at all and really took the edge off that day.

Most of the rest of our days in Quang Tri were flying by in a blur, and even though Christmas and New Year's were approaching, there was no thrill connected to them. I figured both days would be prime candidates for rocket attacks or probes along the perimeter.

While we had flown out to remote sections of I Corps in the late spring and summer hunting the North Vietnamese, the action now was shifting back to Quang Tri, both in the air and on the ground.

"Fort Bolena" had been the subject of jokes and derision in the summer, but now it became a haven, especially at night. When I wasn't flying, I usually worked the night crew. Firefights with the North Vietnamese, who were firing automatic weapons now instead of isolated sniper rounds, became part of our evenings. The perimeter had always been a place where you were careful—now it was a place where you never relaxed.

We got used to hearing the metallic *clang* of enemy bullets hitting the Marsden matting while we were working at night, and we often found ourselves diving for the protection of the sandbagged walls around the avionics hooch.

Somehow, though, we found ways to laugh even when things seemed the worst.

Staff Sergeant Scoggins was in charge of the electricians during the day and his good friend, S.Sgt. Jim O'Connor, was in charge of the radiomen. But at night, two other sergeants, both E-5s on their second enlistments and second tours in Vietnam, were in charge. While things at Quang Tri generally were pretty serious, those two constantly provided us with some comic relief.

Sgt. William Evans was in charge of electricians, and Sgt. Larry Bryant was in charge of radiomen. They both had fantastic senses of humor and were nonstop practical jokers.

On a cloudy November evening around 10:00 p.m., Bryant sneaked up to the side of the avionics hooch with a long two-by-four in his hand. Several of us were gathered around Evans inside as he handed out work assignments.

Bryant threw the two-by-four onto the corrugated tin roof and it landed with a resounding *ka-blam*! Everyone inside, myself included, jumped a foot off the floor, and then Bryant began yelling, "Incoming!"

But as we poured out of the hooch, Bryant was standing next to the blast wall laughing his ass off. That was funny, I admit—but Bryant got his the next night when a real rocket attack was unleashed as most of us were working out on the flight line.

During the first barrage we had jumped into small sandbagged shelters alongside the revetments, and during a lull we headed for the avionics hooch. Once there, Bryant, obviously tense over the number of rockets that were falling, ordered us into the bunker behind the hooch. But as we sat there somebody just had to ask, "Hey, Winter, aren't you on the reactionary platoon?"

"Yeah, I'm on reactionary, but I'm not going out there till this lets up." That's what I thought. Bryant had different ideas.

"Get out of the bunker! Get out of the bunker!" he kept

yelling. He surmised, rightfully so, that I should head to the perimeter in case we were also being attacked by ground. But the usual practice was to wait for a lull in the rocket attack before moving out. Besides, my helmet, rifle, flak jacket, and ammunition were back in my hooch, about a quarter mile away.

But Bryant was insistent that I move immediately. "Get out of the bunker! Get out of the bunker!" he yelled again. Fine, an order is an order and I did as I was told. But I also told Bryant that my gear was back in my hooch.

"There's equipment in the avionics hooch. You can use that!"

Fine, I could. But I asked Bryant to locate it for me. Now, as a sergeant, he couldn't just order me out into the attack without showing some leadership himself. So Bryant came crawling out of the bunker with me, grumbling all the way.

We ran inside the hooch. I grabbed the equipment and was putting the flak jacket on when another barrage began slamming in. Those rockets were big, Russian-made 122mm, and they had a distinctive sound when they came in. The propellant whistled, red sparks flew out the end, and when they hit the first sound was a sharp *crrraaack* followed by the *boom* of the explosion.

When the next barrage hit, Bryant jumped and began yelling, "Back in the bunker! Back in the bunker!"

"But, Sarge," I replied. "I thought I was supposed to go to the perimeter."

"Just get back in that goddamn bunker right now!" Bryant ordered through clenched teeth.

"Okay, okay, I was just trying to follow orders."

Bryant was really upset then, and I was having a hard time controlling my laughter. So were all the rest of the guys, especially Evans, who figured Bryant had been adequately repaid for scaring us the previous night.

I did get back in the bunker and eventually did go to the

perimeter. I spent the rest of the night in a sandy foxhole, waiting for an attack that never came.

Incoming, such as the rounds that night, was one of the strangest things we adapted to in Vietnam. In the early days, when we first arrived, the sound of a rocket exploding would send the entire squadron scrambling for the bunkers.

But after our first attack, many of us were a bit chagrined to hear a taunting voice coming from HMM-262's area.

"It's all over. You can come out now."

Were 262's Marines hiding in their bunkers when the rockets came? No, they were sitting on the roofs of their hooches watching the show.

Did that make them braver or smarter?

No, actually it was kind of dumb, since rockets did fall in the hooch area.

Did 161 follow by example the proper way to react in a rocket attack? Sure. The next time we got hit, we climbed up on the roofs with the guys from 262.

Why? Because we were nineteen- and twenty-year-old Marines trying to establish our bravery in war, and dumb as it may have been, we weren't going to be outdone by the other squadrons.

Life at Quang Tri continued on in that odd combination of anger and laughter, fighting and flying, right up to the day I left. Ironically, one of my last flights with 161 was as a technician on a test flight, not as a gunner. Appropriately, Lieutenant Colonel Niesen was the pilot.

Niesen was checking the new CO out on the '46, and we flew to a spot on the perimeter where we had enough room for maneuvers. Of all the things Niesen did that day, the one that surprised me the most, and best showed Niesen's knowledge of that aircraft, was operating the windshield de-ice system.

Here we were in a country where the coldest temperatures were in the seventies, and no one had used a de-icing system in nearly a year. I hadn't worked on one since the previous winter back in the States and didn't think the system was even operational anymore.

It consisted of an on/off switch, a circuit breaker, and a windshield circuit, similar to rear-window defrosters in modern-day automobiles. Niesen reached up and threw the switch to the "On" position. Sparks immediately flew from the windshield and the cockpit began to fill up with smoke.

Above the heads of both pilots and behind the copilot were consoles that spanned the width of the cockpit and were filled with dozens upon dozens of small, round circuit breakers. They controlled the flow of electricity to every system in that aircraft—engines, radios, navigation equipment, stabilization circuits, and instruments.

The circuit breaker for the windshield de-ice system was one small button in a sea of similar buttons, and for the life of me I couldn't immediately remember exactly where it was located. But I didn't have to because, as casually as if he were turning on the bathroom light in a home he had occupied all his life, Niesen reached to the exact spot where the breaker was located, pulled it, and stopped the spark show.

He then calmly looked over his shoulder and told me to make sure it was fixed once we landed. Again, that man amazed me. With all the things we had to think about in that country, the last one on my list would have been the location of the de-ice circuit breaker.

That was my last test flight as a member of HMM-161, and a few days later, on December 9, 1968, I packed my seabag, boarded a helicopter, and left to join HMM-364.

The sun had come out on the day I left Quang Tri, and for a few minutes the place was brightened. There were plenty of people I would have said good-bye to that last day. But most of them were out flying, continuing the fight, while those of us who were leaving boarded the helicopter that would take us south.

The flight line was bustling as usual, the war was going on as usual, and the world was going to keep on turning. I didn't want to feel sad about leaving so many of my friends, but I did, and I called on that vault of mine, the one I thought was full to overflowing, to absorb my feelings yet another time.

We'd partied the night before, but I didn't really say good-bye to anyone. That word wasn't in my vocabulary. I didn't go around shaking hands and reminiscing, either. Somehow, I felt it wasn't good-bye; it was just "So long." I couldn't have been more wrong.

I would see some of the guys occasionally; I would even be stationed with a few of them in the future. But by the time I left the Marines, the only friend I would see from the old outfit on a regular basis was Doug Braman. Occasionally I would hear from someone, or they would hear from me. But that really was the end of 161 as I had known it, and I've spent years regretting that I didn't take a little more time to say "So long" when I departed.

On that sunny day I just walked into the helicopter and sat down, feeling pretty strange about being a passenger rather than a gunner. I locked my safety strap across my lap, looked out the window one last time, and flew away.

Chapter 23

I had spent two years and two months of my life as a member of HMM-161. I spent two weeks as a member of HMM-364. That squadron and I started off on the wrong foot the day I left Quang Tri, and things never got any better.

HMM-364 had been stationed at Phu Bai during the time we were in Quang Tri, but the day I was transferred, 364 also was moving south, to Marble Mountain.

The only problem with that arrangement was that most of HMM-364's personnel had rotated home, leaving their helicopters behind, and most of their helicopters were "down" for a variety of reasons. Those that could be flown headed south. Those that could fly but shouldn't have did anyway, and some were in such bad shape that CH-53s had to be brought in to carry the '46s out on external hookups.

But while I had concerns with the condition of the squadron we had inherited, the real trouble started as soon as we got to Marble Mountain. We were lined up in a formation, our names were checked off, and we were told to stack our seabags and rifles on the ground. That was the first mistake. In Quang Tri we never walked off and left our rifles lying around anywhere, but this was a new outfit in a new place, so we did as we were told. Then a group of us was ordered to board a helicopter and fly back to Phu Bai.

"To fix helicopters that can't fly?" we asked ourselves.

"No!" was the answer. We were sent to Phu Bai to clean up the mess that 364 had left behind in its barracks. When we arrived there I was surprised to find that 364 had indeed lived in barracks. They had two-story barracks, in fact, and along with that I discovered that they had regular bunk beds with mattresses. They even had Stateside wall lockers.

I had never visited the squadron living areas on my flights into Phu Bai, so I was pretty surprised. After seven months of living in hooches, bunkers, and holes in the ground, I was absolutely amazed at the considerably better conditions so close to our base.

But the real problem I had with 364 was the condition of the barracks they had just vacated. It was knee-deep in garbage, papers, junk of every description.

A six-by had been commissioned to help haul out that mess, and we went to work. Considering that I was about three weeks shy of three years in the Marine Corps, had seven months in-country, and had flown more than two hundred combat missions, I was more than a little upset that my first job at 364 was a garbage detail.

But we did the job as we were ordered, left the place a lot better than we found it, and after about six trips to the Phu Bai dump, went back to Marble Mountain, where I found another unpleasant surprise. Somebody had moved both my seabag and my rifle.

Everything I owned in the world was in that seabag, and that rifle had been checked out to me, so I was understandably concerned. Its serial number was logged next to my name in some armorer's ledger, and if I left Vietnam alive, one of my last duties would be to return it—or pay for it.

I found my seabag about three hours later. I didn't find my rifle for two days. Both were in a hooch on the edge of the Marble Mountain perimeter in an area designated for Zulu Company, the perimeter guard. There weren't enough hooches in the squadron area for everyone who had come in to join 364, so quite a few of us had to stay with the perimeter guard for a few days. It actually wasn't bad, and since we were close to the command bunker we could find out pretty quickly what was going on when we got hit.

A few days after our arrival we took our first incoming rounds. Just after 9:00 p.m., I was walking back to the hooch with Dale Bush, who had come south with me, when we heard an explosion, then sirens sounding, and saw dozens of red trails behind the rockets as they were fired from west of the base. We watched as they began slamming in and then ran for the command bunker when they started walking our way.

The airstrip at Marble Mountain was taking a lot of hits from rockets, and it was a long time before that attack was over. Other nights Dale and I sat on that bunker and watched "Puff" making runs over a huge rock formation just south of us, from which Marble Mountain got its name.

The Vietnamese had some kind of religious shrine at the base of that rock, but they also had VC up in the caves and crevices on top. If they got too active, a strike would be launched against them, and they'd quiet down for a while.

Later, when I began flying out of Marble Mountain, we'd occasionally shoot the place up as we came back from operations. I don't think, considering all the hiding places they had up there, that our bullets did a lot of damage, but we did make them keep their heads down.

Even with the rocket attacks and the bad reception we got on arrival, I didn't mind staying at Marble Mountain. I probably would have stayed in 364 if things hadn't gone from bad to worse on the first morning we spent in the new outfit. The squadron was expected to begin operations immediately, but had a readiness of only about 25 percent. That meant that out of twenty-four helicopters, only six were capable of flying in combat.

But we soon found that quite a few aircraft needed only adjustments to some of the flight systems or minor parts replacements. Besides myself and Dale Bush, several other electricians and radiomen had come down from 161, including Roger Gangi, Sergeant Evans, Sergeant Tom Moore, and a very good and close friend, Ron "Fat" Adair.

Adair wasn't really fat, but we called him that because of Bill Cosby's Fat Albert character. Adair and I could both do better than passable "Hey, Hey, Heeeyyy" imitations, and since the name Adair had the same first letter and the same number of syllables as Albert, we started calling him Fat Adair.

On the first morning we worked for 364, Ron teamed up with Gangi to start replacing parts, Bush started fixing radio problems, and I went out to make adjustments in the flight systems. Within two hours the four of us raised that squadron's readiness from its dismal 25 percent to nearly 70 percent. A few additional helicopters were also close to being in "up" status, and would be as soon as replacement parts arrived.

In Quang Tri, when we worked for Staff Sergeants Scoggins and O'Connor, there was a simple rule to follow. When there is work to do, do it. When you are caught up or have to wait for parts, relax, read a book, play cards, but be available when things get busy again.

Unfortunately, that is not the way it worked in 364. We reached a point where there was no more that could be done until parts arrived. So I found a quiet corner, reached in my back pocket for a book, sat down on the sand, and began to read.

This lasted for about five minutes before I was accosted by a master sergeant, the new NCOIC of maintenance, who started reaming me for "fucking off." I told him I had personally raised the squadron readiness by 25 percent and was just waiting for parts, but he wasn't impressed. At that point I decided I had had just about enough of 364 and started looking for a way out. I didn't have to look far.

In a few days we received word that HMM-164, another '46 squadron that was adjacent to us on Marble Mountain, was going out on ship in January to join a task force. HMM-164 needed electricians.

I saw my chance and took it. I knew quite a few people in 164, having run into them one place or another during my travels in the Marine Corps. Mike Elliot was there, along with some other former members of 161. It wasn't the same as 161, naturally, but it wasn't exactly a roomful of strangers, either, and moving from one squadron to another at that point didn't take much effort.

HMM-164's crew chiefs had also painted replicas of one of my favorite logos on their helicopters. It showed two vultures sitting on a tree limb with one saying to the other, "Patience, Hell, I Want to Kill Something." There was a lot in that line that mirrored my way of thinking. I packed my seabag, said good-bye to 364, and left.

Moving to 164 was good for me in a number of ways, but mostly because I met a Staff Sergeant named Garcia, and because I had a chance to really get to know some Vietnamese people. Garcia had originally been trained as an electrician on fixed-wing aircraft. Every type of aircraft has variations in its electrical systems, and going from fixed-wing to helicopters required some retraining.

Quite a few of the electricians in 164 wouldn't go out of their way to help anyone learn anything, but they were especially rude to "lifers," as career Marines such as Garcia were known. They were "short-timers" who had only a matter of weeks or a month or two at most left in-country, and many had developed acute "short-timers' attitude."

But I liked Garcia, and he was anxious to learn the '46's systems. He'd often ask to go along when I was assigned a job, and he'd ask questions as I went about my work until he was satisfied that he at least had a basic knowledge of the system I was working on. In the long run my help paid off in several ways since Garcia was a man who didn't forget those who helped him, as well as those who didn't, and he repaid his debts, both ways. In my case, he was especially lenient with time off when we weren't involved in a major operation.

Sometimes it would be just an hour or so in the afternoon, when things were quiet, and he'd tell me to "secure" for the day.

"Go to the club," he'd say. "Have a few beers—but be here early tomorrow."

I'd take his advice willingly. The club at Marble Mountain would have been beautiful even back in the States, and it was fantastic compared to what we'd had at Quang Tri. It was made of fieldstone, was round, had a patio overlooking the South China Sea—it was right on the beach, and the only thing that spoiled the view was the concertina wire on the shore—and it had a hundred-foot-long bar, with plenty of ice-cold beer.

It had a jukebox, occasionally a band, and beautiful Vietnamese girls were waitresses. It also was air-conditioned. The first time I went there, a guy who had been in-country about a month was complaining because there was ice in his beer. After seven months in Quang Tri, that was more than I could take so I voiced my opinion of him, which almost started a fight.

That place was pretty wild most of the time, but after so many months up north, I was actually ready for some peace and quiet. Aside from that first encounter, I generally just drank my beer and shut up. About a week later, though, I became the center of attention in the place, but not for raising hell.

I was sitting at a table with about seven friends when the best-looking of the waitresses delivered my drink and at the same time, in front of the other guys, dropped a note in front of me with my name on it. I didn't think she even knew my name, so I was a bit surprised as I opened it to read it.

Her name was Phan, and she merely was thanking me for having some manners—I still said "please" and "thank you" when I ordered my beer—a rare quality in those days. The waitresses in many cases were the first women some of the guys had seen in months, and for most of us they were definitely the first we had been near on a regular basis. Some guys just couldn't handle it, and to say they acted like animals would have been putting it nicely.

The note said, "Dear Ron, You aren't like the others here. Thank you for being nice, Phan."

Of course, the rest of the table thought it was an invitation to a sexual rendezvous, so their queries and comments went on for quite a while. I was told that Phan had received her college education in Hue before the Tet Offensive blew that town to hell, and I soon found that she could speak English, French, and Vietnamese fluently. She had long, straight, black hair, beautiful eyes, and was incredibly pretty.

I'd seek her out when I went to the club and talk to her when she got a break. But it never went any further than that, and I think the friendship would have gone to hell if I had tried to make something more of it.

She worked there primarily because the tips were so good, Phan said. At that time the average income for a Vietnamese farmer, in American dollars, was about fifty dollars per year. Many of the waitresses were making thirty and forty dollars a night at the club, a phenomenal sum, so they put up with the Marines in exchange for giving their families a standard of living they'd never known before.

After a couple of weeks, Phan got a job at the PX selling film and was liberated from the animal den. I'd still stop and talk to her every couple of days or so.

I kept her note for a long time, but it got lost along the way somewhere, which I regret to this day. It wasn't my biggest memento of the war, but it was a remembrance of a friend, and a little piece of proof that I kept some semblance of sanity in that place.

I never met Phan's family or was allowed to see her life outside the base, but I did know that she wanted two things—to be free as Americans are, and to see the war end. At least she got half her wish.

When my time off wasn't being spent at the club, I liked to go out in the Da Nang area and see the sights, such as they were. Usually Fat Adair or Gangi would go, too. We'd hitch a ride down to what we called the "four corners" where the south road went back to Marble Mountain, the north road to an area called Red Beach, which also housed a small base called Camp Tiensha, the east road to the China Beach R&R center, and the west road down into Da Nang City.

From there we could pick and choose where we wanted to go. The intersection was a busy place, with military convoys coming and going, a marketplace where civilians sold food and vegetables, a refugee resettlement area known as Cabbage Patch, where makeshift huts had been thrown up to house those displaced by the war, and dozens of street urchins who would sell you anything that wasn't tied down—and rip you off at the same time.

I had first gone there back in the summer when I got in-country R&R out of Quang Tri. I was walking up to the gate at China Beach when I was surrounded by about twelve kids, ranging in age from six or so to about eighteen, all of whom were yelling and tugging at my sleeve.

Just in time I realized that all but one were tugging from my left side while one—actually the largest of the bunch—was behind me on the right, slitting my trouser pocket with a razor, attempting to lift my wallet. Another had already slit my shirt pocket and was trying to get my cigarette lighter out.

I smashed my elbow into the face of the one trying for my wallet, breaking his nose and bloodying him pretty badly. They all backed off then and called to another guy, considerably older, who had been lounging across the street. He apparently was the leader, looked to be in his late teens or early twenties, and was supposed to watch out for his troops.

He started across the street toward me, to show how tough

he was, I guess. I just swung my M-16 down, pointed it straight at him, and switched it to full automatic. I looked him straight in the eye and said, "Come on. See if it's worth it."

He stopped dead and started backing away slowly. The kids he had working for him cleared out, too. After that I carried my wallet in the front of my trousers, between my fly and my groin. That was one place the kids never grabbed.

My one loss from that incident was my lighter. It was a Zippo, and I'd had it engraved by a kid at a stand on the side of the road. The engraving was a picture of Snoopy lying flat on top of his doghouse holding a sign that read FUCK IT.

I was mad that I'd lost it, but it was easy enough to replace, and I just had another kid on the side of the road engrave another one for me. I had two such lighters. The second said, LIVE BY CHANCE, LOVE BY CHOICE, KILL BY PROFESSION. U.S. MARINES. They didn't come home with me either, but I wish they had.

During my trips out to Da Nang, I had met a Vietnamese Marine master sergeant named Nguyen, who lived with his family in Cabbage Patch. We weren't supposed to go in there, it was completely off-limits, but whenever I was around he said I was welcome in his house. So I'd duck through the wire, run through the twisted alleys, and eventually come to his house. He was a decent guy who had been fighting the communists since they were called Viet Minh and the French were in Vietnam.

"I kill many VC," he proudly told me one day, making an imitation of an M-16 in action, going, "Boom, boom, boom!"

He had been born in Hanoi but had given up his home and moved south in 1954 when the country was partitioned. He hated communism, didn't want to be a communist, wanted to live a free life, and had dedicated his life to fighting or dying as a free man.

He was the kind of guy the reporters never did stories on.

Every time I visited Nguyen he fed me, gave me a place to sleep, drank beer with me, and told stories about the way things were in his country. He had a wife, a very pretty daughter about my age named Mai Li, whom I became friends with, and a son about thirteen.

I picked up a lot of information on Vietnam from that man and even learned a bit of the language. It wasn't always easy to communicate since his English was just a shade better than my Vietnamese. I was at his house the day former President Eisenhower died. Ike was a man who was known all over the world, and I gathered from the way Nguyen reacted that he really felt bad about such a historic figure dying. But at first I couldn't understand him.

He kept saying, "Asin hover, fini—he dies."

I kept trying to figure out who the hell Asin Hover was until Nguyen said, "President, American president. General Asin Hover."

Then it hit me. "I-sen-hower!" That I understood.

Whenever I stayed with Nguyen and his family, I'd leave some money, usually about twenty dollars in MPC—military payment certificates—to help out. I was pulling down about three hundred dollars per month between my base pay, combat pay, flight pay, and no income tax, and had left a lot riding on the books. Even though twenty dollars was a lot to them, it didn't seem like much to me.

We were paid in MPC because the government didn't want greenbacks making their way into the communist money supply. MPC looked like monopoly money, and the design was changed every few months or so to keep the locals off guard.

Usually the word got out before the exchange took place—you'd have to go to the pay officer and turn in all the money you had for new money—and the mamma-sans who ran the bars and whorehouses got theirs exchanged without missing a beat. Once in a while, though, stories would go around about a local businessman or woman missing the exchange and getting stuck with thousands of dollars of worthless MPC.

Nguyen was pretty sharp and plugged into the American system pretty well, and I never heard of him missing the exchange.

He kept letting me come to his house for the remainder of my tour. After 164 went out on ship, first onto the USS *Tripoli* and then the USS *Valley Forge,* Staff Sergeant Garcia would let me have a few days off at a time in between assaults and operations.

I'd hitch a ride to Marble Mountain on one of our helicopters, then down to the corners and Nguyen's house. Garcia would give me a time when I'd have to be back, and in between I'd visit and learn about the war from the people who were living it in for more than thirteen-month tours.

Among the many lessons I learned was an especially important one from a bunch of little kids, some no more than three or four years old. You'd see them on the side of the road, outside the wire surrounding Cabbage Patch, or on the other side of Da Nang by another refugee area known as Dog Patch, from the L'il Abner cartoon.

They'd grab you as you walked by and pimp for their sisters or whoever was putting out that day. "Hey, GI. Hey, Marine. You want to boom-boom my sister? Five hundred p, man, come on, she's a virgin. Five hundred p."

Five hundred p stood for 500 piasters, which was the equivalent of five dollars American money.

Of course, their sisters weren't virgins, but at that point it didn't matter. They needed the money. Over the years I've met a lot of people who have had everything in their lives handed to them on silver platters, who act as though they deserve it, and who look down their noses in disgust when I tell them about little kids who learned to pimp almost as soon as they learned to walk.

I heard enough derogatory remarks about those kids, their sisters, and the people in general while I was there. But I think that people who have never been in a position of total need—where every meal isn't guaranteed, and housing and clothing and schooling aren't guaranteed, and every night is spent worrying about the incoming or the outgoing or the VC or the Americans—could learn a lesson from those little kids on the streets, or their sisters, or their parents, who depended on them in a world gone haywire.

In America the dollar rules, and the marketplace, where it's required that you sell anything of value for personal profit, is the measuring stick of success. Quite often in the Vietnam of 1968 and 1969, the only thing of value to sell, whether it was for a meal or the price of some cheap clothes or a piece of tin to mend a hole in a shanty, was your sister, or daughter, or wife, or yourself.

And more than once I heard those little kids calling out to passing Americans to share a few moments behind the wire for a few of their dollars. But to my amazement, they would do it not only in Vietnamese, their native language, but also in English, and sometimes even in French. They could switch between languages without missing a tone or inflection, and they knew what they were saying in each one.

I don't know how many American three-year-olds can understand the concept of pimping for a meal, let alone do it in three languages. And I don't call what they were doing sleazy, or ignorant, or low-life. I call it survival, and those three-year-olds had already become masters of the art.

Chapter 24

There were five of us in the taxi, heading from Travis Air Force Base in California to the airport in San Francisco. We had gone through customs and now were headed to our homes. We didn't know each other, but for the moment we were saving a few dollars on the ride.

Just outside the gate of the air base, we saw a kid hitchhiking on the side of the road. He looked to be about sixteen, had long, blonde, greasy hair, and was wearing several strings of beads.

He flipped us the bird.

"Welcome home!"

The war had ended quickly and quietly for me. After more than a year of counting days and crossing off dates on my short-timers' calendar, it was over. The months had flown by, and I received my orders back to CONUS (Continental United States), the World, Mom, home, round-eyed women, and apple pie.

But I wasn't all that sure I wanted to go. Besides a more intimate exposure to the country and the people, my months in HMM-164 had also given me exposure to a type of soldier who is often written about now, but rarely was heard of then—the multitour man.

Where I previously had thought that seven, or nine, or eleven months in-country was big-time, I had found myself in the company of Marines who had been in Vietnam for twenty months, twenty-four months, thirty months, and had no intention of doing anything else until they were discharged. Suddenly I wasn't sure that I wanted to return to the States and its accompanying nonsense. The war was going on, it would continue after I left, and there were people in Vietnam who really wanted us to be there, to help.

But I had also made promises back home that I felt I should honor. I had dated extensively on my last leave, primarily with one person, and had said that if I returned and all was the same, we'd get married. I had thought, back in those days before I got to Vietnam, that everything would follow a standard pattern, and that I wouldn't change. Coming home, getting out of the service, finding a job, getting married, and living happily ever after all seemed to fit that pattern.

But I had changed. The war had changed me, the people had changed me, and the guys I flew and fought with had changed me. I had been giving serious consideration to staying on for another tour. Several of the guys who had been in HMM-161 and moved to HMM-164, including Bob Thompson, who was flying gunner with me nearly a year earlier in my first firefight, and Steve Brown, had already decided to stay for another six months. We had been doing a lot of flying, and I had become as acquainted with The Arizona as I previously had been with the DMZ and Khe Sanh areas.

In early January 1969, HMM-164 had embarked on the USS *Tripoli,* a helicopter carrier built from the keel up specifically to house troops, helicopters, and squadron personnel. We were part of a task force that included another helicopter carrier—the USS *Okinawa*—landing ships, destroyers, and the battleship USS *New Jersey.*

Our job was to position the task force along the coast and mount operations against enemy emplacements and troop concentrations when they were discovered by Recon teams in the field.

The *Tripoli* was a good ship and I liked it, but it rotated back to the States after we'd been on board only a month. We had to disembark, fly in to Phu Bai, stay there a couple of weeks, then embark on the USS *Valley Forge.*

The *Valley Forge* was also a helicopter carrier, but like the *Princeton,* it originally had been designed to house naval fixed-wing squadrons, not helicopter squadrons and infantry battalions. It was much more cramped—we were stacked five-high in the sleeping quarters—and living conditions weren't the best in the world.

The hammock I claimed was next to the top and Brown had the one above me. On ship it is advisable to get as close to the top as humanly possible because if someone above you gets seasick easily, sleeping in a storm can become very unpleasant. Brown was heavier than I, and if he was in his hammock, I couldn't turn over in mine because there wasn't enough room. At least he didn't get seasick.

If one person in that compartment caught a cold, everyone caught a cold, and at one point the surgeon general of the Pacific Fleet inspected the ship. We were told he had condemned our living area, but it wasn't as if they were going to call off the war and send us home just because he had.

In late February we sailed south to an area near Chu Lai, where we were told the Viet Cong had a major stronghold and hideout. The target area was the Batangan Peninsula, a finger of land that jutted into the South China Sea. It was to be a multiservice operation.

On board with HMM-164 was the 3d Battalion, 26th Marines, and the 2d Battalion was on the *Okinawa.* There was to be a helicopter assault on one side and an amphibious assault on the tip. The Korean Marines, with whom we often worked and respected immensely, were to hit another side, and the U.S. Army's Americal Division was supposed to block the end of the peninsula so the VC couldn't escape.

The night before the operation, the *New Jersey* and the destroyers began pounding the peninsula, and some of us sat out on the *Valley Forge*'s catwalks for several hours to watch. The *New Jersey* was exactly one mile across the water from us. When a broadside was fired, the night sky would light up and we would count, "One-thousand-one, one-thousand-two, one-thousand-three, one-thousand-four, one-thousand-five," and then you'd hear, and feel, the sound. *Ka-blam, ka-boom, boom, bam, pow, bang,* however you wish to describe it, the sound was impressive, awe-inspiring, tremendous, violent, destructive.

We'd listen to those big shells, sixteen inches across, weighing as much as a Volkswagen Beetle, roaring across the night sky, then hear the distant muffled *boom* as they hit some target on shore. Each time the *New Jersey* fired, we wondered how anyone could be alive onshore.

The assault began around 6:00 a.m.—0600 military time. Earlier, before mounting the machine guns, I had gone down to the mess deck for breakfast. A meandering line of Marine infantrymen clogged the passageways, and as I neared the head of the line, I began receiving more than a fair amount of none-too-good-natured complaining.

As a flight crew member, I had chow line privileges—meaning I could skip the line and go straight to the head—but that didn't sit too well with those in line. Along the way I was hearing a lot of talk about what the infantrymen were going to do to the Vietnamese once the operation was under way. There was a lot of street-type talk and a lot of bragging.

The 26th Marines had been among the defenders at Khe Sanh and later were involved in an operation named Meade River, where they had killed a huge number of NVA troops. They had captured weapons and supplies and had done well. But they also had taken casualties, and as I progressed along the chow line, I realized that many of the infantrymen were young replacements—new guys, with their hair still cut in boot camp style. In many cases I figured I had more time in-country than they had in the Corps.

At the head of the line one guy gave me some lip, and I turned on him without saying a word. He was a private, and he saw two things when I turned—the gunner's wings on my chest and the corporal chevrons on my cover. He shut up immediately, and I grabbed a tray for breakfast.

An hour later the launch was under way. It went off without a hitch. The landing was made without difficulty and the focus began to shift toward resupply operations. Then the call came for medevacs, and more medevacs, and more medevacs. It wasn't fierce opposition or well-entrenched troops that prompted the calls.

The Batangan Peninsula had not seen American troops for several years, and in the meantime the Vietnamese communists had littered it with minefields. There was also a rumor that at least one field had been left by the French fifteen years earlier.

It didn't matter who put the mines there, a company had entered a minefield, started tripping mines, and the number of wounded began mounting immediately. According to another rumor, a green lieutenant had kept the troops moving through the field rather than stopping and making them probe their way out with bayonets.

Probing the dirt for buried mines was one of the basics we had been taught in infantry training, and it was inconceivable that it would be ignored. But the number of wounded showed that something had gone terribly wrong. The sick bay on the *Valley Forge* was filled in no time, and an area was cordoned off on the hangar deck to hold the overflow. We were told that a similar situation was developing on the *Okinawa,* and that didn't take into consideration the number of wounded being taken to the hospital ships.

As the bodies continued to accumulate, so did the horror stories. An entire squad had been wiped out, survivors were blown up as they carried the wounded to safety, and helicopters were landing right in the minefields to pull the wounded out. As each new incident was reported, my sense of amazement continued to grow, but I was speechless when we were told that a young infantryman died from shock on the way to the ship in a helicopter, from a piece of shrapnel that had pierced his leg. The wound normally wouldn't have been considered that serious, and he had an older corpsman, known in the squadron as "Pappy," working on him.

But despite the knowledge an experienced corpsman accumulates and the hardest of work, the Marine couldn't overcome the shock of seeing his friends cut down so quickly. All the bravado from that morning's chow line was gone now. The new guys had learned about war almost as soon as they landed, and most of them had yet to fire a shot in anger.

On a trip down to the hangar deck for ammunition I saw the wounded, who had been grouped together on stretchers behind hospital privacy screens. Mines cause the most horrible wounds, with no rhyme or reason to the way intestines are ripped open, limbs are blown off, facial features are permanently disfigured. Most of the guys on the hangar deck had less serious injuries, but they were still hurting.

Eventually all the wounded and dead were hauled out and the operation continued. I heard that the grunts found miles of tunnels, food, weapons, and medical supplies, but that the main force of VC had slipped through the Americal Division lines, either during the initial assault or the night before when the *New Jersey* was pounding the peninsula.

As far as the operation was concerned, I considered the actions of our pilots and crews to be among the bravest I had seen. Landing in a minefield and getting out alive is no small accomplishment. But naval aviation training teaches Marine and navy pilots how to land on ships, even when they are tossing and pitching on unsettled seas, and I guess that training had prepared them for other dangerous types of landings also.

Since we had left the States, I had seen a number of pilots make excellent landings on ships in terrible conditions. And I have yet to see anyone equal Colonel Niesen's dramatic mid-Pacific rescue in 1968. If I had to be on an aircraft in an emergency, I'd prefer it had a Marine pilot. Whether dodging artillery at Khe Sanh or landing in minefields on the Batangan Peninsula, our pilots had always shown themselves to be the ultimate professionals.

The operation at the Batangan was one of the worst I participated in as far as casualties went, and in retrospect it posed some unique problems for the pilots and flight crews. But, like everything else by then, it was handled as though minefields and extraordinary numbers of casualties were everyday occurrences.

It also was the last major operation for me. As it wound down, so did my activity. Garcia, who had gotten me promoted to corporal in February, continued his practice of giving me free time in Da Nang. I'd spend a week or two working, and then have a day or two on land.

I had a close brush with death on one of my last flights in April, but was saved by the professionalism of the crew chief. His name was Whitey, he had more than thirty months in-country.

We were supposed to ferry the commanding officer of the 26th Marines out to firebases so he could check on his troops. We flew off the ship and were about a mile from Marble Mountain, still over the water at 5,000 feet, when I heard an unfamiliar sound and saw Whitey jump up from his seat. The engines were programming back to zero RPM for some reason, and we suddenly started dropping like a stone.

The colonel was sitting on the port side of the aircraft, and the cord for his helmet was plugged in on the starboard ceiling over my head, so it stretched across the interior of the cabin. Whitey was just behind the cockpit, by the starboard entranceway, and he ran for the rear.

In one swift motion he grabbed the cord in one hand and the colonel's helmet in the other and ripped the cord out of its socket. The colonel's head bounced off the wall behind him. Whitey opened the engine compartment doors in a flash and grabbed the fuel programmer rods in his hands. He manually brought the RPMs back up to 100 percent. It all happened in about ten seconds, and in that space of time we had dropped a good thousand feet. If Whitey hadn't been so experienced, hadn't known exactly what to do, and hadn't done it immediately, it isn't likely we would have survived that drop toward the ocean.

We flew into Marble Mountain with Whitey still working the engine controls, and the entire crash crew, complete with foam-making trucks, was lined up on the runway waiting. The colonel was out in a flash, and we set to work to fix the problem. An hour later we were airborne again as though nothing had happened.

Throughout those months I continued to see Nguyen, Phan, Mai Li, and my friends at Marble Mountain, and the weeks and months slipped right by. I agonized over the decision to stay or leave, but somewhere around the end of February, I was told I had already passed the deadline for extending, and the decision was made for me.

During the first week in June my orders came. I packed a box with some souvenirs, including a set of ivory, gold-inlaid chopsticks I had purchased in Hong Kong and my HMM-161 Squadron cruise book, and mailed it home. It had to go through the Fleet Post Office in San Francisco and never made it to my home.

I lost a lot of memorabilia in that box, and getting ripped off by someone back in the States didn't make coming home any easier. On my last day I went to the fantail of the *Valley Forge,* took out my lighters, the one with Snoopy saying FUCK IT and the other with LIVE BY CHANCE, LOVE BY CHOICE, KILL BY PROFESSION. U.S. MARINES, and lit one last cigarette with each of them. Then I threw them into the South China Sea.

I figured they wouldn't be appropriate and wouldn't be appreciated back home. I was right, but that was one of the stupidest acts of my life—just plain stupid. I didn't realize at that point that a time would soon come when I would have wanted anything from my time in Vietnam to keep forever.

When it was time to leave, I said some good-byes, hefted

my seabag, boarded a CH-46 for the last time, and flew into Da Nang. Roger Gangi was with me, as was Rick Landers, a crew chief from Virginia who also had been with us ever since New River. We stayed overnight, boarded a jet, and left for Okinawa. When the plane took off, I didn't look out the window, didn't look down, and didn't look back.

We stayed in Okinawa for two days, getting ready for the World. We went through a bunch of administrative tasks and partied in the NCO club one night. They had a special on bottles of pink champagne, and the corks popping in that place sounded like a firefight. Landers, who always had been a firecracker in his own right, livened that place up considerably.

The last night, Roger and I went into town, had a couple of drinks, and raised a little hell. The next morning we headed for the plane home. They lined us up in alphabetical order, but at the last minute I was bumped from the plane so some guys who had emergency leave could go home. Roger and Rick Landers made it on board.

Twelve hours later I got on the next plane out, and somewhere between Okinawa and Japan found I knew at least one person on board. It was the recruiter, the sergeant from the supermarket back in Wynantskill! Call it what you will, sheer chance or poetic justice, he was the last person I expected to see on that plane.

We talked for a while, and then he got off at our refueling stop in Japan. He didn't get back on board when we left. My journey had started thirteen months earlier at New River, in the company of more than two hundred other members of HMM-161. I made the last leg home in the company of a planeload of strangers, and I never felt more alone.

I had a strange feeling inside and didn't want to talk to anyone. I kept trying to sleep, and the stewardess kept waking me to see if I wanted anything. I had believed we would come home together, victorious, celebrating. After all that we had done, I believed we should have.

The war might continue, but I couldn't help thinking we had made a substantial contribution to winning it. The army was moving into many of the areas where we had fought, bringing its larger number of troops and support units, enlarging the bases, taking over security, and giving the place an air of permanency. The South Vietnamese Army was getting more involved, and as far as I could see the North Vietnamese were getting their asses kicked on all fronts.

It seemed as though it would only be a matter of time until it was over. Somewhere over the ocean, on the way up to Alaska, I jolted out of an uneasy doze and remembered with a horrible emptiness inside that I had never told Nguyen, Phan, or Mai Li good-bye. I should have, and regretted that I didn't.

Worse than that was another feeling that I couldn't quite place, a sense of not doing the right thing. I couldn't shake the belief that I should have stayed, should have continued until it was really over, not just until someone said it was okay to go home.

I had flown three hundred missions as a door gunner, hundreds of additional hours on test flights, had worked seven days a week throughout the tour, either on helicopters, perimeters, mess halls, or battles, and had seen enough of war to know what it was about. I had dealt with death, and I had cheated it.

We had done so much in Vietnam, had worked and fought so hard. We had lost friends and repeatedly taken chances ourselves, but never shied away from the job we had to do.

Doug Braman had flown more than 1,000 missions, the highest number in our squadron, and was cited for bravery in a battle south of Khe Sanh in February. Al Munoz flew more than 900 missions and had been wounded. Most of the crew chiefs, since they flew full-time, also had been closing in on the 1,000-mission range.

It all added up to a tremendous amount of work, a tremendous amount of dedication, and outright courage. There should have been more at the end than a ride home alone.

But while I had a sense of missing out on something, I was also tired by then, beyond exhaustion, and another part of me really was looking forward to going home, if only for the rest. "It will turn out all right," I told myself. "It has to."

But as hard as I tried, I still had the sensation, both when I awakened and in my dreams, that I had left all that was important to me, and marked the very best of me, behind in Vietnam.

It was receding at 600 miles per hour and could never be retrieved.

PART III

Chapter 25

I was standing behind a huge glass wall at Bradley International Airport in Windsor Locks, Connecticut, looking out over the runway, watching jets taking off and landing. An old sense of longing made my insides feel empty and I was wishing I could get on board and go with one of them. I don't remember why I was there in the first place, but as I stood lost in my reveries, I slowly became aware of a minor commotion at the most distant passenger gate.

Looking in that direction, I was snapped into instant attention. The commotion was being caused by three CH-46 helicopters taxiing to parking positions on the flight line. I couldn't believe my eyes. They were Marine Corps helicopters!

It was a bright summer day in 1977, and the sun gleaming off the windshields and windows temporarily kept me from reading the squadron markings on the side. I started making my way down to the passenger gates, hoping for a better look, and vaguely wondering whether I would know any of the crew members.

Just as I arrived at the gate nearest the helicopters, the doors to the flight line burst open and a noisy group of a half dozen Marines came through, headed toward the coffee shop. They were wearing green utility trousers, leather flight jackets, green utility covers. Almost instantly I realized that I recognized some of them. No, not some of them. I recognized all of them!

At the same time, they recognized me. They were all from HMM-161, and as I glanced out the window toward the helicopters, I finally could see the HMM-161 markings on the sides. There was a noisy reunion, and as some of them hurried off for coffee, I tried to figure out how they had all ended up together again and why they were now in Connecticut. They all looked the same. They hadn't changed, not one bit.

I felt conspicuous. I had changed. I was older, a little soft around the middle now, from too many years of sitting at a desk, too many nights staring into space, remembering—always remembering. It had been a long time since I had hefted .50-caliber machine guns, boxes of ammo, and lugged radio gear around the flight line. There had been too many nonproductive years—at least from my point of view. But I was so glad to see them!

It was a happy reunion, but it was short, and as suddenly as it started, they had to leave.

"Come on with us," they kept saying as they headed out the door. "Don't stay here, come on."

I wanted to. Believe me, I wanted to go with them. But something was holding me back, and as I walked back to the observation window, I felt that tremendous sense of loss and sadness again. It was that same feeling I had experienced on the flight home from Vietnam so many years ago. It caught me by surprise because I thought I had successfully put it away, in that old vault of mine where I used to store bad feelings.

I watched as the engines were started and the rotor blades began turning. As they began to taxi toward the runway, I had another feeling, too, a very strange feeling. I realized during the reunion that among the group were some of the people I had thought were dead!

In a way it made sense. Most of the time in Vietnam, when a helicopter went down, the crew was rescued, or bodies were recovered, by infantry in the area. If they were badly wounded or dead, Marines from other squadrons as well as HMM-161 took them to hospitals, or to the morgue at Da Nang.

Frequently our knowledge of what had really happened out there was as much a matter of conjecture and rumor as it was news from official statements. So it wasn't impossible that someone we thought had died had actually been wounded and survived.

I'd been shocked to see Bill Frantz there. I had thought I was seeing things when he came out of the crowd, and I had even told him, "Man, I thought you were dead." I'd been so happy to see him.

But he just looked at me for a few seconds, then turned and walked away, not saying anything. When he reached the door he looked back, waved for me to join them, and headed back to the helicopter. It had me baffled as I watched them lift off, heading west, fast, the way we used to when leaving a hostile zone in Vietnam.

They were almost out of sight and I was turning to leave when I heard a scream from others who had been watching. Simultaneously there was the sound and concussion of an explosion. I turned and saw a cloud of black smoke rising from the area where the helicopters had headed.

I ran out of the building and headed for the crash site as fast as I could. A fence was in the way, and a small knoll, and I couldn't see what had happened. People were yelling, running along with me, sirens were wailing, and above it all I could hear explosions, screams, wounded and dying men.

I was within sight now, and people were hemming me in. I kept trying to get through, kept yelling at them.

"Let me through! *Let me through!* I know those helicopters. I can help. Please let me through."

A tremendous pillar of black-and-white smoke, just like the one at New River in 1967, when Mike Vicknus had died, was rising straight up in the blue sky. I was still hemmed in and I was still yelling.

"I know those helicopters. Let me through. *Let me help*!"

I was so angry! So frustrated! People were dying right in front of my eyes and I couldn't do anything about it. It seemed as though everything around me was deliberately preventing me from helping them.

I kept yelling, *"Let me through! I can help! Let me . . ."*

I shot up in my bed, my heart pounding. The room was cold and pitch-dark; there were no helicopters, no fires, and no people. It wasn't the summer of 1977, it was mid-January 1978.

I was in bed in my home in East Haddam, Connecticut, not at the airport, and it had been a dream. But it had seemed so real! The faces, the conversations, the sounds, the smells, the emotions, all were so incredibly real.

My God, I hadn't thought about those people in years. Why now?

I had felt so sad inside, so terrible in the middle of that dream, so wretchedly helpless as my friends were dying, that tears were running down my cheeks.

I hadn't cried in Vietnam. Not once. I hadn't even cried in 1973 when my brother Larry was killed in a car wreck, at least not publicly. So why now? Why had this dream come along after all these years to break into that vault of feelings that I thought was safely put away forever?

I tried rolling over and going back to sleep, but it didn't work. I tossed, turned, and stared into the darkness, but I couldn't get 161 out of my mind. Finally I went out to the living room. The wood stove wasn't putting out enough heat to offset the chill, so I opened the damper and put a few more logs on.

There was a lot of snow on the ground and a full moon helped light the outside to a semblance of daytime. I heard my son Kevin, who was seven then, stirring in his sleep. I looked in, but he was just having a dream of his own and was already back in a deep slumber.

Sara, only six months old, cried softly. Maybe she'd heard

me stirring. I went into her room, tucked her blankets around her, and kissed her good night. I padded out to the kitchen, checked the clock—2:04 a.m.—thought about having a cup of coffee, decided against it, and grabbed a beer instead. I went back to the living room and sat in my rocker, watching as the fire grew, feeling its warmth, thinking.

It had been a long haul since Vietnam. I had come home as I said I would and made good on my promises. Two months after I got back I was married. Three months after that my wife was pregnant. A year and a couple weeks after I was married, Kevin was born.

I had been stationed in a unit called Headquarters Squadron at the naval air station in Norfolk, Virginia, when I got back, and there couldn't have been a worse place for me to go. The whole purpose of that squadron was to maintain two chrome fixed-wing aircraft that flew generals to Europe or the Caribbean for NATO maneuvers. It was full of high-ranking enlisted men, most of whom hadn't gone to Vietnam yet, and didn't want to.

A half dozen of us from 161 had been sent there, and since those who hadn't gone were jealous of those of us who had (but not jealous enough to ask for orders overseas), they made life miserable for us to compensate. There were more master sergeants, gunnery sergeants, and staff sergeants in that place than you'd normally see in three squadrons, and a lesser number of lower-ranking enlisted men to do the dirty work.

So we spent a lot of time sweeping and swabbing hangar decks and shining the chrome on those airplanes. But Vietnam wouldn't let go all that easily, and even in Virginia it had a way of intruding.

It happened in September, and came in the form of a letter from Hong Kong, roughly three months old, bearing a familiar address in the left-hand corner.

It was from Anna, a girl I had met there at a place called the Muskee Bar. I had gone there once in October 1968 for three days as part of a rest program for flight crews with high numbers of missions. She was a short, very pretty Chinese girl with shoulder-length black hair, and she had kept looking at me as I sat in the bar with my beer. Eventually we got together and she took me all over Hong Kong, Kowloon, and the New Territories for the next three days.

She was my age, a lot of fun, and provided a welcome oasis in the desert that was the war. She wrote at least two letters to me each week after I returned to Quang Tri. In February, when I was given formal R&R, I had gone back and spent a week there. She had taken me to her mother's home for dinner, to the Sha Tin floating restaurant for a special meal, to movies, nightclubs, the San Francisco Bar on Hong Kong Island, the Star ferryboat a hundred times, and again she took my mind off the war for a few days.

The last time I was in Hong Kong I had told her I was thinking of staying in Vietnam for another tour, so she continued writing for several months. After I left Vietnam, I stopped writing. After a while she did, too.

But then that day at mail call, a month after I was married, the letter came. The envelope was a gentle shade of purple and it carried the subtle scent of her perfume. It caused quite a bit of discussion in the squadron. I went inside the avionics shop on the second floor of the hangar and walked to the rear, where the windows overlooked the flight deck and seaplane ramps outside. I opened the letter and read slowly.

"I miss you," it said. "But I haven't heard from you for so long." The script was neat, feminine. I remembered it so well, and I remembered her, usually laughing, sometimes very serious, holding my arm as we walked the streets of Hong Kong at night, or just sitting at a favorite table in the Muskee Bar as Simon and Garfunkel sang "Sounds of Silence" over and over on the jukebox.

"I'm sorry," it said. "If I don't hear from you by the end of the month, I won't be writing anymore."

I checked the date again. The letter was way overdue, and

the deadline had long since passed. I couldn't have done anything about it anyway. I put the letter back in the envelope, held it just below my nose, inhaling slowly and lightly, remembering her perfume and a lifetime of good times packed into ten days.

Then I slowly tore the letter in half, did it again, dropped it into the wastebasket, and walked away. And once again I couldn't escape the feeling that I was in the wrong place, doing the wrong thing.

If I had any lingering doubts about feeling out of place there, the personnel in Norfolk made sure they were taken care of. A gunnery sergeant who wore a huge pair of gold radio operator wings even ordered those of us who had been door gunners to stop wearing our combat wings on our utility uniforms.

Gunners' wings, earned in combat, could be worn on any uniform. But peacetime radio operators' wings, which could be earned in the States, could be worn only on a dress uniform. He couldn't wear his wings on his working uniform, so he didn't want us to, either.

I told him I'd fought to put those wings on my chest, and he'd have to fight to take them off. So the gunny made a stink about it until he was informed that he was trying to counter a direct order from the commanding general of the 1st Marine Division. That shut him up, but he still made life a pain.

With that kind of reception for a homecoming, I didn't give a lot of thought to making a career of the Marines. I was discharged on January 9, 1970, made a trip back to Wynantskill to get a few things in order, and headed for Connecticut, where I had a job in the Experimental Department at Pratt & Whitney in East Hartford.

After being highly trained on the CH-46, after knowing electrical systems, hydraulics, engines, and airframes, after hundreds of hours on test flights, after troubleshooting damaged systems in the air during firefights, Pratt & Whitney paid me three dollars and fifty cents per hour to move instruments from one laboratory to another. They even let me wrap and store cables at the end of each shift.

The bosses said if I did real well at that job, eventually I'd get promoted and move up to plugging the cables in. What a deal!

I found out quickly that regardless of what we had learned in the service, the private sector was giving the good jobs to our contemporaries who had stayed behind and finished college. They had degrees, and even though we may have had a wealth of experience that no degree could match, the system was geared for that piece of paper.

We had been penalized inside the service for our time in Vietnam, and now we were being penalized even worse in the civilian world. Career-wise I figured I was at least four and possibly as many as six years behind people my age who had found a way to stay out of the service.

But I had no choice, and no options for myself at the moment. A baby was on the way, and there was no insurance to pay for the hospital costs. So I kept going to work, even though I hated every minute of it. I would much rather have been in Vietnam.

In the summer I enrolled in a two-year engineering college and applied for a transfer to the third shift. In September, I started school and began working from midnight until 7:00 a.m. Classes ran from 8:30 a.m. until 4 p.m. five days a week. With homework and normal day-to-day duties, I found myself getting about fours hours of sleep out of every twenty-four. I was injured at work in 1971, laid off, put on compensation, and when that stopped, worked at odd jobs ranging from liquor store clerk to truck driver.

I sold vacuum cleaners and used cars—in short, I did what I had to for survival. But I stayed in school and eventually the two years passed. In 1972, I graduated with my Associates Degree in Electrical Engineering.

I worked for a year, first as a technician, then as a junior engineer, and finally decided that sitting behind a desk charting the course of electrons was not anywhere near as much fun as flying in helicopters. It wasn't the electronics job I had liked so much in the Marines, it was the flying!

So I did the only thing that seemed logical at the time. I quit my job, reenrolled in college—the University of New Haven—where I signed up for a degree in English Literature, and reenlisted in the Marine Corps!

I was accepted into the officer candidate program—nobody said anything about flat feet this time—and was scheduled to take the OCS Platoon Leaders Class training course during the summer of 1974 in Quantico, Virginia. I went and completed the course with a very high class standing. But after returning for my last year in college, I decided against accepting a commission. There were a lot of reasons behind that decision, not the least of which involved the situation in Vietnam.

There wasn't one, at least as far as the Marine Corps was concerned, and interest in that country seemed to be fading quickly. I missed the camaraderie of my old unit and the sense of purpose. It just wasn't the same the second time around.

After I graduated in 1975 with a B.A. degree, I continued working for a local fish and game club, guiding hunting and fishing parties, stocking streams, and cutting firewood. I did some freelance writing, and in March 1976 was hired as a reporter for *The Hartford Courant.*

I wouldn't have anticipated doing that kind of work for a living, especially with the example some of the media people I had seen in Vietnam had set. But we all have to eat, and I think I did a better job as a reporter because I knew how it feels when the media doesn't tell the truth, and reporters write their opinions instead of facts.

At any rate, it had been a busy eight years since I had left Da Nang, and I hadn't thought that much about it for a lot of those years. Well, I didn't think I had thought about it. But if that was so, why did I now find myself sitting in my living room, in the dark, drinking a beer and wondering about it all? Probably because the real truth is that there hadn't been a day in all those years when I didn't think about Vietnam at least once, if only for a second.

There were a lot of reasons why it kept creeping back into my mind. Doug Braman and I had stayed close, and his home wasn't far from mine. We didn't always talk about it, but it did slide into our conversations occasionally. I also happened to be watching the news one day in 1972 when the North Vietnamese unsuccessfully invaded the South, right through Quang Tri.

A photographer had film of the evacuation of the airstrip, and as I watched with mixed emotions, I saw the water tower, the one the officers got their clean water from, burning and crumbling.

People also would bring Vietnam up every once in a while, unexpectedly, and that could trigger some memories. As I became acquainted with professional people, other college students, and office workers, I began running into an occasional outburst of disbelief when I said I had been to Vietnam.

"*You* were in *Vietnam*?" would be asked with a look and tone of incredulity. Then they'd just stare at me, as if I were an animal that should have been confined in a zoo. That was usually followed with some incredibly intelligent remark such as, "You don't *look* like one of those guys!"

What, I wondered, was a Vietnam veteran supposed to look like? We were, and are, people, just like everyone else. But the media had been hammering out the drug abuse story, and once that started, everyone was tarred with the same brush. If you had been to Vietnam, you killed babies, burned villages, raped little girls and old women, and were now a whacked-out drug freak. So I did my best to repress Vietnam, consciously or unconsciously, even if it did come up occasionally.

But after 1975, when our government let Saigon fall, let the South go down to the communists, left all that equipment and all those people behind, and treated everything we had done, and all the deaths it had caused, as if it were all insignificant, I really clammed up.

Vietnam also had never been brought up in my house, even though I would have liked to talk about it once in a while. There was a universal attitude that it was considered a bad subject. The night I got home I said something about the war, and just the mention of that place brought an instant silence. Someone in my future in-laws' family changed the subject, and it stayed changed for nearly a decade. Less than twenty-four hours after I arrived home, as I was sitting in the bar of a local restaurant waiting for a table, a long-haired guy wearing a peace sign and love beads snuck up and sucker punched me in the face.

I didn't get hurt and he paid for it, but it was very strange nonetheless.

About the only person who ever discussed it with me was my dad. It was funny how he and I were getting along so well. Whatever had been our problem initially no longer was part of our relationship, and occasionally we'd discuss his war and my war in-depth. I guess it was a case of him learning more and getting a lot smarter for every year I aged.

In fact, he used to tell me, "You know, when you were eighteen you didn't think I knew anything. Now that you're in your twenties, I've gotten pretty sharp."

Outside of Dad, however, no one else in the family wanted to know about Vietnam. My medals were stuffed away in a drawer somewhere. I would have liked to display them, but considering the way the war was regarded, I think the point would have been missed.

Over the years I had been progressing in school and my career, but things hadn't been all that steady in my marriage. We had separated in 1974, right after I returned from the summer at OCS, and reunited in 1975 just before I graduated from college. Then I started the journalism career, bought a house in the country, and settled into the complacent lifestyle that was expected of me.

But while I was outwardly playing the game that was expected of me, inside I was terribly unhappy. The kids helped alleviate that somewhat—I was close to both of them. But there always seemed to be a sense of emptiness inside, as though in fulfilling everyone else's expectations of me, I was ignoring my own.

I knew inside that the rocky times weren't over. They were just in a lull. I wasn't sure why they would start again, or when, but it was getting harder and harder to see the years slipping by with no sense of purpose or accomplishment.

I had been sitting in that chair for nearly three hours, rocking, putting wood on the fire occasionally, and thinking about all that had gone by. Why was I sitting alone in the middle of the night drinking beer and remembering? Where did that dream come from anyway? Why now?

The moon had gone down sometime in that period, and the darkness outside was changing to the gray of dawn. I got up, patrolled through the house, stopping in every room, peering from every window. It was as if I was walking fire watch again.

I noticed as I looked out on the snow that I had a clear field of fire in virtually every direction. The nearest tree lines were fifty feet away, and with the snow on the ground everything stood out clearly. I remembered the bunkers and the white sand at Quang Tri, and I wondered if that had been in the back of my mind when the decision was made to buy that house in the first place.

I went back to bed, slipping in on my side, staying there, out of reach, out of touch. I tried to sleep but it didn't come easily.

The horizon was streaked with crimson as my eyelids finally started getting heavy. And when I did fall asleep, it wasn't deep or refreshing. I kept dreaming. And in the dreams I saw helicopters, machine guns, battles, and a pair of long-dead eyes staring back at me.

Chapter 26

The guard at the gate was a tall lance corporal. He was lean, young, and looked like the perfect Marine. He stopped our car, talked to us a minute, checked my driver's license, and then waved us through.

On the other side of the guard station was a causeway, and on either side of the causeway, salt flats. I felt charged with anticipation—and apprehension—and had a strange tingling sensation along my spine as we proceeded toward the buildings on the other side. It was July 1983, but I had felt that same sensation once before, in January 1966.

That time I was riding across the causeway in a bus, headed for recruit training at Parris Island. Now I was coming back, as a visitor. It was inevitable that I would return here. For all those years when I had tried to put the Marine Corps and Vietnam out of my mind, they really were just below the surface, waiting. For a while I had been so busy with my life that all else was pushed deep inside, seemingly forever.

But after life had settled into a routine, Vietnam and my time in the Marine Corps began reasserting themselves. Dreams, sometimes nightmares, would come and go. Or I would be working in the garden behind my house and stop suddenly, motionless, when Connecticut Air National Guard helicopters flew overhead on their weekly training missions.

Once, as I stood at my kitchen sink, I felt a familiar vibration, and without even thinking ran to the back door and out into the yard. From the tree line to the east a flight of four CH-46s suddenly appeared, flying about 500 feet above ground level, fast, in perfect formation.

I had no idea where they came from or where they were going, but they were Marine helicopters and nothing else mattered. It felt as if every nerve in my body was screaming for them to stop, hover over my yard, send down a hoist cable, and extract me. By 1980 my marriage was again foundering, and in 1981 we separated, this time permanently. In the end, after a hard-fought divorce, I walked away, scarred but intact, with joint custody of my kids and a new start on life.

A more aggressive acknowledgment of my time in Vietnam and its role in my life was to be part of that new start. The dedication of the Vietnam Veterans Memorial in Washington, D.C., helped motivate me. I asked for and received permission from my editor to write a lengthy article on 161, interviewing Bill Frantz's family, other relatives, Doug Braman, and even tracking down Al Munoz in Texas.

The article was released on the *L.A. Times/Washington Post* wire services and appeared in newspapers nationwide, and I received calls and letters from as far away as Alaska. One of those calls was from Don Vaughn. The reunions with Munoz and Vaughn were long-distance—but they were real this time, not dreams, and we began making plans to bring 161 back together someday.

I attended the dedication of the Wall, and while it was emotional, I didn't get to spend as much time there as I wanted, primarily because of my duties writing about it. But I did have one moment that gave me that old sense of belonging, of being part of something special.

It came just before the dedication speeches commenced, as a military band started playing the various services' anthems. They played "Anchors Aweigh" for the navy and got a nice round of applause. They played the songs for the air force, the coast guard, and the army, and each time got another nice round of applause.

I quietly told my companion, "Watch what happens when they play 'The Marine Hymn.'"

"What do you mean?" she asked.

"Just watch," I repeated.

The last strains of "The Caissons Go Rolling Along" were just dying away, and the accompanying applause was dying out when, with just a pause, the band struck up "The Marine Hymn."

And from out of the hundred-thousand-plus crowd gathered before the memorial, a roar erupted that was sustained throughout the course of the hymn. She looked at me with a perplexed look on her face and asked, "How did you know?"

I had a feeling of pride in me that was so powerful it threatened to burst my chest, and I was afraid to answer her because I didn't want to show how much it meant to me. But I did manage to say, "They're Marines."

There was nothing more to say, and she asked no more questions. I stood there, listening to the rest of the hymn and remembering when I had started on that journey to Parris Island, so very long ago. Whatever it was I had been seeking, I had found, somewhere along the line, and that spontaneous response to our hymn made it all quite clear to me.

My reawakening on Vietnam was causing some major changes in my life, but my companion that day also was responsible for other changes that coincided with all this activity. Her name was Jennifer and she had taken a job at the paper, in the same office where I worked. We got to be friends, then began dating, and along the way she made what everyone else thought was going to be a fatal mistake. She asked me about Vietnam.

She said she'd delayed for two weeks before bringing the subject up, because others in the office told her it was a bad idea. But, instead of the explosive reaction that some had expected, I just started telling her about it, in bits and pieces over the course of a year or more.

She got the full benefit of thirteen years of hoarded war

stories. Sometimes we'd sit quietly in front of a fire, talking in general, historical terms. Sometimes she'd get a sentence or two, or perhaps just a word in response to a question. And occasionally, sitting in my truck in our yard, listening to midnight radio and sipping from a bottle of scotch, she'd get a free-ranging discourse. At times I'd go on for an hour or more about heroism, betrayal, politics.

I told her of the feeling of omnipotence that accompanies a low-level, high-speed flight into a hot zone with a .50-caliber machine gun blazing out the window. She learned that some days I miss that feeling horribly and wish that somehow I could reach back in time and have it again. I told her that when I face the truth, that it is gone, and never can come back, I feel empty inside, and sad beyond description. She learned that having experienced war, I not only know its horrors but also have a sense of fascination with the overwhelming power and destruction I encountered there.

I told her I am not ashamed of going to Vietnam. I'm proud of it. We did our best to keep that country free, and for a time we did. If ever there was a question of whether we should have gone, it was answered in Cambodia when the communists took over, and in South Vietnam when our allies were sent to reeducation (concentration) camps, and on the South China Sea when boat people, trying one last desperate time to be free, were raped and murdered by pirates, without a word of protest from the peace movement.

I believe the free world never should have stood by and let any of those atrocities occur. Above all, Jennifer learned that having become a Marine early in my life, there is nothing else that I have ever encountered that has as much control over my feelings and actions, even to this day.

What she learned did not always come easy, but as hard as it was, she stayed, and when the time was right, asked more questions, bringing out more of what was locked inside. I explained about the spark of rage deep inside me that occasionally flares when I think too much about it. But it is a rage without a target, because those who created it have all disappeared, into their own lives and careers, or into the bureaucratic morass of our national government, and I can't reach them, and I can't focus that anger on them. It dies as quickly as it flares, but when it comes, it is best to leave me be for a while.

Jennifer accompanied me to Washington for the dedication, and we decided that if I really was going to come to grips with the Marine Corps and Vietnam, it wouldn't be a bad idea to go back to Parris Island and take another look at my heritage.

Which brought us to that causeway on a steaming July day, back where I'd started on a warm January night. It had been brutally hot on the trip down I-95. We didn't have air-conditioning, and the kids kept passing pieces of ice up to me from our cooler so I could stay alert.

But we had a nice, cool room waiting for us in Beaufort, South Carolina, and the trip was worth the aggravation. We were well received by the public information officer, a major named James Vance, and his assistant, Capt. Keith Oliver.

They assigned a lance corporal to guide us around the island. We saw the rifle range, the obstacle course, and the new Women Marines battalion. We saw the new barracks for the male recruits, air-conditioned and housing four platoons on a single floor.

Initially I thought that things were getting a bit easy for Marine recruits, until I realized that air-conditioning in the summer can be used the same way heating is in the winter—to keep the training cycle going when weather conditions are adverse.

The recruit receiving barracks was still there and the yellow footprints were still on the pavement out front. We even gagged it up and took pictures of Kevin, Sara, and Jennifer standing on them. We met some drill instructors and some of the higher-ranking enlisted men who were involved with administering the training. They joked and offered to get Kevin a haircut, their way, even though he kept his pretty short to begin with.

We were given freedom to travel about the island, but I was most interested in the 2d Recruit Training Battalion where I had been assigned. We walked down the old company street, and it didn't take much imagination to remember Starbuck, Sparks, and Hale, guiding the platoon through close order drill, calling cadence as we marched.

But when we got to the end of the street, I was disappointed to discover that our old barracks had been torn down, only a month earlier. It seemed to take something out of the visit, especially since the temperature was so high that no one was training or marching.

Marine bases have a system of flags, starting with green and ending with black, that change as the weather gets hotter. Depending on the flag that is flying, the base can go from 100 percent activity to 100 percent inactivity. A combination of high humidity and 100-degree heat brings the black flag, and by late morning it had been raised. That was as disappointing as not finding my barracks.

I had been telling my family for weeks that the sound of a Parris Island drill instructor calling cadence or chewing out a recruit who had made a mistake would be an unforgettable facet of the visit. Then, just as I thought we'd be leaving unfulfilled, I heard that sound, the unmistakable tread of a Marine platoon marching—lefts and rights in unison, sounding as though only one very heavy heel was hitting the pavement with each step.

Maybe the temperature had gone down or maybe someone hadn't been told it was a black flag. It didn't matter. They were marching, and the drill instructor was calling cadence. It was beautiful!

He apparently had one recruit who couldn't get a position correct because I heard him order, in that deep drill instructor's growl, "You'd better get that *daamn* elbow in! I've been telling you about that elbow all *damn* day, private!

"You come see me when we get back to the squad bay! If I see that elbow sticking out one more time, I'm going to bite the damn thing *off!*"

Now THAT was a drill instructor. Then I felt better.

Parris Island had changed in some ways, but not in the ones that mattered. Starbuck, Sparks, and Hale were no longer there, and hadn't been for a long time. But there were others to take their place and continue the job.

There had been something in me back in 1966 that responded to the Marine Corps, with its harshness and constant challenges. I had been one enthusiastic Marine when I graduated from Parris Island, and while my interest in a career as a Marine had waned, my pride in serving only grew as the years passed.

I had felt a sense of accomplishment, and a sense of contributing. I had also come away from Parris Island with the feeling that I had endured a major test of my physical and mental abilities, a test that would buttress me as I encountered other obstacles in life.

It only took the sound of a drill instructor's voice, and the remembrance of that order—"See me when we get back to the squad bay"—to remind me what it was like to be challenged and rewarded for a job well done, or singled out to account for your mistakes. It was a worthy challenge, and not only had I survived, I had succeeded.

That reminder was what I really had come for. It gave me a measure of peace of mind, and I was satisfied.

We said our thank-yous and good-byes and headed north along Route 17. There was more to my time in the Marines than Parris Island, and more to my journey. We had also made arrangements to visit New River. No longer an air facility, it now is a full-fledged Marine Corps Air Station, with two Marine air groups stationed there, double the number from my days.

We stayed overnight in Myrtle Beach, South Carolina, and finished the trip up Route 17 into Jacksonville in the morning. Five miles south of Jacksonville, about three miles from the air station, I pulled over, watching silently as several flights of '46s passed overhead. I felt kind of happy watching them, a little choked up, and a lot like I was finally coming home!

At New River a lieutenant named Norma Stewart, from the base Public Information Office, gave us red-carpet treatment. I saw my old barracks where I lived while assigned to 161.

The flight line had doubled in size to accommodate the second air group, and a new hangar had been built. New barracks had been constructed for the crews. All signs of the area where the CH-53 had crashed in 1967, where Mike Vicknus and twenty-one other Marines had died, were long since obliterated, and the only trace of that day was deep in my mind.

Another '46 squadron occupied our old squadron area at the hangar now, and in many ways things there looked exactly the same as they had the day we left. The squadron offices on a second level above the hangar deck were still used for the same purposes. Even Sgt. Maj. John Goodfellow's office, where he handled the squadron's day-to-day administrative affairs, meted out advice, occasional discipline—and once had Lance Corporals Braman and Winter standing tall, explaining why they were three hours late coming back from weekend liberty—hadn't changed, except for the furnishings.

Lieutenant Stewart took pictures of Kevin and Sara sitting in the cockpit of a '46 while squadron personnel gave me a rundown on its latest modifications and improvements. We even went up in the control tower and watched the controllers as they guided aircraft into takeoff and landing positions.

By the time we finished lunch at the officers club, and toured the Naval Air Technical Training Center where I had received my classroom training, I was feeling pretty good about the trip. But there still was a nagging uneasiness inside me, and there was only one place I felt I could come to terms with it.

It was caused, I suppose, by the fact that, as nice as everyone was to us along the way, Vietnam was a long-dead issue for most of them. Many of the younger officers hadn't been in long enough to serve there, and the enlisted men, who had been in grade school when the last American troops were withdrawn in 1973, could only relate to the 1979 hostage rescue attempt in Iran.

No one remembered the day 161 gathered on that flight line, ready to make our final launch from New River. No one remembered the families gathered to see us off, the smiles, the tears, and the fears.

They did remember Colonel Niesen. He had made quite an impact during his time in the Marine Corps and was spoken of often during my visit. But they didn't remember the day that twenty-four CH-46s thundered into that clear North Carolina sky, heading west in flights of four. They didn't remember the people who had left that day, and they didn't remember the ones who hadn't come back, and never would.

I had found most of what I was looking for there at New River, but that spark of continuity, the remembrance of the people I had served with, was necessary for my trip to be successful. There was one more stop I would have to make.

Again we said good-bye, and then headed toward Washington, D.C., and the Wall. But that leg of my journey would take another four years to complete. Oh, we stopped there that summer, but it was late, everyone was tired, and while as usual, it was emotional, we were mostly concerned by then with beating the rush-hour traffic out of the city.

Jennifer and I went back again in 1984 to cover the dedication of the statue of the Three Servicemen, but again, my duties as a reporter kept me from having time for my own feelings. I met Joe Carcasio there, an old friend from 161 who was staying in the same hotel I was, and we promised to keep in touch.

Later there were other trips that helped bridge the gap back to the days in New River and Vietnam. In 1984, I went back to my hometown, spent a weekend with my old friend Bob Soloyna and his family, and looked up John Messick. We'd all grown up since we last saw each other, but in many ways we were still the same.

Before we went to visit John, I called and reminded him of his promise—to buy me a case of beer if I stayed away from drugs in Vietnam. I hadn't seen him since 1968 in New River, and he said he'd forgotten. But an hour later, when I went to visit him, John had a case sitting on his porch, waiting for me.

But it was in November 1986, the day after Thanksgiving, that I made another journey to the Wall and finally found what I had been looking for. Jennifer and I had long since been married, and as usual we went together and took Kevin and Sara with us. We went to the Marine Corps Museum and Archives in the navy yard, visited the Lincoln Memorial, and toured the Smithsonian Institution.

Then I went back to the panels, which by now I nearly knew by heart, stopping at each one, remembering each person. There were so many. Sharp, Helmstetler, Brandes, Frantz, Cheek, Ferrazano, Scott, Powell, Sweet. On another panel farther along was a name I had found there in 1982, while looking for someone else. William H. Bazemore, the new guy who had shared Thanksgiving dinner, and made one day in Vietnam slightly better for me, had died in April 1969.

Tom Lenz, another electrician, had died with him. Tom had joined 161 back in New River, just before we left for Vietnam, and above everything else wanted to come home a hero. He volunteered for Recon missions almost exclusively. On a bad day in February, he and Bazemore flew together, and died together, after their helicopter was hit by an RPG.

I had written about him in 1982 and tracked down his

mother, Elvira Schneider, in Yoakum, Texas. She had told me of her worries over smuggling Lone Star beer to Tom in packages from home, and I told her how I remembered him sitting back, sipping on a warm can of it every so often.

She told me how he cared so much about the car he'd left at home, the one he'd bought while still in high school. After Tom died, she had cleaned it out to sell it, and found a bottle of his beer under one of the seats. She put it away in a closet and kept it there, unopened.

Mrs. Schneider had given her only son to that war. And for a long time no one had cared, or remembered. I stood by those panels, thinking about 161, all its work, its dedication, its sacrifices, and especially its people.

We weren't the unfortunate sons of the nation's poor swept unwittingly into that conflict through some fluke of birth. We were Marines, volunteers, educated for the most part, at least through high school and in many cases college. We had believed in that cause, and only lacked the ability to see into the future, to see the day our nation's leaders would turn their backs on us, and then blame us for their failures.

We had taken our chances, and all of us had paid the price in one way or another. I realized as I stood there that another name should have been on the wall, another member of 161 who had succumbed to the war.

Fred Young, a skinny wisecracking corporal from Virginia, a good friend who always had a smile and a way to make you laugh with his jokes, had died in December 1983. I found out about it two months later, when I called his house after spending nearly a year trying to find him.

The small nucleus of 161 members who wanted a reunion had been growing, and I'd felt good about finding Fred. It was only when I called, expecting to hear a wisecrack, that I learned I was too late.

His wife, Kay, left to support three children, said it was a form of cancer. She attributed it to Agent Orange. The VA wouldn't recognize his death as service-related, and I'd done what I could to help her out.

Fred had received his high school diploma while in the Marines, and after the service he went to college and ultimately earned a Master's Degree. He had become a teacher at the same high school he had dropped out of to join the Marines. He'd done well, and deserved much better than he received from his country.

I thought a long time about Fred, wondering if any of the other guys had met a similar fate, before moving on to the one last panel I had to visit.

It was on the east side of the V, indicating he had died before most of 161 went to war. I went to panel 14E, sought out line 121, and found the name. It was no surprise. I had known since 1967, ever since I had seen it in the back of *Leatherneck* magazine, where they had a space reserved for the heroes, that it would be there.

I knelt and traced out the letters, remembering the citation for the Silver Star.

"For conspicuous gallantry and intrepidity in action."

I hated seeing it, but all things considered, I guess he'd rather be remembered for fighting for his country.

"Serving as a patrol leader . . ."

"Led an eleven man reconnaissance patrol deep into Viet Cong controlled territory. With professional skill and diligence he positioned the members of his patrol to the best advantage . . ."

"Exercising sound tactical judgment . . ."

"The patrol was fiercely attacked by sixty Viet Cong . . ."

"Aggressive fighting spirit and initiative . . ."

"Served to inspire all who observed him . . ."

"Disregarded his own personal safety and unhesitatingly exposed himself to the withering small-arms fire . . . until he was mortally wounded by enemy fire."

"Contributed directly to the survival of the patrol."

It keeps going, but it keeps hurting. This was the man I

followed, the man who represented the epitome of the professional Marine.

"Outstanding courage, resolute leadership and unswerving devotion to duty reflected great credit upon himself, the Marine Corps and the United States Naval Service.

"He gallantly gave his life for his country."

The letters spelled R-O-B-E-R-T F. S-T-A-R-B-U-C-K.

I knew it would be there, but it still ripped into me like a knife when I saw it. His death was a reminder of everything I had ever believed in, and everything that had turned out so much differently than I had expected.

We had been portrayed as losers. The country spent decades believing without question that somehow we had let them down, that somehow we hadn't done enough, even if they couldn't pick a time or place where we ever lost.

But they'd never met Starbuck or any of his men. They never met Colonel Niesen or any of his men, either.

I knelt for a long time, remembering the people I had served with, the people I had met, the people who only wanted to be as free as we were. I thought about all our battles, all our victories, and how we had believed they would contribute to a final victory. I thought about 1975, the fall of Saigon, and all the years after.

I remembered the last time I saw Starbuck, on graduation day at Parris Island. I knew, instinctively I guess, that I had been in the company of a very special person there. I'd felt let down when he didn't come around to see us off the next morning. I'd wanted to thank him, to let him know in some small way that the job he'd done over the previous two months had an impact that would carry far, far beyond that island, and even the Marine Corps.

I'd wanted to say good-bye—even if it didn't agree with his view of the Marine Corps method of doing things. The opportunity had been lost, and like so much else, the words had been locked away in that vault of mine, the one that finally had started to release its secrets.

After a while I slowly stood up. I really didn't want to. There was a power to that wall, strength in those panels with those names that could keep me rooted to that spot. But I gathered my own strength and headed for the end of the monument.

Strangely, as I left the deep darkness of the vortex and the lists of names grew smaller, I felt a sense of escape, as though the grip that place and that time had on me was weakening, at least for the moment.

Along the way, toward the end, my head cleared the top of the monument, and I could see beyond it, to the mall and the streets nearby. I had a feeling of breaking free.

I remembered sharing a similar feeling with Doug Braman, back in December 1968, during the monsoon season. We were finishing up a day of flying, and before heading back to Quang Tri our pilots went straight up until we broke through the clouds.

From the cold, dark, and dangerous grayness below, we suddenly found ourselves exposed in the warmth of a Vietnam sunset.

All around us was the top of the cloud cover, with an occasional mountain poking through, like islands in a frothy sea. The setting sun bathed it all in a crimson glow.

It was beautiful beyond description, and we tried to capture it with our Instamatic cameras. We weren't successful on film, but the memory has never left either of us.

I had the same feeling as I watched the activity around the memorial. Below, there was war and death, hate and betrayal. But above it there was another facet of human existence, a facet that reminds us of the continuity of life. There is hope, even on a battlefield, and there is life, even after horrible death.

Vietnam makes me sad when I think about it, and it sometimes makes me angry. But not all things related to the military, and my experience there, are negative. Some of the bad, which we in our youth saw as just another part of the service, in fact only reflected life.

There also are many good things to remember, not the least of which are the friends, the camaraderie, the sense of involvement and accomplishment, and the lessons we learned.

Starbuck had been a good teacher. He had taught us self-reliance and dignity. He also had taught us to persevere, to set goals, to work toward them, and to never quit until we reached them. Starbuck said you have to apply those lessons for virtually everything you do in the future, and you have to keep working, living up to the same set of standards, if the rest of your life—in the military or as a civilian—is to be successful. Above all, he had taught us to survive.

They were valuable lessons, and I hadn't forgotten them. The goals of Vietnam are behind us now, but within easy reach of our memories. The lessons learned during that time can be applied, as life goes on and different obstacles are encountered, as long as they are kept in perspective.

But now it was time to deal with the life I had built in the many years since I had left Parris Island, New River, and Quang Tri.

I reached out my left hand and pulled Kevin and Sara close. They didn't like it and wanted only to walk alone. Kevin was checking out some girls, and Sara wanted to do cartwheels on the sidewalk. They wanted their independence, and all those reminders of death made them uneasy.

It was overwhelming, and not a simple thing to explain. I couldn't blame them. I reached out my right arm and draped it over Jennifer's shoulder. I didn't say anything and she didn't ask anything.

We made our way through the crowd, coming finally to that place above the wall, where life goes on. I was feeling pretty sad, but I knew that I had to continue, to put the past behind me, even if it was only temporarily.

Back at Parris Island, Starbuck had told us, "When things

are so bad that they're too tough for everyone else, I smile, because then they're just right for me."

And as hard as it was, I forced a smile. Inside I thought I would explode. But I kept walking, one step at a time. I could see the football games being played on the mall and the children running to the Lincoln Memorial.

I knew I could leave and go on with my life, but I also knew that I would be back—many times. I knew that no matter how often I returned, the feeling would always be the same.

I will remember life, and death, and sacrifice, and unsung heroes. I will never forget Bill Frantz, or Ken Brandes, or Fred Young, or any of the others. I will never forget what they meant to me, or why we went to that faraway place and fought a war.

I especially will never forget Starbuck. I know that Vietnam will always be with me, but I also know I'll never let it destroy me. I wasn't defeated then, I won't be defeated now.

I squared my shoulders and prepared to move on. There was no more to say then, no more to remember. But still, I hesitated, one last time, for just a second, before I stepped away to start the journey home.

I looked back, to panel 14E, line 121, unable to make it out clearly in the distance, but knowing by heart what was there.

And, after all the years of memories, and all the years of waiting, I finally told Starbuck, "Thank you—and goodbye."

Epilogue

On September 30, 1988, former members of HMM-161 who had served during its two tours of duty in Vietnam gathered in Reston, Virginia, marking the first time that most of them had seen or heard from each other in twenty years.

The reunion culminated five years of work—tracking down old friends, many of whom had moved thousands of miles from their original homes, setting a date, finding a location, making arrangements, and handling all the little details that take time and attention. In the end it was worth every bit of effort.

When the formal events began, one hundred former members of HMM-161, spouses, and friends were on hand. Among the retired officers and enlisted personnel who attended were Col. Paul W. Niesen; Col. David Elam, who had succeeded Niesen at Quang Tri; Col. Reinhardt Leu, our group commanding officer at New River; Brig. Gen. Edward Parnell, who'd held the same position at Quang Tri; Lt. Col. Joseph Felter and Lt. Col. James Loop; CWO Donald Lambert; Sgt. Maj. John Goodfellow; and 1st Sgt. William Scoggins.

We'd also found Scoggins' old friend Jim O'Connor, who had retired as a master sergeant and worked for Federal Express in Memphis. He'd wanted to come, but what initially was called a family matter that kept him away was later revealed to be a fatal bone cancer. We were able to talk with Jim on the phone, but never saw him again.

The weekend was emotional to say the least and had its share of surprises. We found Lt. Col. Al Doktor, formerly Lieutenant "The Doc" Doktor, stationed at Headquarters Marine Corps, and he found Chuck Songer, who had been wounded in 1968 flying into the DMZ with Colonel Niesen. Eugene Lee, a staff sergeant and crew chief on Niesen's aircraft the day Songer was wounded, also was there along with several of our former staff NCOs.

There were some pleasant surprises, such as finding Paul Bevil, our friend who had been wounded in the summer of 1968 and not heard from again. He lost most of his heel and experienced recurring difficulties from his wound, but was well into a career as supervisor in a printing plant in Georgia.

Tom Breuss, one of my best friends from New River and my companion on many a weekend escapade, had stayed in and retired as a master sergeant. Immediately upon retirement from the Marine Corps, Tom took a position with Boeing Vertol, returning to New River as a technical representative on CH-46 helicopters.

We found Ron "Fat" Adair building fire engines in Colorado, Dale Bush working as a security inspector for the post office in Syracuse, Al Munoz employed in the oil fields near Wharton, Texas, and Roger Gangi a high school principal in Georgia.

Former crew chief Chuck Palmer had gone into police work, as had many others with whom we served. Sgt. Maj. John Goodfellow was well into a second career, this time as head of security for Duke University in North Carolina. There were enough pilots, mechanics, crew chiefs, electricians, radiomen, hydraulics men, and metalsmiths to fly a CH-46 to Reston, take it apart, put it back together, and fly it out again.

It was a weekend to renew old acquaintances, retell old war stories and shared experiences, and most important, to remember who we were. We discovered that along with universal pride, baggage from Vietnam was still hanging around the necks of many who served in 161. There were regrets, recriminations, and doubts, most resulting from the homecoming we'd received and the many years of distortions voiced in the national media by those who had opposed the war.

We didn't have any walking time bombs or severe post-traumatic stress cases, despite what many in the media would have had America believe, and many issues our comrades were facing had been amplified out of proportion by time and isolation.

Post-Vietnam often was dealt with the same way we took pre-Vietnam, with that old grain of humor. A case in point was crew chief Ed Irwin's comment, "Well, we're all older, fatter, and balder now." In many cases that's true, although most of the officers and senior NCOs were already fully grown when we were together and really hadn't changed much. Those of us who were in our teens and early twenties still had some growing to do after Vietnam, and we'd changed the most.

But when the wisecracking and discussions on outward appearances were through, there remained another facet of our relationship to explore, one that carried across the decades without changing. Tom Morrison, a crew chief from Illinois, hit it dead center when he told us, "I've had lots of acquaintances since then, but I've never had friends like the guys in 161." Virtually everyone agreed with him.

Yet, I was astonished to find that some people I was very much looking forward to seeing again weren't sure of the reception they'd receive. Bill Scoggins said toward the end of the weekend that he thought those of us who worked for him in avionics might not want him to attend. Scoggins had been in charge of doling out flight assignments to electricians who volunteered to fly gunner, and since several electricians were killed, he felt responsible.

In a way that's understandable. During a service at the Vietnam Veterans Memorial, I read the list of those who had died during HMM-161's two tours in Vietnam. Getting through that list, and the subsequent playing of taps by a Marine Corps bugler, without loss of composure, was one of the hardest things I've ever done. Yet not one person who attended the reunion believes other squadron personnel were responsible for those deaths. That responsibility lies with the politicians who sent us there, and those who allowed Vietnam to fall.

I was equally surprised to find that Scoggins was twenty-nine when we were in Vietnam, only nine years older than I had been. The officers and staff NCOs had seemed so much older then, not because of their looks but because of their experience. When I think of all we did and were required to do at such young ages, the enormity of what our leaders took on at their ages is all the more impressive.

Scoggins had been around the world and back since Vietnam and even served under Colonel Niesen again, as a civilian this time, working for Bell Helicopter in Iran until the Shah was overthrown. He settled in Florida and, like others from 161, had been carrying an unnecessary load on his shoulders.

But, as Bob Monk said, "There's not a man in the world I respect more than Bill Scoggins." Monk, from Kosciusko, Mississippi, a good friend and fellow electrician, used to engage in endless debate about me being an "incurable Yankee" and him being a "diehard Grit."

But we were friends the whole way and both ended up as writers and journalists. He and Allen Herlocker had stayed on in Vietnam for an extra six months, probably the last two members of our version of HMM-161 to be together.

At 1:00 a.m. on a Sunday morning, as the reunion was winding down, in a hotel room jammed with electricians and radiomen drinking beer and talking, Bob was eloquent in expressing the deep sense of brotherhood that sustained us through all the years of isolation, and that we all hoped had finally come to an end.

But the story of HMM-161 did not end there.

We thought, after that first reunion in 1988, that the isolation and questioning about Vietnam was finally over, and with some good reasons. We'll never forget our time together there, but we figured that if occasionally that remembrance became too painful and we needed someone to talk to, then a friend we can count on is only a telephone call away, not a dim face in a receding memory.

We had found one-fourth of our original squadron for the first reunion and continued the process of finding more. That's the way Marines do it.

An unexpected, but welcome offshoot of our decision to reunite was coming back in contact with the active-duty squadron. After our Washington reunion, the first Gulf War broke out, and HMM-161 was sent to Kuwait to participate in the fighting.

With help from Headquarters Marine Corps, we contacted the commanding officer and soon were sending packages from the States bearing goods to help ease the stress of combat. Since then there has been regular contact with HMM-161, and it has added service in the Iraq War to its battle streamers as well.

Irony of ironies, the modern-day squadron is still flying the same CH-46 helicopters that we worked on nearly forty years ago. At the time, many in Marine aviation said the '46 would never last. But another entire generation of Marines is still using them.

They have been updated with more powerful engines and the latest electronics, but the bodies are the same, and we even hear from time to time of crews finding old patches, occasionally made from tin beer cans from the sixties, that cover bullet holes from battles back in Vietnam. I can't help but feel an overwhelming sense of pride when television news clips from the war zone show the '46s still in action.

After waiting so long, our first reunion seemed to go by incredibly fast, so we held a second reunion in Kansas City in 1991. We had continued to add to the roster of those who had been located, including pilot Tom "Marty" Martindale and my comrade from avionics, John Zanercik.

But missing forever was Colonel Niesen, who had died of a heart attack a year earlier. His death was a huge blow, and we were grateful that his widow and daughters attended to spend some time with us. Paul W. Niesen was a very special man who rose to the occasion as he encountered it. He was intelligent, dedicated, had a tremendous work ethic, was brave and formidable in battle, and inspired his men as much by his faith in us as by his own actions. He was dedicated to his family as well as his Marines, and they showed us they were equally proud of him.

There have been many occasions in my post-Marine career when, faced with a difficult decision, I asked myself what the colonel would have done and tried to act in that fashion. He has continued to be an inspiration long after our time in the Marines ended. I can't think of a better testament to the man we followed, literally to hell and back.

As the years crept by we have had smaller reunions, in Las Vegas, Reno, and Pensacola, Florida, sometimes as part of much larger reunions that evolved from other Vietnam-era Marine squadrons joining together.

With each passing year the death toll continues to mount, as I suppose is to be expected. Most who have passed on are the older members of the squadron, career Marines who already were in their late forties when we served together. But not everyone falls into that category.

On the afternoon of December 12, 1996, I received a call from an acquaintance in Colorado, who lived next door to and was good friends with Ron Adair. He told me that Ron had come home from work the previous Friday, December 9, and hadn't been seen since.

His neighbors went to his house and found Ron on his kitchen floor. He had put a pillow under his head, and a pistol under his chin, then pulled the trigger.

I don't know why Ron killed himself. The only connection I could make to anything was that he ended his life on the anniversary of the date HMM-161 was broken up and dispersed in Vietnam. He left no message of explanation for us.

I had talked with him on the phone a few weeks earlier and he had told me of his dissatisfaction with the increasing population where he lived in Colorado, that he was considering moving to Wyoming, where there was more country and good trout fishing. We made some general plans to get together for a fishing expedition in the coming years. I had thought those phone calls and the occasional reunions were enough to get us all through our dark moments. I was wrong and I regret it.

A winter storm kept me from making the trip to his funeral, but Dale Bush and Allen Herlocker did attend to represent the squadron. But it is not Ron in his grave that I will remember.

Besides his "Hey, Hey, Hey" Fat Albert impression, I will always remember his steadiness in a firefight when we flew a mission together in 1968. Ron was the port gunner, I was starboard, and when the shooting started we both were engaged.

I was doing my usual "in your face" out the starboard gun position, but couldn't help but notice the volume of fire coming from Ron's gun behind me. It was steady, methodical, unemotional, and so effective. I told him afterward that I believed you could write a rock 'n' roll song to the beat. His coolness under fire was absolutely inspirational.

I miss Ron. I miss his phone calls and the opportunity to see him occasionally. I regret that we never made that fishing trip together, and I can't help but wonder if there wasn't something more I could have or should have done that would have prevented him from taking his life.

I have no idea what he encountered in the dark of night, what ghosts and demons he faced in solitary moments, whether they were related to Vietnam or something entirely different. Maybe life had just stopped being an adventure and instead became too much of a burden. I don't know why he didn't call. But I do know that Ron's death wasn't just a loss to his family and friends, it is a loss to America.

Ron was not a physically imposing man. But he was smart—in Quang Tri, besides being a top electronics technician, he had devised a way to fix a recurring flight control problem on-site, eliminating the need to send scarce parts to Da Nang for reworking—and had received a commendation for it. He was cool under fire and had the heart of a Marine.

In the end, that is what mattered, and that is why I was proud to call him a friend. And it is people like Ron who are so desperately needed by America if this country and freedom are to endure. Whatever else may have been involved, America's treatment of Ron and many others like him after our return from Vietnam has to be a factor in his ultimate decision to end his life.

While I don't want to dwell on the negative, there is one other death that should not go without mention. In August 1999, Dad died, only about six weeks after being diagnosed with cancer. He had suffered a brain aneurysm about ten years earlier and, despite recovering nearly completely, was never really himself again.

Only a few weeks before the cancer diagnosis, he had gone for a routine checkup and been given a clean bill of health. But he knew he wasn't feeling well and went for a second opinion. By the time he was diagnosed it was too late.

He lived eighty-three years, had crossed the ocean between Scotland and America four times by his eighth birthday, served his country in war, had made a good living, and raised a good family. I last saw him in July 1999, about a month before he died, just before an unsuccessful attempt at chemotherapy that ended up doing more harm than good.

He was still up and around, but obviously not doing well. I think we both knew the end was near, but no one was speaking of it. When I left his apartment, I shook his hand and said thanks and good-bye. He just said, "I'll see you." We left it at that.

Dad had never returned to his native Scotland, but in true Highland tradition, a piper played at his funeral, and he was carried to his grave accompanied by the strains of "Bonnie Dundee" and "Scotland the Brave."

Like it or not, the Old Man was an integral part of my Vietnam experience. I don't really think he pushed me in that direction, I think I was destined to be there and he was destined to be himself, which pretty much ensured I'd fulfill my destiny.

More so than my father, however, the deaths of Colonel Niesen, Ron Adair, and others from HMM-161 symbolize what Vietnam has become in my life—a continual stream of conflicts. I will always be proud of what we accomplished and how we carried out our missions, but that pride is offset by pain over the way we were treated by our country and the loss of so many capable people, both long ago and continuing to the present.

Fortunately, there are mitigating factors. There has always been life in the face of death, and for me it has come in several forms. My older children, Kevin and Sara, are grown now. But Jennifer and I had one more child, our daughter Heather, and she has benefited from my long-ago decision to explore my Vietnam experience more thoroughly and openly.

For starters, some of my medals now are encased and displayed on a wall in our home. Heather knows that I served there, what I did, who my friends were, and what it meant to me. She knows that her father goes to schools and community groups to talk about history and warfare and what my exploits have in common with the next generation. She sees much more involvement from me on the community level in patriotic affairs such as Memorial and Veterans Day ceremonies. And she regularly invites me to her elementary school to participate in annual Veterans Day activities. If I forget, she does not.

Vietnam is no longer hidden away and not discussed. It is a matter of pride for our family and our friends.

While Kevin and Sara may have missed that when they were growing up, they too take advantage of my experiences and call regularly to settle debates or disputes when someone makes blanket statements about Vietnam or its impact on present-day politics that they believe are wrong. Heather will grow up knowing more about Vietnam and its place in American history than her brother and sister did, but they already know how to apply that knowledge to their lives.

Yet, every time I believe I have put Vietnam in its proper place, something comes along to reach out and pull me back. I am not complaining about that, nor is it meant to be negative. I have come to the conclusion that Vietnam will always be with me and part of me, and that as time passes I must deal with new issues as they surface.

The primary lesson I have learned and that I hope to pass on is that Vietnam is an integral part of my life, and has shaped how I approach many of the challenges faced in later years. But it isn't my entire life.

Despite the conflict and contradictions, I believe that in the final analysis, Vietnam was worth it. That was not immediately apparent, but in the end, after President Ronald Reagan put the Soviet Union's feet to the fire and drove them into bankruptcy, Vietnam's place in the overall victory of the Cold War became much clearer.

I believe that when you examine Vietnam as a solitary event in American history it is easy to lose sight of its importance as one piece of a much larger puzzle. Nonetheless, in Vietnam we did far more than win all the battles, only to have the politicians and bureaucrats overturn our efforts.

We kept an ally free for at least a decade longer than would have been the case otherwise. We gave nearby countries, such as Thailand and the Philippines, the time and opportunity to build their armed forces, their governments, and their economies, making it harder to turn those populaces toward communism.

During that period the Soviet Union was the primary exporter of the communist philosophy, and it was the Soviet Union, not China, that bore the largest share of the cost of confronting the free world. China had taken it on the chin from our forces in the Korean War, and America's veterans of that fighting also have been neglected and disregarded.

But taken together with many other efforts that persisted through the Cold War's forty-plus years of conflict, Vietnam, Korea, the continued American military presence across Europe, and our willingness to challenge communism across the globe proved too much for a failed experiment in forced economics.

In the end, President Reagan's eight years of military buildup finally drove the Soviet Union into collapse. But it was a long and costly victory.

I told my son after he had grown to adulthood that there are many reasons why Vietnam is perpetually referred to in the negative, especially in the national media and by politicians who use the word to evoke images they believe will help their cause.

The truth is, millions of people perished in Southeast Asia after the U.S. and its allies left. A million South Vietnamese took to virtually anything they could find that would float, at least temporarily, and hit the South China Sea in an attempt to reach freedom anywhere else.

Hundreds of thousands were imprisoned in concentration camps that the world media euphemistically referred to as "reeducation camps," following the communist spin of the time. Some estimates put the number who died there well in excess of the number of Americans killed during the war.

The communist Khmer Rouge slaughtered 3 million Cambodians while the world sat back and did nothing. The communists, in a methodical purge of anyone who had the temerity to think differently than allowed by their ideology, decimated hill tribe populations in Vietnam and Laos that had supported the U.S. and democracy.

I guess no one really wants to look at that carnage and say

they were responsible for the lack of action that permitted it to occur. But it did, and it did because we turned our back on an ally who trusted us, and believed in us. When I say "we," I mean the United States as an entity, not those of us who fought to prevent that tragedy.

I have no quarrel with people who honestly believe in peace and work for it to flourish. But I also am acutely aware that there are others in this world who see peaceloving people as nothing more than prey—weak and vulnerable.

Some of us have to be warriors so the others can live freely. I have never asked anything of those who seek peace except that they respect the actions of those of us who secure their freedoms, as we respect their quest for a better world.

In saying that, I also must point out that I believe the so-called peace movement of the late sixties and early seventies was a disgraceful farce perpetrated by people who had either lost or never had any idea of the notion of sacrifice. Despite all the noble proclamations of the time, the movement essentially dissipated with dissolution of the draft, revealing its true self-centered, selfish core.

Even though war continued to rage in Southeast Asia and millions were dying, I don't remember any of the American "peace activists" flying to Phnom Penh to stand on the steps of the capitol building and challenge the Khmer Rouge to stop the butchery, or confronting the communist tanks in front of the South Vietnamese presidential palace.

I don't remember hearing of peace delegations going into the jungles of Laos to support the hill tribes or find "common ground" with the communist Pathet Lao. All I heard from the peace movement after the draft ended was a deafening silence as millions of innocents died horrible deaths.

I believe that human nature being what it is, few if any will stand and take responsibility for what happened after we left Vietnam. Most will simply deal with it silently, or continue to harangue those who served, using long-since discredited arguments that have no meaning or relevance. It is all they have left.

But so long as they live, and so long as our national and world media are dominated by people who contributed to the decision to abandon our South Vietnamese allies, the truth will remain an underground message spread by dissidents—those who served and believed in the cause.

When the Iron Curtain and Berlin Wall came down, truth started to emerge. In time the communists will be gone from Vietnam, too, and more truths will be told from those left behind. A simple form of that truth is that after World War II, the nature of warfare changed. No one wants to face nuclear annihilation, so now we fight against ideologies, forces that work without large armies and that recognize no national borders.

Judging from the attacks of September 11, 2001, we will continue to face these new enemies, and their altered tactics, and defeating them also will be long and costly. But we have to realize that there is no common ground. They want nothing less than the communists did, total domination and subjugation. If there is a lesson to be learned from Vietnam, it is that the government must be far better at articulating the nature of the fight and how long it will take to win it to retain popular support.

The World War II generation is nearly gone, and the warfare of that generation is all but gone, too. If America and worldwide democracy are to survive, the populace has to understand that the methodology for fighting and winning is different now. And there no longer should be a question of whether to take the fight to the enemy on foreign soil, because now it has been proven that if we don't, the enemy will definitely bring the fight to us.

Defeating the ideological foes we now face will take military might initially, but once the battlefield is secure we will be faced with changing the attitudes of those who believe our destruction is a holy mandate. This could take generations of toil and education. America and our allies should know this and commit to it.

I have never accepted that belief that the people who served in Vietnam so valiantly, so heroically, deserve to be relegated to a victimized netherworld where those who opposed the war condescendingly refer to us as misguided, or misled. We were neither, and future generations of warriors should be spared a similar fate.

I tell my children that for a brief time in my life I walked with heroes and giants, was privileged to be included in their company, and to be called "Marine," using the highest definition of that word. I saw humanity in its most noble form in the most inhumane of circumstances, and I will always remember the strength, the courage, and the sacrifices I witnessed.

I know that I was not a hero. I have never considered myself as such. But I knew heroes and witnessed their exploits. For that I will be eternally grateful, and I will never allow their deeds to be sullied while I have the means to tell the truth.

But I believe the ultimate truth of Vietnam and our participation there will not be widely understood until all who undermined our efforts there, as well as those of us who fought, are long gone.

When there are no more egos to salve, no more careers that can be affected, no more political battles to be won or lost based on participation in the cause of Vietnam, then the full story will emerge. Then historians will be able to objectively review our time there and pass on to the civilian and military leaders the lessons that can be used to truly prevent "another Vietnam."

Then, I believe, our contributions to a free world will be understood and appreciated. Then the Vietnam War, and Vietnam Veterans, finally will be accorded their rightful place in the history of America.

SEMPER FIDELIS

Appendix A

HMM-161 Squadron Personnel (Squadron's Second Vietnam Tour)

LCpl S C Abele
LCpl R C Adair
LCpl M J Aichele
LCpl D E Allen
Cpl J M Allison II
Lt J F Andrews III
Capt P F Angle
LCpl J A Athey
LCpl R L J Axberg
Cpl M W Bachert
LCpl D K Baker
Cpl G C Baker
Capt J W Baker
Cpl W F Baldwin
Maj R W Barber
Sgt J E Barlow Jr
LCpl F A Barth
LCpl C A Basinski
LCpl W H Bazemore
Cpl C L Beasley
LCpl P B Bevil
LCpl D Bilbrey
Lt B C Blair
Cpl R A Bletz
CWO W J Bolena Jr
Maj J L Bolton
Maj W Boone
Capt M K Boykin
SSgt O H Boysen
LCpl D M Braman
Cpl K N Brandes
LCpl F C Breese
Cpl T J Breuss
LCpl C G Brewer
SSgt J A Britton
LCpl S K Brown
Sgt L R Bryant
LCpl L W Busato
LCpl D J Bush
Cpl J E Byrne
GySgt A D Cadiente
Sgt D L Cannady
Cpl J Carbone
Cpl J W Carcasio
Cpl C R Carr
Pfc B W Carter Jr

Sgt D L Centers
Sgt J M Chandler
LCpl R M Cheek
Sgt F J Cichowski
Cpl J D Clapper
Sgt J N Clark
LCpl S D Clem
Cpl W Cody
Lt D C Collins
Lt T L Collins
Capt B F Conner
LCpl D L Cornell
MSgt R C Coryn
GySgt O J Cote Jr
Sgt R L Craven
LCpl J D Cross
Maj M L Crowdis
LCpl N D Curl
LCpl A L Cutting
Cpl W B Daigle
Pfc J W Davidson Jr
Cpl J R Deniston
Sgt L E Depperschmidt
GySgt R A Derrick
LCpl P J Despard
Pfc R A Dietrick
Lt A M Doktor Jr
LCpl J S Dolan
LCpl M W Doubet
Cpl B A G Douglas
Lt R E Dueker
LCpl J C Duncan
Sgt C C Dykes Jr
Sgt R C Eaton
SSgt F Ebron
Cpl J W Edwards
LCpl R E Eichhorn
LCpl E Enas
Pfc A L English Jr
SSgt E R Eno
Cpl R G Evans
Sgt W E Evans
Lt W R Fabinsky
Capt R H Fahrner
Cpl W C Fell
Maj J L Felter
Pfc C R Ferrall
Cpl J R Ferrazzano
GySgt W P Forsythe
LCpl M L Franklin
LCpl W D Frantz
Lt R A Frech
Capt G J Freese
Cpl R L French
Lt C Galavitz
Cpl M S Galvin
Cpl J D Ganey
Cpl R F Gangi
LCpl G Garland
Cpl L A Garmus
LCpl R P Gill Jr
LCpl D W Gines
Capt R C Glover
Sgt Maj J H Goodfellow
Sgt L L Gray
SSgt D R Green
LCpl W R Gruby
Sgt W H Haffa
LCpl L H Hahn
Cpl D W Haire
Cpl J L Harnly
LCpl P E Harvey

Cpl D W Heath
Lt M D Helmstetler
LCpl W Hennessey
Lt C D Henricks
LCpl R A Herlocker
Capt B J Herron
LCpl C B Higgins
GySgt M A Hills
Lt W T Hitchcock Jr
Cpl J H Hollifield
Pfc H R Howland Jr
Cpl G L Huggins
Sgt G L Humphries
Cpl E R Irwin
GySgt M E Johnsen Jr
Sgt B W Johnson
LCpl K B Johnson
LCpl M L Johnson
SSgt V R Johnson
LCpl L C Jones
LCpl C E Jumper
Lt R D Kaiser
Cpl D F Kalafate
Cpl J Kennedy
Lt N T Kirk
Sgt E B Kohler Jr
CWO D E Lambert
Cpl K D Lampe
Cpl R C Landers
Cpl P W Lanier
Cpl R T Latimer
LCpl A S Latina
Cpl A Leal
LCpl G L Leamer
SSgt E W Lee
LCpl T W Lenz
Capt G F Litchfield
Maj J S Loop
SSgt G W Lord Jr
Capt P M Mack
LCpl F J Mackay
Pfc D A Magnone
Cpl K A Mahlum
Sgt B L Mandel
Lt T A Martindale
Capt H E Massey
Sgt G A Masters
GySgt E J Matt
LCpl C L Maupin Jr
LCpl R J McDowell
Lt M M McElwee
Cpl J J McKinness
Cpl R W McMillen
Cpl J W Merritt
Lt J F Meyer
Cpl K R Meyer
Cpl P J Mikula
LCpl J G Miller
Capt R E P Miller
Cpl W N Milner Jr
Cpl J D Mitchell
Pfc R S Monk
LCpl F E Moore
Sgt T P Moore
LCpl A M Morris Jr
Cpl L T Morrison
LCpl A J Morrow Jr
Lt G W Moser
Lt R W Mullins Jr
LCpl A Munoz Jr
Lt L F Muranyi
LCpl C L Muth Jr

SSgt C Nelson
Sgt G W Nelson
Col P W Niesen
Sgt J A Novak
SSgt J M O'Connor
Lt J R Odom
Cpl R M O'Donnell
Lt K R Olson
LCpl J R Osburne
SSgt C D Overstreet
LCpl F Palladino
Cpl C W Palmer
Capt G W Parker
Pfc J M Parker
LCpl G L Parmenter
LCpl R L Patterson
GySgt J L Payne
LCpl L D Pearcy
Lt F A Penning
SSgt H D Pingle
LCpl R E Posey Jr
Capt J L Powell Jr
LCpl J C Prescott
Lt J A Prombo
LCpl R S Pushe
Capt D P Reichert
LCpl B L Reiss
LCpl N H Richards
Capt C T Riel Jr
Maj C D Riordan
LCpl J L Rivera
LCpl R E Rivera
Cpl R J Robbers
Cpl D Rose
LCpl G A Rude
Cpl M J Saley
Cpl X E Sanchez
LCpl W Sarellana Jr
LCpl J C Sass
Capt P M Schafer
Lt K D Schagat
Cpl R J Schumaker
SSgt W H Scoggins
Cpl T C Senften
Pfc T P Shafer
Cpl C Shannon
Capt L S Sharp
SSgt J S Sheppard
Cpl J A Shoultes
LCpl S M Shuey
Cpl J A Siegel
Capt W N Simmons
Maj R N Simpson
Cpl G E Sinner
LCpl D A Slankard
MSgt R R Smidley
Pfc D L Smith
Capt T H Smith
Lt J D Snyder
Cpl B J Soignet
Cpl F Somer
Lt C R Songer Jr
SSgt V Sooto
Cpl J J Sorenson
Cpl J A Sprague
Sgt J L Staggs
SSgt B W Stalcup
Cpl S J Stanick
Cpl G L Stanley
LCpl J J Steckbauer
Cpl B E Stiles
Lt T J Sullivan

Lt J N Sweet
LCpl J E Talton
LCpl J C Taylor
Sgt W N Thomas
LCpl M K Thompson
Pfc R L Thompson
Pfc T L Thompson
Sgt F M Tolley
SSgt J A Towle
Sgt R L Tracy
LCpl D W Vaughn
Sgt K R Villwock
Sgt N K Wall
Capt M T Warring Jr
LCpl S J Watkins
Pfc D L Weidner
Cpl R E Weiss
LCpl W A Wertz
Sgt W A Wild
Cpl R K Wilkerson
Sgt P D Wilkes
Sgt R Wilkins
GySgt G E Williams
Cpl R Williams
LCpl R D Williams
LCpl A G Wilson
SSgt P A Wilson
LCpl R E Winter
Cpl J C Withrow
Lt M J Witsell
SSgt W A Woodard
LCpl T E Yeck
Sgt B Young Jr
Cpl F D Young
Pfc A J Zamiska
LCpl J E Zanercik
Sgt K R Zimmerman

Appendix B

HMM-161 Killed in Action

Last Name, First Name	Rank	Branch	Capacity	Incident Date (yr, mo, day)
Akins, Donald	Cpl	USMC	Crew chief	690602
Antonelly, Charles	Cpl	USMC	Maint	651106
Barr, Allan	1stLt	USMCR	Co-pilot	690423
Bazemore, William	LCpl	USMC	Gunner	690422
Belknap, Ronald	Cpl	USMC	Gunner	660808
Benson, Martin	1stLt	USMCR	Co-pilot	700206
Brandes, Kenneth	Cpl	USMC	Crew chief	680822
Cheek, Robert	LCpl	USMC	Crew chief	681017
Chemis, Charles	GySgt	USMC	Crew chief	651017
Chmura, Michael	Cpl	USMC	Gunner	651017
Creed, Edward	HM3	USN	Corpsman	660625
DeCraene, Alan	1stLt	USMC	Pilot	700216
Doeden, Nicolaus	1stLt	USMCR	Co-pilot	650606
Ferrazzano, John	Cpl	USMC	Gunner	681017
Foster, Curtis	Pfc	USMC	Crew	650606
Frantz, William	LCpl	USMC	Gunner	681017
Garringer, Jan	Cpl	USMC	Crew	700216
Green, Arthur	LCpl	USMC	Crew	660925
Griffith, Dale	Cpl	USMC	Gunner	690607
Helmstetler, Michael	1stLt	USMCR	Co-pilot	680619
Henricks, Charles	1stLt	USMC	Pilot	690323
Hertz, Allen	1stLt	USMCR	Co-pilot	650606
Hesson, Danny	LCpl	USMC	Gunner	691010
Hutton, William	HM2	USNR	Corpsman	690314

Last Name, First Name	Rank	Branch	Capacity	Incident Date (yr, mo, day)
Lenz, Thomas	LCpl	USMC	Gunner	690422
McBee, Carl	LCpl	USMC	Crew	650606
McKay, Gerald	1stLt	USMCR	Pilot	650606
McNally, Paul	Capt	USMCR	Pilot	650606
Morin, Donald	LCpl	USMC	Crew chief	700216
Parker Jr., Vernon	Cpl	USMC	Crew	660925
Powell Jr., Joseph	Capt	USMCR	Pilot	681017
Reiter, Dean	1stLt	USMCR	Co-pilot	660925
Sampsell, Joel	1stLt	USMCR	Co-pilot	700216
Scott, Dayne	HM2	USNR	Corpsman	681017
Sharp, Lufkin	Capt	USMCR	Pilot	680619
Stahl, Donald	Sgt	USMC	Crew chief	660625
Sweet, James	1stLt	USMC	Co-pilot	681017
Tracy, Gary	Cpl	USMC	Crew	650606
Wiese, Robert	Cpl	USMC	Gunner	700216
Wilson, Frank	Cpl	USMC	Crew chief	650606